Our Yankee Heritage

OUR YANKEE HERITAGE

New England's Contribution to American Civilization

By

CARLETON BEALS

Essay Index Reprint Series

 BOOKS FOR LIBRARIES PRESS
FREEPORT, NEW YORK

STANDARD BOOK NUMBER:
8369-1593-3

LIBRARY OF CONGRESS CATALOG CARD NUMBER:
73-111814

PRINTED IN THE UNITED STATES OF AMERICA

Contents

Our Yankee Heritage

I. The New England Way

JOHNNY APPLESEED, that strange and beloved St. Francis of the American West, who went forth from New England to fill the Ohio country with flowering fruit trees, is a symbol of the role of Yankeeland in the life and growth of the United States.

Many seeds that he planted had already been tried and tested. They bore within their genes the handiwork of patient horticulturists in the corner of the country from which he came.

Not many years ago, Luther Burbank produced marvelous new plants and flowers. Hybrid corn is remaking the agricultural map of the world. But even before the American Revolution, the nurseries of New Haven were developing new apples, plums, and peaches. Nathan Beers and others who took the lead have long been forgotten, but their horticulture and their trees moved across the land.

All the New Englanders who went west scattered seeds of one sort or another. They took with them their churches and schools, their free town meetings, their skills and industries.

The story of New England has been told many times in many ways. This account tells of some of the men and women, their backgrounds and their lives, who did much to build those institutions and habits of New England that became important for the whole country. It tells of some of the important ideas and inventions, the great documents of freedom, the love of education, the explorations and trade that especially contributed to the building of modern America. It seeks to describe how some of those ideas and ways of life came about; how they grew and put down roots and became sturdy; how later they were spread across the country.

It was a process by which a new land, with different soil and climate, long nurturing a different race and strange plants and animals, shaped the men of old Europe into new beings, and how these new "Americans" took hold of the resources they found "in American ways" to create a better and freer life. It is the story of the interplay between human beings and the American earth, each remaking the other.

From the handicraft skills of early New England, adapted to utilize the special resources of America and answer the needs of people in an entirely new world, came the first important inventions, the laborsaving devices, the little shops and mills on rushing New England streams, that were to grow into great industries there and in the West.

The vast continent could not be claimed until men had learned the true ways of the American earth and what they could do with it. The continent could not be subdued—not even most of New England itself—until the newcomers had worked out the ideas of government and freedom without which their society could not expand and grow and move dynamically westward. First, they had to shake off the strait jacket of feudal Europe, the old class distinctions, the narrow sectarianism, the age-old instruments of oppression before they could take hold of the new land and tame the western wilderness. Not until the necessary foundations had been laid and a free, vital society had been shaped could they cope with that enormous empire.

It took more than a century and a half—a period almost as long as the history of our independent republic—before they could begin to accomplish this. Thereafter, the industries and ideas and institutions of New England continued to nourish the whole land long after the founding of the free nation. They still do.

2

The Englishmen who, with their families, crossed the dangerous ocean in frail boats, suffering hardships and risking death in an unknown wilderness, came in order to worship God as they pleased and to find wider opportunities.

In spite of the persecutions of the Established Church and His Majesty's constables, it took enormous courage, however great their desire for liberty, to tear up family roots that had gone down for generations and abandon home and country to set forth on an adventure the outcome of which was so hazardous and doubtful.

But the break with Church-State authority had already been made, secretly or publicly, and those who had crossed the channel to Leiden in the Low Countries a dozen years before the *Mayflower* were already "well-weaned from the delicate milk" of their mother country and "nursed to the difficulties of a strange, hard land." "All great and honorable actions," as their young leader William Bradford put it, "were accompanied by difficulties. . . . They knew they were Pilgrims."

Resolute, fortified by their fervent convictions, they had had experience in facing new, difficult conditions, were already flexible in adjusting themselves to survival under unfriendly circumstances. Even so, the New World enterprise called for far greater courage and resourcefulness.

The determination to set forth on another adventure to still another foreign land, this time "a howling wilderness," was not made out of "newfangledness or other such like humour." The members of the Leiden congregation, which supplied the first emigrants, were growing older, children were not getting ahead in the Low Country, families were beginning to break up, the very existence of the devout little congregation was menaced. War threatened, and religious liberty was in danger again.

The congregation sought a place to live where, in time, conditions might be "better and easier," where they would have complete liberty, and where others "of like faith" could join them. The New World, whatever the hardships, offered such a fresh opportunity for freedom and for "propagating and advancing the gospel of the Kingdom of Christ."

Thus they were encouraged in their desperate enterprise by being part of a close-knit congregation, largely isolated from the society around them, almost like a medieval brotherhood, like a ghetto set up in an alien population. In England their fellow congregations were clandestine; services were held in secret cellars on the portals of which at any moment the iron-tipped staff of the law might strike and where the lantern of arrest might swing in their eyes.

In the New World, they were soon called upon for still greater readjustments; indeed, they were obliged to make themselves over into a new image. They brought with them, besides tools, food, seeds, and animals, the ideas and habits of old England, plus what they had learned in Holland. Some of their seeds withered in the new American soil. So did many of their ideas. Part of their heritage helped them. Part of it became an obstacle in taming the new land and surviving. They could not immediately shuffle off old habits and ideas that hampered them in taking hold of the new earth and making it fruitful. They learned to do so more readily with their hands than their brains—a practicality and opportunism characteristic of American life from that day to this.

In the beginning, they were wary of this vast new continent. They would have lacked the knowledge and equipment to grapple with it boldly, even had there been more of them. The first settlements clung fearfully to the shore and a few river valleys. When they stared across the broad, dangerous ocean that separated them from the civilization that, in spite of its cruelties, they had known and loved, they felt great yearning; they had terrible hours of homesickness. It took time before they could look steadily and gladly at the firm rocks under their feet and really feel that this was their home forever, their land, their country.

They were greatly sustained by their joy in their new-found independence. Already the Lord had "delivered them from the hand of the oppressor." Whatever happened here, He would hear their voices. His mercies would "endure forever." They were a deep-feeling people in whom the pendulum between grief and joy swung wider than in persons safe and secure, not seeking a new way of life.

But from the first moment when they waded through the icy Cape Cod waters to the shore, they had to devote most of their thought and energy to surviving in this strange, fear-some land, which, as they looked at it from the decks of the *Mayflower*, seemed to bear out their worst terrors—"a hideous desolate wilderness," wearing "a savage hue," probably "full of wild beasts and wild men" in unknown "multitudes."

They were to suffer frightful calamities during the next few winters—more than half of them perished—but their fears were increasingly replaced by wonder at the amazing new trees and plants, the birds and fish and animals, all the wide majesty of the new land. Little by little, from the Indians, from experience and experiment, they learned to reap good crops, to build better houses, to eat new foods—to be Americans, not merely transplanted Europeans. Gradually their roots went deeper into the stony but verdant countryside.

It took time. Though by 1640 some 20,000 settlers had emigrated from England, it was nearly a century after the landing before the human and material resources of the newcomers became ample enough to settle all Connecticut and Rhode Island; the settling of western Massachusetts took longer still. Even when the hour of American independence struck, only fringes of Maine, New Hampshire, and Vermont had been occupied.

Nearly two centuries, from the time of the initial settlement, went by before the springboard was strong enough or the vision and confidence great enough for any determined leap across the Appalachians. Not until then were the knowledge, tools, techniques, animals, seeds and progeny, the institutions of freedom, available for the monumental task of swiftly taming a continent.

3

It was in the earlier "dark ages" of struggle in stormy New England that people learned to seize hold of the American earth, utilize its riches, and know its blessings. During those formative years, they developed the know-how of frontier settlement: efficient ways of clearing the land and planting;

how to lay out towns, build homes and civic edifices, record property titles, and encourage free enterprise.

New England, with its small freeholdings owned by free men, was the laboratory for the whole country. There, new methods were tried out, new tools made, new forms of political and social organization developed. There was the cradle of security, liberty, and industry.

Many of the new things learned were very simple, and these remain as bright jewels in the beloved legends of early America: the "stirring-off" time for maple sugar when the spring sap began to run—that and raising bees in grass-rolled hives were important; for sugar, having to be imported, was expensive. The very first settlers told of their turkey dinners, succotash, cranberries, blueberries, pumpkins, Training Band drills, "Proxin' Day" when the people cast black and white beans to elect town officials and held their annual fair to barter their homemade brooms, hand-woven linens, crude iron tools hammered out in barnyard forges, and whittled objects from spoons to spinning wheels.

They set in motion many of the great forces that were to shape the future nation. New Haven on Long Island Sound was the first "western" cattle town—"herds of a hundred or more"—though no brawling, bar-lined place. Within twenty years after settlement, Morocco Lane, running along West Creek, was famous for its skillful tanners and leather craftsmen. By then the town was already exporting to far places meat, hides, leather goods and shoes, harness, saddles, buggy slings, jackets, brass-riveted beer mugs. There, as in Farmington and other "frontier" Connecticut cattle towns, were worked out techniques of feeding, breeding, veterinary care, branding, and recording brands that subsequently served the great cattle and dairy industry of the Far West.

Somewhat later, a footsore New Haven tavern keeper devised the first right and left shoes in man's history. People, accustomed to sharp-pointed "straights," long derided them as "crooked" shoes. "Host" John Miles was forgotten when his comfortable shoes came into use after the Civil War.

Plymouth colony developed the first techniques of Indian trading and the fur trade, of preserving and shipping skins and furs that later gave rise to the fur enterprises of Roxbury, Springfield, and Litchfield, then Vermont, upper New York, and the Great Lakes, and finally served the great industry that rose in the West and made pack peddler John Jacob Astor an important name in American history.

On the very first vessel after the *Mayflower*, Plymouth shipped out lumber. All the New England colonies exported planking, clapboards, beams, wainscoting, shingles. Quickly they learned the art of felling and cutting up trees, of sliding them to the rivers. The early records are full of stories of logging down the Kennebec and Housatonic, and this, too, required special tools and skills. Before long, Bangor, Maine, became the lumber capital of the world.

It took time to devise the best gadgets for splitting off shingles and to learn how to do it smartly. The simple saw-pit method of cutting up tree trunks soon gave way to up-and-down power saws, then circular saws on every little stream, finally to the building of factories to make saws and axes. Presently the sound of powered planers shrieked through the tall timber. All sorts of new tools—adzes, axes, lathes, pot augers, planes, scrapers—were devised to work wood.

The lumbermen swept west in boot-stamping crowds. They stormed like blazing locusts through the forests of western Pennsylvania; they ripped away the best of the Wisconsin woods; and they moved up to the Lakes, where they wrestled Paul-Bunyan-style with mighty Vikings—the Swedish and Norwegian settlers—who also knew lumber; for a thousand years they had known it. The day came when near replicas of Connecticut towns, with Cape Cod houses and central greens, appeared deep in the Minnesota woods, at the very headwaters of the Mississippi. Much of that lumber trade had been learned originally among the chestnuts, oaks, hickory, maples, cedars, and elms of New England hills.

So it was with many things, many new industries. Just as New England developed the skills necessary for successful frontier settlement and the know-how for the later industrial might of America, so did it learn to pattern free government corresponding to the flexible needs and opportunities of the great new continent. It was not easy, even if everybody craved freedom, to cast aside rigid medieval and ecclesiastical methods; too often, old abuses were duplicated and perpetuated; but step by step, obstacles to free representative government were removed. These men who worked in the practical vineyard of liberty were growing new plants of political life the like of which the world had never seen, the fruits of which it had never tasted. Sailing uncharted seas never before explored by mankind, they and they alone had to avoid the reefs and ride out the storms. The attempt was sometimes dangerous and disastrous, and the muskets of freedom were sometimes routed by the poison darts of the medieval mind, the superstitions of many dark centuries. Freedom under law and order was not handed to America in the form of a full-blown rose; it had to be planted, cultivated, and grown, grafted and regrafted—perfected. That, too, was the New England way. Not until New Englanders became free Americans could they set out with others to reshape the continent successfully. During those two preliminary centuries, they worked out the pattern of free institutions, the constitutions, laws, and governmental superstructure necessary for the proper enjoyment of order, liberty, and progress. The divine right of kings could no longer prosper in the wide, untrammeled space of America. The New Englanders were self-made men, and only a self-made government could satisfy them.

Here then was a fivefold process in the settlement and growth of New England: (1) adaptation to the American earth and its resources, and utilization of them in a new "American" way—a process of becoming American not European; (2) the working out of necessary techniques and the accumulation of the essential capital for taming the frontier; (3) the development of original skills and new products; (4) the development of free institutions, without which the continent could never have been settled and developed so swiftly; (5) the carrying of these skills, the know-how, learning, and institutions, across the land into the West.

Mostly this occurred step by step: little inventions of new tools for the hand and new tools for the brain, the spirit, and society. Just a combination candlestick and pigskin scraper; a machine to dip matches, thus doing away with carrying the hot coals that were responsible for the accidental burning down of many houses; a mortised lock, making life and property more secure; new textile and shoemaking equipment; an apparatus to cut pearl buttons; a machine for making coins; a mechanical corn-planter; a new kind of school desk; new styles of fishhooks, harpoons, and grappling irons for boats. Very early, New Englanders started the conservation of certain trees. Within twenty years, they had set up regulations for standard quality and purity of products, for weights and measures and packaging. In the same way in the less tangible sphere, step by step, new town committees faced unprecedented situations. Perhaps a new town office was created; trial by popular jury came along and, after something more than a century of effort, full tolerance everywhere for all religious societies.

But sometimes the change-over was sudden, far-reaching, dramatic, brought about like a great flash of light by some individual or a single group, either because the new way answered an important or pressing material or spiritual need, or because the moment was ripe for integrating a vast amount of prior knowledge and experience that had been steadily accumulating. These more dramatic discoveries were bold milestones on the road of more prosaic, less-noticed efforts; they were the brilliant result of steady experiment and growth.

Such a dramatic achievement was the formulation of the Mayflower Compact before the Plymouth settlers set foot on Plymouth Rock.

II. New England's First Town

BEING THUS arrived in good harbor, and brought safe to land, they fell upon their knees and blessed the God of Heaven who had brought them over the vast and furious ocean, and delivered them from all the perils and miseries thereof, again to set their foot on firm and stable earth, their proper element."

Thus William Bradford, yeoman leader of the *Mayflower* Pilgrims, told how he and his companions first came ashore in America, November 11, 1620, on the Cope Cod sand dunes near Provincetown.

It had been a terrible voyage, sixty-five days of tempests and near death. The shrouds were broken, sails rent, seams opened in the oaken ribs. They barely managed to push the buckled main beam of the ship back into place by "a great iron screw," brought out of Holland, and had gone scudding on through lashing gales under bare poles.

Now they faced a bleak winter shore, an uncharted wilderness, where they had never intended to settle, on which they had no permission to settle. They would be under no direct authority; they had only themselves to rely upon.

They faced not only a dangerous venture but trouble in their own ranks at a time when they had to stand together or perish. Some favored the daring change of plans, made during the voyage, which had brought them to this forlorn shore rather than to the Hudson River, where they had a patent from the Virginia Company to settle. Others were filled with dismay and bitterly opposed to this complete plunge into the unknown darkness of the almost unknown continent.

Differences had arisen even before they had left England. They had sought the "King's broad seal" and guarantees from both the Archbishop and the Virginia Company that they would enjoy "liberty in religion." All they were able to obtain was a promise they would not be molested if they "carried themselves peaceably." Many believed this to be a very "sandy foundation," and such a "flat schism" rose that one Pilgrim said discouragedly, "To speak the truth . . . we are more ready to go into a dispute than to set forward a voyage."

The argument continued through the long trip. After sighting Cape Cod, the vessel had turned south to reach the Hudson, but dangerous reefs and storms—perhaps these were only an excuse—forced them to steer north. When it was definitely decided to settle in New England, the dispute took a sharper turn. Some argued, since here on Cape Cod they would be wholly on their own, every man could do as he pleased, no one would have power to command him. The indentured servants would "use their liberty."

But the forlorn shore and their fears of this unknown world and its perils sobered them. If they were to survive, they had to work together. Here they expected to spend the rest of their lives, and from the start, they quickly realized, they had to establish an authority all would accept. And so, as the *Mayflower* rode at anchor off Cape Cod, before exploring their new domain, they discussed the best course to follow during the difficult times ahead.

Their lessons in church democracy and independent church covenants stood them in good stead. In their congregations they had learned to discuss differences amicably for the most part and to accept the will of the majority without coercion or defiance. In their long struggle for religious freedom and in their Netherlands exile, repeatedly they had had to solve unusual contingencies. This was the most serious they had ever faced together, and they had to break new ground. Out of sheer necessity, they had to create a government—their own government.

After due discussion, a document was drawn up that found favor, and forty-one adults stepped forward and affixed their scroll-like signatures, almost like picture writing. It was a ceremonious act, carried out with formality—therefore a tie more binding.

The Mayflower Compact declared that they had come "for the Glory of God and the Advancement of the Christian Faith and Honour . . . of King and Country." As loyal subjects of their "dread Sovereign King James," they agreed to "Covenant and Combine" themselves "into a Civil Body Politic" and, for their "better ordering and preservation," to "enact, constitute and frame such just and equal Laws, Ordinances, Acts, Constitutions and Offices . . . as shall be . . . meet and convenient for the general good of the Colony," unto which they promised "all due submission and obedience." Such was the Mayflower Compact.

Meticulously they observed all proper forms. One eye was directed at their own imperative needs and desires, the practical realities in their situation. The other was directed at the land they had left. Their compact had to be so worded as to establish their new independence yet not alarm the authorities back in England. It avoided stated aims of religious freedom, for a separatist church was sedition and rebellion, and set forth dutifully their full allegiance to the Sovereign. The very act of making out such a document, even its careful wording, marked the unique character of their enterprise. For all the polite phraseology, it was a breaking of precedents. Though it tipped its hat to their "dread Sovereign," it was a new document, with a new idea, made for a new society. Only free men, accustomed to independent ideas, could have penned such words.

Those first *Mayflower* people, painfully trying to meet an urgent need in accordance with their deep convictions, were probably only vaguely, if at all, aware of the importance of the little paper they signed, or that each signer would be assured of a certain near immortality. They were merely trying to settle their own pressing problem, an actual situation, in a reasonable, fair way, and the result was fair and reasonable, a working compromise between authority and freedom.

It was, it so happened, much more than that. Behind it lay a great new philosophy of enlightenment, something born of their long struggle for political and religious freedom, their rejection of all authority that did not derive from free opinion and free association. It was part of the stirring of a new economic age, of the printed word, of the dissemination of knowledge among all men. The Mayflower Compact was thus a precursor of the spirit of the new age and, as such, was rooted in basic principles of self-government, so that those principles became more important than its specific provisions or its specific provisos or its guarded phraseology, for it permitted, among their things, not only change and growth, but an orderly method of change and growth.

Thus was the first document of self-rule made in America, a covenant for majority administration, for liberty under law. It was to help shape political life for generations, not only in Plymouth, but in Maine, New Hampshire, Vermont, and western Massachusetts. Its concise concepts, tooled to an almost diamond sharpness, like most great but simple documents, were to serve free men all along the open frontier. A condensed doctrine of political freedom, designed for practical use, it became part of the enduring American experiences, the cornerstone of democratic representative government that would rise stone by stone from the further experience and aspirations of the people of the entire continent.

2

After the death that first spring of Deacon John Carver, the first Plymouth governor, William Bradford was chosen; except for five years, when he asked to be relieved, he served for the rest of his life. He had helped make the practical arrangements to settle in America. He had helped formulate the Mayflower Compact. He directed the course of settlement, guided the first steps of the colony in work and righteousness, helped make it secure by friendly relations with the Indians. Most of the story that has come down to us was recorded by him.

He was born at Austerfield, Yorkshire, in March, 1590, the only son of a yeoman farmer and a shopkeeper's daughter. His father died when he was a year old; his mother soon remarried, and he was raised by his grandfather and uncles, who, in due time, put him to work in the fields.

When only twelve, moved by the word of the Bible, he joined a prayer and discussion group at William Brewster's house on the Bishop's Manor in nearby Scrooby. Brewster was well-to-do and had long been active in the Royal diplomatic service.

In 1606, the Scrooby people, calling themselves "Saints," had organized a Congregational church. It was "the breaking out of the light of the gospel in the honourable nation of England." But thereafter young Bradford had to suffer "the wrath of his uncles" and "the scoff of his neighbors."

Soon "hunted and persecuted" on every side, the Saints suffered "bloody death and cruel torments, imprisonments, banishments and hard usages" and resolved to escape to the Low Countries, a "desperate adventure," for it was a strange land where they "must learn a new language" and get their "livings" they "knew not how."

Those first to go, in 1607, sold their homes and chartered a vessel. They embarked secretly at night, but were betrayed— seized and thrust into small boats. "Cat-poll" officers "rifled and ransacked" their belongings and searched "to their shirts for money, yet even the women further than became modesty." The prisoners were made a spectacle of "to the multitude which came flocking on all sides to behold them."

Next spring a Dutch ship was hired. On the approach of an armed troop, the captain hurriedly weighed anchor. The men, already come aboard, were frantic for the safety of their families on shore, and they had "scarce a penny," only the clothes on their backs.

A dreadful storm drove them to the rocky Norway coast. Great seas swept over the foundering ship; "the water ran into their mouths and ears, and the mariners cried out, 'We sink!

We sink!' The passengers cried, 'Yet Lord Thou cans't save!' whereupon the ship did not only recover . . . the violence of the storm began to abate."

Those left behind, "their poor little ones hanging about them, crying from fear and quaking with cold," were hurried from one justice to another. To imprison so many women and children would cause everybody to "cry out," yet none had homes any more; there was no place to go. In the end, the constables were "glad to get rid of them . . . on any terms."

"All gat over at length, some in one place and some in another, and met together again . . . with no small rejoicing."

A free church was set up in "fair" Leiden. Brewster, with a large family to support, taught Latin and became a printer, publishing books banned in England. Bradford earned his living as a weaver and, in spare time, learned Dutch, French, Greek, Latin, and Hebrew. He accumulated a fine library, which he took across in the *Mayflower*.

A dozen years later, when the decision was made to remove to the New World, William Bradford was one of those chosen to make practical arrangements. Though the charter obtained was far from satisfactory, sympathetic Merchant Adventurers, headed by Thomas Weston, a London ironmonger, were induced to provide money and supplies on a joint-stock basis, the debt to be paid back in seven years, capital and profits to be divided proportionately.

The first Pilgrims, a party of thirty, embarked at Delftshaven July 22 on the sixty-ton *Speedwell*, "open and leaky as a sieve," and they rode out with the tide, "which stays for no man." In Southampton they chartered the 180-ton, 64-foot *Mayflower*, "a sweet wine-ship." Seventy-one others joined them, including women and children, fourteen indentured servants, and hired artisans. Captain Myles Standish was employed as military leader. William Bradford came aboard with his wife Dorothy May, whom he had married in Amsterdam in 1613.

They set sail in the two vessels August 5, 1620, but twice

had to put back into ports to repair the *Speedwell*. Even then, sea water "came in as at a mole hole," so they had to cram themselves and all belongings into the *Mayflower*. Half their food was used up before they got started, and they had to sell three or four score firkins of butter to pay the bills.

"We shall not have a month's victuals when we come into the country," moaned one leader, "and will know the gasping of hunger-starved persons."

3

In the wide, placid Cape Cod harbor, where "a 1000 saile of shippe" could ride, there was the "greatest store of fowle that ever we saw." Whales played hard by. "If we had instruments & means to take them we might make a rich returne, which to our great grief we wanted. We might have made three or foure thousand pounds worth of Oyle." That would more than have paid off their indebtedness.

But under the leaden winter sky, the land looked gray and empty and menacing. The "mighty ocean" that had tossed them so badly now shut them off from the civilized world. Their religious beliefs, for which they had suffered so much persecution, shut them off even more than the ocean did. They felt great loneliness. Here were "no friends to welcome them nor inns to entertain them or refresh their weather-beaten bodies," no houses or towns to repair to "for succor." This was no "fine Pisgah" from which to view "a more goodly country to feed their hopes." The dismal prospect sorely tried their courage.

The first day ashore, clad in iron corselets, the men gripped their flintlocks and swords apprehensively and plodded single-file behind blustering little Captain Standish. The forlorn rolling sand reminded them somewhat of the "downs of Holland."

Inland from the bleak shore, they grew more encouraged. The earth's crust was black, "a spit's depth" of it, and the woods were dense with oaks, sassafras, pines, birch, holly, ash, and walnut. The juniper firewood that they carried on their backs to the ship through nearly a mile of icy water was sweet and burned still more sweetly, providing them with their first hot food in weeks.

On Monday, a bitter-cold day, they carried the women ashore to wash clothes and hauled out the big shallop—stove in during the worst storm—so they could help John Alden, the hired cooper, repair it.

Two days later, Captain Standish led a party to explore farther. They took along a few "bisket" and Holland cheese and a little bottle of "aquavite." Toward the ocean side, they sighted half a dozen "Savages" who ran into the woods and "whisled" the dog they had, to follow.

Setting out at dawn the next morning, the explorers struggled through thorny thickets that tore their "armour to shreds. . . . We came into a deep valley, full of brush, wood graile and long grasse . . . we saw a deer and found springs of fresh water . . . and sat us downe and drunke our first *New-England water* with as much delight as ever we drunke drinke in all our lives."

It was like a sacrament that was to tie them and their children and their children's children to this new American earth and its flowing springs for all the years to come. This moment of thirst and tiredness provided their first strong note of pleasure in their new home, their first deep emotional link with the new land. Thereafter, as they came upon more marvels, joy and wonder eased away more of their dour foreboding.

They passed Truro Pond, "a musket shot broad, and twice as long," and came upon sandy Indian mounds. Pawing under an old mat held down by a wooden mortar, they found a broken bow and rotted arrows. "We put in the Bow againe and made it up as it was, and left the rest untouched, because we thought it would be odious unto them to ransacke their Sepulchres."

Near cornfield stubble, in other mounds "newly paddled with hands," they found "divers fair Indian baskets filled with

corne," some in ears, yellow and red and mixed with blue—
"a very goodly sight," the first Indian corn they ever had seen.
They called the place "Corne Hill."

In great excitement, they filled their pockets with as much
as their heavy armor permitted, and two men, using a pole,
carried off all they could in a huge ship's kettle "out of
Europe," which they found there. And so, "like men from
Escol," told about in the Book of Numbers, they carried back
"the fruits of the land" to show their brethren, who were
"marvellous glad and their hearts encouraged."

Corn, too, was another everlasting tie with the American
earth. Without those precious kernels they would never have
survived the first dreadful winter or those to follow. The "seed
of all seeds," bearing the Taino Indian name "maize" and
given to the first men of earth by the Aztec gods and "the
seven bright maiden stars," was to become the greatest of all
American crops in the heyday of America's greatness. So, the
corn and water of Cape Cod, fruits of the new soil, started the
continuing process of making Europeans over into Americans.
Thus, in time, were men's lives shaped to the new continent
and their brains built to master new freedoms.

4

They kept searching for the best place to settle. Twenty-
four Pilgrims and ten sailors, led by Captain Jonas, waded
through the freezing water. It was blowing violently and snow-
ing, and for two days they struggled through the drifts and
camped under pine trees, miserable, wet, and cold, but able to
appease their ravenous "Soldier's Stomacks" with three fat
geese and six ducks.

They went up a river to "Corne Hill" to get the rest of the
maize. It was "God's good Providence" that they knew where
to look, for snow covered the ground, frozen so hard they had
to "hew and carve" it with their "Curtlaxes and short swords."
They got about ten bushels, enough for spring seeding, and
also found Indian beans and wheat.

Captain Jonas had to take fifteen sick men back to the *Mayflower* in the shallop. Some died.

The remaining explorers came upon more graves with utensils, trinkets, beads, and a fair-haired skeleton embalmed with red powder. In deserted tepees of bent young saplings "like unto an arbor" and double-lined with straw mats, they found "wooden Bowles, Trays & Dishes, Earthen Pots, Hand Baskets made of Crab Shells . . . an English paile or Bucket." The baskets, "curiously wrought with black and white in pretie workes" were filled with venison ("fitter for the Dogs than us"), parched acorns, fish and boiled herring, silk grass and tobacco. The tobacco was also to provide another important New England crop.

A week later, Captain Standish with ten Pilgrims and eight sailors, took the shallop six or seven leagues along the shore. It was "cold and hard weather," and freezing spray glazed their clothes, "like coats of Iron."

On shore a dozen Indians fled. They had been cutting up "a great fish like a grampus . . . two inches thick of fat like a hog." It was a blackfish, often cast up on Cape Cod sand bars for easy taking, and this New World gift was also to provide sustenance during dark days ahead when there was no bread or meat.

That night, as usual, they made a barricade of logs, stakes, and thick pine boughs against the cold wind and enemies, and posted sentries. In the morning, just after they had taken their armor and guns to the shore and were back in camp eating breakfast, they were attacked by thirty or forty Indians. Arrows flew thick among them. "The cry of our enemies was dreadful . . . 'Woath woach ha ha hach woach.' "

The "Savages" were driven off. The Pilgrims examined with great curiosity the spent arrows, tipped with copper, deerhorn, or eagle claws. This place they called "The First Encounter."

They sailed on fifteen leagues into snow and darkness, finding no place to land. The wind howled, the sea grew rough, their rudder broke, and the mast splintered into three pieces.

By lusty hand-steering and hard rowing they managed to round what was to be named Gurnet Point, got through roaring breakers off Squaish Head, and rode out the night of driving rain in Duxbury Bay in the lee of a "strange iland" later known as Clarke Island after a *Mayflower* pilot.

It had no inhabitants, and they rested through the Sabbath. On Monday, December 11, they landed on the mainland, this time (so fanciful legend had it more than a century later) on Plymouth Rock. Marching into the land, they found cornfields, running brooks, and woods with the same trees as on the upper Cape, also cherry, plum, and other fruits. They were amazed, later on, by the abundance of wild strawberries. Sorrel, yarrow, brook lime, liverwort, and watercress grew wild; there was "a great store of leeks and onions," also "strong flaxe and Hempe." Their excitement and pleasure increased.

The locality abounded with excellent fowl and fish—"Skote, Cod, Tarbot and Herring." The mussels were the "greatest and best we ever saw." "Fish-hooke"-shaped crabs and lobsters were "infinite." The clay, smooth as soap, "no better in the worlde," was excellent "for pots."

They decided to lay out the town here on high ground the Indians had cleared for cornfields, where there was a brook, pure bubbling springs, and "a great hill, on which we poynt to make a plat-forme, and plant our Ordinance which will command all about; from thence we may see into the *Bay*, and farre into the sea, and we may see thence *Cape Cod*." Such was Patuxet—"At the Little Falls"—the Plymouth of the New World.

The explorers hurried back to those on the *Mayflower*. The news of their fine discovery "did much to comfort their hearts." But in Bradford's absence, his "dearest consort," Dorothy May, had fallen overboard and been drowned.

5

The *Mayflower* was brought into Duxbury Bay on December 16. At first storms kept them on board, unable to prepare shelter onshore, but all Saturday, the twenty-third, they felled trees. On Sunday William Brewster held double services—"plain in what he taught" but very moving. Monday—Christmas Day—they continued their work ashore, "some to fell timber, some to saw, some to rive, some to carry, so no man rested all day." They started their communal house —"The Rendezvous"—high on the hill and laid out the sloping town in a double row of nineteen holdings, one for each free male adult. On January 9, lots were drawn.

"We agreed that every man should build his own house," for all would "make more hast[e] than working in Common." Thus was individual initiative, free enterprise, and private property first put into practice in America. Thereby a pattern and a method were established for laying out later New England towns—a system of surveys, town planning, and homestead allotments that carried on as an instrument of frontier settlement to the Northwest Territory and beyond. Free land and individual holdings helped make a free system.

But that was no easy winter. Weak from scurvy, for weeks without bread or corn, for a while without even meat or fish, most of the Saints fell ill, sometimes two or three died in a single day. In the worst stretch, only seven persons were on their feet. The latter "spared no pains night or day," but with "abundance of toil and hazard for their own health," fetched wood for the sick, "made them fires, dressed them meat, made their beds, washed their loathsome clothes, clothed and unclothed them." No one showed more love "unto their friends and brethren" than did William Brewster and Myles Standish. "Myself and many others," wrote Bradford, "were much beholden in our low, weak condition."

Nearly half the crew and half the 102 passengers died. Only twelve of the original twenty-six heads of families were left— in all, nineteen men and thirty-six women, children, and servants.

But on March 3, the wind turned south, the mist lifted, and

"birds sang in the woods most pleasantly." The backbone of the hard winter had been broken. Spring was approaching.

By April 5, enough of Jonas's crew had recovered for him to haul in the anchor and sail away. As the *Mayflower* vanished across the far reach of waters, the folk watching from the high Rendezvous beside their cannon turned again to their homes and fields—alone now in their wilderness settlement. Beyond their doors stretched the continent of mystery and danger—all America.

Fair weather brought new tasks and hopes. They put in garden seeds and turned the soil to plant corn. Upon this crop depended whether they would survive another winter. They were helped by Indian friends.

Three years before this, an epidemic, started by sick French prisoners, had wiped out every man, woman, and child of the Patuxet tribe that had resided at Plymouth. All over New England, Indians had died "in heaps" till the living could not bury the dead. "The bones and skulls upon the several places of their habitations," observed Thomas Morton, a new settler to the north, "made such a spectacle . . . it seems a new-found Golgotha." This calamity gave the Indians little stomach to oppose the newcomers, which was most fortunate for the "Saints," so badly stricken that first winter.

All during those long months of hunger and "The Great Sickness," the Indians had skulked about, causing the suffering Pilgrims continuous alarms. Once tools were stolen, but no serious trouble was experienced.

In March, a tall naked Indian, with long hair and only fringed leather about his middle, strode into camp and in English asked for beer. He was Samoset, and he had had dealings with earlier explorers.

They threw a horseman's coat about him, fed him, put him up for several nights at Stephen Hopkins's house, then sent him off with a knife, bracelet, and ring, telling him to return with others.

He brought in half a dozen Indians daubed with black and

white stripes and designs and clad in deerskin cloaks, except the leader, who wore a wildcat skin. The stolen tools were ceremoniously returned. "They did eat liberally of our English victuals," then sang and danced "after their manner of Antiks." They were sent off with trinkets.

On Samoset's next visit, he brought Squanto, a Patuxet, who spoke even better English. He had been kidnaped in 1614 by Captain Thomas Hunt to be sold as a slave to the Spaniards, but escaped to England, where he lived for some years. He came to "New Foundland" in an exploring vessel, skipped ship, and made his way overland to Plymouth, where he found that all his people had perished in the great plague and that Englishmen were living in his old home.

The great Sachem Massasoit of the powerful Wampanoag tribe was hard by with sixty braves. Edward Winslow went out to parley, with gifts of knives, a copper chain, several jewels, a "Pot of Strong water," and a quantity of "biscuits and butter."

Massasoit came in unarmed with twenty followers. The governor greeted him with "Drums and Trumpet . . . and some few Musketiers," and the two leaders kissed each other's hands. The sachem was taken to a new house being built, where a green rug and cushions were laid out, and was served meat and strong drink, which made him sweat.

Peace was arranged; a document was signed that provided that no injury be done by either side, stolen property be restored, offenders delivered up for punishment. "If any did unjustly war against him, they would aid him; if any did war against them, he should aid them." Such was the first American-Indian peace treaty—a military alliance—and for years the Pilgrims walked in the woods as safely as in England itself. The treaty provided a pattern for many future peaceful arrangements with the original inhabitants, and though the centuries to come were filled with bitter conflicts, and treaties were shamefully broken, they represented an effort essentially part of the American way of life—to solve difficulties on the basis of agreement, fair play, and legality.

Squanto, no longer having any people, insisted on remaining at Plymouth, his place of birth. He showed the Pilgrims how to set their corn and fertilize it with fish at the time the oak leaves were as big as a mouse's ear, and their corn grew tall and fat. But the English seeds that they planted gave scarcely any yield.

He showed them where to get eels, "fat and sweet," so numerous he merely had to take them up with his hands. He taught them where and how to catch fish and shellfish, how to store them; how to procure other products of land and sea; and he piloted them through the wilderness "to unknown places for their profit." As Bradford put it, he was "a special instrument sent by God for their good beyond their expectations."

In September he took them to Massachusetts Bay to trade for beaver. The Tarentine Indian women were so eager for the settlers' wares that they stripped off their beaver coats, though "with great shamefacedness (for indeed they are more modest than some of our English women)."

Such trade became all-important. Merely by tilling the soil the Pilgrims could never pay off their indebtedness or purchase goods necessary for survival and comfort—shoes and clothes; guns, powder, and shot; pitch, tar, and rope; hoes, scythes, and axes; drugs and spices. Fishing, the fur trade, and industry promised them their only sure fortune.

They soon had a sizable shipment ready for export when the *Fortune,* the first vessel to come over after the *Mayflower,* put into port. It brought thirty-five more settlers, "lusty young men" who came empty-handed and put such a strain on the colony that rations had to be halved. But on this vessel the "Old Comers" shipped out hogsheads of beaver and other skins, "gat with a few trifling commodities," aromatic sassafras (another important New World product), good walnut lumber, clapboards, and wainscoting.

As the years passed, the cutting of lumber, important for the lucrative West Indian trade, became a source of wealth for all New England. Many a floor in Old England and the Bermudas was laid with stout New England oak; many a wall was sheathed in New World pine or chestnut; many a sturdy mast and spar in His Majesty's Navy came from the tall, straight firs of Connecticut and Maine. Lumbering, begun in New England, and later carried to the Northwest, speeded up home-making and the building up of the continent.

The gathering of tar and pitch and other forest by-products for ships, for wainwrights, arms makers, and leatherworkers, for the coopers, distillers, and meat packers, also became an important industry.

The British Navy considered these New England products as vital for empire defense, for there was danger that other sources might be cut off by the Turks. This led, a few years later, to a notable decision in matters of religious controversy, when King James I, at a moment of intense persecution, set aside the decision of his own Privy Council, dominated by arbitrary Bishop William Laud, to coerce the Massachusetts government and churches. Royal authority declared that empire defense took precedence, that it was of great importance that people emigrate to New England, that one of the chief reasons they did so was that there they would be free from religious persecution. Unfortunately this was a wisdom more often forgotten than remembered.

When the Plymouth people built their first schooner-rigged pinnace, or "pine-tree" boat, another important industry was launched. In due time, New England vessels, their trim shapes subtly influenced by streamlined canoes, crossed the seas, rounded the capes, whaling and sealing in Arctica and Antarctica, and voyaging across the Pacific in the China trade, or down to Africa for slaves. Fabulous profits poured into all New England, and such vessels helped pace the expansion of the nation to the shores of the Pacific.

Plymouth set up a trading post on Buzzards Bay, on the

south shore, to traffic with the Dutch from New Amsterdam and with fishing and cargo vessels from Europe. They also established inland posts. Defying Dutch guns on the Fresh (Connecticut) River, they slipped upstream with a prefabricated fort below decks and set up a trading post at the junction of the Tunxis River at Windsor. On the Kennebec River, far north in Maine, they outfitted another post with corn, cloth, implements, knives, and trinkets to trade for furs, and, three years later, a second post on the Penobscot River.

These enterprises taught them how to fend off the Dutch and French, how to deal with the Indians. They acquired skill in handling and preserving pelts—knowledge handed along the frontier, which later served Far West fur traders.

Such undertakings enabled the Pilgrims to come to grips with their new world and adapt their lives better to its products, its demands, its opportunities.

There were setbacks. A shipment of beaver skins went down off Virginia. The Turks daringly seized one laden vessel within sight of Albion's shores. Several fishing and saltmaking ventures proved disastrous. The Penobscot post was robbed, then seized, by the French, and the gunboat *The Great Hope*, hired at big expense, failed to recover it. The Connecticut River post was taken over by Massachusetts settlers.

Nor were difficulties confined to western shores. The London Merchant Adventurers were greedy, scarcely honest, and Isaac Allerton (William Brewster's son-in-law), the colony's own agent, juggled accounts, charged high interest and commission, and trafficked in goods entrusted to him, for his own profit. He embarked on personal fishing and trading enterprises, but charged any losses to the colony. Eventually disowned, he went to New Amsterdam and later erected a fine harbor-front mansion in New Haven colony. He became the first merchant prince of the New World.

Alarmed by ever growing obligations in spite of their hard work, the settlers bought out the London investors, for £1,800 and assumed the £600 company debts. Eight colonists, headed

by Bradford and Standish, underwrote the agreement in return
for a trade monopoly and an annual tax on each shareholder
of three bushels of corn or six pounds of tobacco. Thus was
another American process of private corporate industry inaugurated.

From time to time, lawless or immoral elements had to be
punished. Small, scattered settlements to the north and roving
adventurers committed depredations, causing trouble with the
Indians that endangered Plymouth's long-standing peace.
Several malcontents, not enjoying proprietary rights in Plymouth, agitated, not without reason, for a more democratic
system. They were roughly treated and banished. They carried
their freer ideas to the new settlements along the Connecticut
River.

But on the whole the simple Mayflower Compact served the
first Pilgrims well. Reinforced by two patents from the Council of New England, headed by Sir Ferdinando Gorges, which
had been granted the entire area between the fortieth and
forty-eighth parallels "from sea to sea," the original agreement
enabled them to live in harmony and bend their efforts to the
major tasks of building their homes, tending their farms, and
engaging in commercial pursuits.

In 1636, the document was implemented by the "Great
Fundamentals," which set up a General Court, with two
deputies from each town (new settlements adjacent to Plymouth) chosen by the freemen assembled with the governor
and his assistants. This provided the world's first written
constitution, a pattern soon followed in Connecticut along
more liberal and independent lines.

Every activity in Plymouth was interlaced with religious
sentiments. The going-up to church services, at first held in the
Rendezvous, was a solemn occasion that greatly impressed
Dutch trader Isaac de Rassiers when he came over on a visit
from the Buzzards Bay post with a flourish of trumpets.

The worshipers, he observed, "assembled by the beat of the
drum, each with his musket or flintlock, in front of Captain

Standish's door. They have their cloaks on and place themselves in order, three abreast, and are led by a sergeant without beat of drum. Behind, comes the governor in a long robe. Beside him, on the right, comes the preacher with his cloak on, and with a small cane in his hand, and so they march in good order, and each sets his arms down near him."

In November, 1621, when their harvest was in, they celebrated "Thanksgiving," the first in America. Governor Bradford sent four men out fowling "so we might after a more special manner rejoice together." In a single day as much fowl were killed as, "with a little help beside, served the Company almost a week." To help celebrate, King Massasoit brought five deer; he came with ninety men, whom the Pilgrims "entertained and feasted" for three days. Thus did another unique American institution come into being.

During the celebration, the Pilgrims practiced arms, so it was also the first formal "Training Band," or militia, day. This —the first citizens' militia—also set the future pattern for New England town-meeting exercises for centuries to come and was to be incorporated into the life of all America.

So was a society born, so did it rejoice, so did it prepare to defend itself, and in so doing, this tiny first settlement initiated many of the enterprises and institutions characteristic of American life for so many generations: a pattern of majority rule, a concept and practice of free enterprise, individual home ownership, a citizens' militia, Thanksgiving, typical American dishes, and new remedies and drugs from American herbs; the starting of American fishing, saltmaking, fur trading, lumbering, and shipbuilding. In Plymouth was begun the necessary adjustment of Europeans to the demands and opportunities of the new continent.

III. Rhode Island: Cradle of Liberty

THE EXODUS FROM England continued, not merely Puritans and Pilgrims, but others seeking broader economic opportunities or political freedom.

In June, the year following the Plymouth Rock landing, a Captain Wolcott came over with twenty proprietors, many indentured servants, and ample supplies to start a successful plantation near the southwest corner of Boston Harbor at what was called Mount Wollaston, later Quincy.

The feeling of independence was strong, and when Wolcott began selling off indentured servants to Virginia, the colony was seized by settler Thomas Morton, who had been a lawyer at Clifford's Inn in London. He renamed the place "Merry Mount," freed all the servants, and with them set up a successful joint trading enterprise. The gay, lax conduct at Merry Mount so grated on the more Puritan Plymouth settlers and others coming to the Boston Bay area that some years later Morton was seized to prevent his colony from becoming a refuge for runaway servants. He was charged with harboring immoral elements and selling guns to the Indians. His successful beaver trading was a thorn in the flesh of all the other settlements, and he was accused of adhering to the Book of Common Prayer and high-church practices. He was forced to go back to England. Shortly he returned as a secretary to Isaac Allerton, boldly living in the latter's house in Plymouth. He was thrown out of the town and went back to his old Merry Mount haunts.

In 1624 a group, the Dorchester Company, settled Gloucester on Cape Ann, an enterprise that turned out badly. Those who stuck it out, led by Roger Conant, moved on to Salem. Other groups settled north of Plymouth and around Boston Bay. In 1628 John Endecott took a large group to Salem and acted as governor for the New England Company, with general jurisdiction in the Massachusetts area. He had a number of set-tos with Morton.

The most determined settlement was made by the new Massachusetts Bay Company, which succeeded the New England Company. By an oversight, no mention was made in the Royal Charter of where the annual company meetings should be held, and this made it possible to set up headquarters in the New World, with the result that company government was gradually transformed into independent commonwealth rule.

Eleven ships were outfitted at Southampton. The first four, including the flagship *Arbella*, bringing the first governor, John Winthrop, left England March 29, 1630. The main settlement was set up at Shawmut, or Boston, and successive contingents chose to settle at Charleston, Watertown, Roxbury, New Town (Cambridge), Mystic, and Dorchester.

On the whole these were families of more substance than those at Plymouth, and few had made an open break with the mother church. But one of the first official acts of John Winthrop and his magistrates was to seize Thomas Morton a second time, burn his house, and banish him from the New World.

Among the first comers to Boston was Reverend Roger Williams. In England he had taken no open stand against the Church and its distasteful conformity oaths, but the doors of advancement were closed to any with his ideas, and he decided to emigrate to the New World as the lesser evil. He left England reluctantly, with great sorrow, only because, as he wrote, he was "pursued" out of the land by Bishop Laud, for he could "not accept the national church or ceremonies beyond God's will." It was "bitter as death," when he rode "Windsor way" that year of 1630, to take ship at Bristol.

But a great load of tribulation was lifted from him. In Boston, among friends and sympathizers, he felt the freedom and challenge of this wide-open land where life could be remolded nearer to the soul's desire. As assistant at the Boston church, he labored in the spirit of the Psalms: "I am my beloved's and my beloved is mine; he feedeth among the lilies." He worked to convert the Indians and was consumed with curiosity about the language and customs of these simple "Children of God." He won their full confidence.

All too soon, he found that his ministerial associates had little of his all-embracing humanitarianism. The new leaders were intense, dogmatic men with no comprehension of religious tolerance. The minds of men were not made free by the mere act of crossing a great ocean—quite the contrary. Deprived of familiar personal supports of society and half-frightened by the demands of the new environment, if anything their minds grew more rigid and intolerant. Authority became even more inflexible after the arrival of arbitrary Reverend John Cotton, who was head of the Boston church. The lilies soon became gilded images in high places, and Williams's eager glow faded away. Soon, Roger discovered, independence of opinion had less chance in small, tightly knit Boston than in England, and punishments were equally severe.

The charter, he made bold to remark at a time when men's tongues were already hushed by fear of authority, gave too much power to the magistrates, the council chosen by the representatives of the landed proprietors, and that power was being abused. Among other things, they rewarded themselves with large tracts of land. Though the people had come for freedom and new opportunities, the tight little theocracy that took over control, resting on a tiny minority of church-member landholders (a charter violation that persisted until 1664), had unabridged power in all moral, spiritual, political, and economic matters and could override the representatives of the restricted number of voters.

The magistrates' power was somewhat modified in 1641 by Nathaniel Ward's Code of Laws, the *Body of Liberties*; and in 1644, though suffrage remained restricted to a few settlers, a bicameral legislative system, with very restricted rights, was set up. But all Massachusetts, dictated to by Boston, was to remain a hidebound "Bible Commonwealth" until the final terrorism of the witchcraft trials at the end of the century caused a general revulsion and brought about needed reforms.

Williams also criticized the Church. It was still "implicitly national," with the same old "abomination of worship," its disciplines, as in England, enforced by the constables and the whipping post.

With growing conviction and courage, he moved toward open opposition to the Massachusetts regime, already meting out frightful physical punishments. After some years, he was haled before the Magistrates' Court for "fallacious opinions" and refusal to conform.

2

Roger Williams was born in London about 1600, son of James, a merchant tailor, and Alice Pemberton, of the lesser landed gentry of St. Albans. Very early he heard "the call of Christ" and for twenty years was "persecuted in and out" of his father's house.

The famous jurist, Sir Edward Coke, noticed young Roger practicing shorthand by taking down excerpts from the sermon at St. Sepulchre Church and got him admitted to Charterhouse School. Roger's studious habits won him a "gentleman's" scholarship at Cambridge, and he registered at Pembroke Hall on June 29, 1623.

By then, the university, ceding ground to the rising merchant class, had widened its curriculum beyond church law and medieval disputation to include the classics, geography, and history. Even so, its studies, which John Milton called "sowthistles and brambles," scarcely matched the grandeur of the age of Bacon and Descartes. Roger bemoaned that they were limited to the "old Seed-pots of all Pietie" and that professors trimmed their "faces and colour to the Prince's eye and Palate."

By imposing an oath of conformity, heresy hunters at Cambridge sought to smell out church reformers in order to throw them into jail and mutilate them. Men with independent religious beliefs were provoked to rebellion or reduced to hypocrisy. Many people began fleeing to the Low Countries or the New World.

Williams was obliged to swear that he believed in the King's supremacy in spiritual matters and that he accepted the Book of Common Prayer and the Thirty-seven Articles of Faith as God's inspired word. He conformed with a wry grace and took his baccalaureate. He studied two years more but never completed work for a higher degree because of the "Popery of Laud," which with ever greater ferocity was reducing teachers and students to timid taciturnity.

Unwilling to swear falsely again, Williams took a post at Otes as private chaplain in the household of young Sir William Masham, a member of Parliament and unsympathetic to Laud.

He fell in love with whimsical Jane Whalley, protégée of Lady Judith Barrington of the neighboring manor. Jane was a sister of Edward Whalley, the judge who later fled to the New World charged with attempted regicide. Lady Barrington frowned on Williams's suit, and he had to bow to her decision with "resignation." As a minister of the gospel, however, he tried to save her soul, "choked with worldliness," by informing her that the poor were as much God's handiwork as the rich, that her candle was "twinkling" and "her glass" was "run." Lady Barrington forbade him to set foot in her house.

He dared not accept a more lucrative post, for his deep convictions would soon provoke punishments by the Church and the authorities. Troubled by his break with the powerful Barringtons, his loss of Jane, and the persecution that threatened him, he was stricken seriously ill.

After his health improved, he married Mary Brainard, a lady's maid. Once the presumptuous young cleric had found his proper level, Lady Barrington became gracious again.

He began to consider emigrating to America and attended a meeting at the Earl of Lincoln's house of persons interested in the Massachusetts Bay enterprise: John Winthrop, going as governor, and Thomas Hooker and John Cotton, renowned for their daring sermons.

Cotton, from Boston in Lincolnshire, a thoroughgoing Calvinist who merely wished to substitute his own harsh intolerance for that of Laud, found Roger's arguments in favor of religious freedom "sandie." Later, Williams remarked humorously, Cotton was to find them not sandy but "rockie."

3

The "Rock" soon disturbed the Boston hierarchy with his stanch ideas of democracy in Church and State. Tension mounted. Williams hearkened to the Book of Corinthians: "Wherefore come out from among them, and be ye separate ... and touch not the unclean thing." He took a position at the more liberal Salem church. Governor Winthrop protested to Salem for having hired him "without advising the Council."

Williams then went for two years as an assistant to the Plymouth church, outside Massachusetts' jurisdiction, where Separatist ideas were stronger. He continued to work with the Indians and became a close friend of the leading sachems. But when he criticized Bradford, Standish, and others for appropriating Indian lands without compensation, the atmosphere grew chilly, so he went back to Salem, as full pastor this time, once more against the wishes of the Boston authorities.

His smoldering differences with Cotton and Winthrop broke into open flame when they attempted to impose a "Resident's Oath." Williams came out boldly against it.

By this oath every settler was obliged to swear to submit without question to the authority of the magistrates or suffer immediate banishment. This abject civil and religious conformity meant the suppression of all free inquiry. The Resident's Oath cut two ways: against those who wished to adhere to Anglican ritual and also against those seeking Congregational independence. Ironically—as banished Thomas Morton had perceived and stated—the oath was a form of sedition against the Crown and the High Church. In the other direction, it was an aggression against every free-minded settler and against the mind and spirit of man.

In the case of Anglican sympathizers, since no open break had occurred with Laud's church, the issue of nonconformity to local religious practices that did not correspond to those in England was rarely raised; they were accused of "moral turpitude," "abuse of the Indians," or property violations. But the local authorities used the full power of the established church, whose ritual they themselves did not follow, to suppress those who advocated church democracy, variants of the creed, Separatism, or freedom of conscience.

The oath now put all such parties, Anglican and Separatist, on the spot. Williams argued that the oath mixed the things of Caesar with those of Christ. "Do not take the name of thy God in vain" by calling on him to "witness the oaths of nonbelievers." This was back-handed advocacy of religious freedom. Williams considered it "an abomination" to invoke God's name in swearing allegiance to any earthly government by "fallible" men. All human rule was but "a drop in the bucket" of the "eternal purpose." The oath, an unholy effort to buttress the privileged position of the magistrates and the clergy, was an act of worship being used for unworthy political ends. This was a mockery of religion, a defilement of God.

The purpose was to establish another intolerant and exclusive "national church." The State, Roger contended, had no right to interfere with religion except to safeguard every man's right to choose and practice the religion of his conscience. The imposing of "uniform" church discipline by police punishment was contrary to Congregational freedom. It was contrary to the Christian faith.

Early in 1634 he was summoned before the court and, according to Winthrop, clearly "confuted." This meant he had to make a humiliating confession of error or be punished.

4

The leaders who purged Williams were honest, self-right-
eous men who believed that they alone knew God's will, that
all else was sinful and heretical. This mania for absolute
conformity made them jealous of the slightest divergence in
religious or political opinions. The flimsiest accusation by a
pious or malevolent neighbor might result in a public flogging,
ear-cropping, tongue-slitting, and banishment. In performing
such cruelties, the authorities were merely enforcing "liberty"
and carrying out "God's will" with zealous rectitude.

Their arbitrary cruelty was the product not merely of rigid
convictions, but of deep fears. They were in perpetual terror
lest their iron-fisted rule be overthrown by Royal decree.
Greedy private interests, such as powerful Sir Ferdinando
Gorges, with strong court backing and the sympathy of Bishop
Laud, were trying to set aside the Massachusetts government.
They spread outrageous tales regarding the deviations and sinful practices of the Massachusetts churches. Thomas Morton
was busy night and day bringing charges against the colonies
before the Privy Council. He had written and circulated a
brilliant and witty book about the New World and his own
experiences with the "Saints." He, too, poured into the ears of
high prelates and the British authorities tales of laxness in
ritual, lay preaching, civil marriages. To soften such attacks,
the Boston magistrates ruthlessly squelched all who sought
religious liberty. They passed the British pressure right down
the line. Any rational thought was considered dangerous to
the survival of the Boston theocracy, and free spirits like Williams were offered up on the altar of appeasement to the
Crown and to Bishop Laud.

The fears that produced such spiritual and corporal cruelty
had even deeper elementary causes. The Massachusetts newcomers were uprooted men facing a dangerous new environment they could not comprehend or love. They feared the
Indians. They feared the Dutch and French. Above all, they

feared the wilderness—its hidden terrors, its power to wean men away from obedience—and they set up arbitrary regulations to block interior settlement. Conditioned to life in a tight little island, they found the vast new continent a colossal nightmare, peopled with monsters. To make the Boston area into another tight little island, they imposed artificial uniformity, like children fearfully drawing the curtains to keep out the dark. They were not able to appreciate or develop the great new empire within their grasp. Their faces were set backward, away from national destiny.

"We must be knit together in this work as one man," wrote Winthrop pompously in his *Model of Christian Charity*. They also called on their Lord for help. Any affront to Him menaced their safety, might bring down on their heads not only Indians and witches but the British Privy Council. Since, as Williams put it, "they could hardly believe God would suffer Mr. Cotton to err," an affront to Cotton became an affront to God. They did not wait for God to do the punishing. Loyalty was confused with abject obedience and mental abdication. Men of ability were crushed or driven out. The harshness the authorities exercised merely created worse situations, which seemed to justify and require even more harshness, though they themselves had created the situations. The faith of the "Saints" became rigid and brittle, an armor, a juggernaut, not a creative way of life.

The more bigotry and cruelty they exercised, the more cloudy their judgment became. Their fears became tinged with ugly superstition. Even brilliant, austere John Cotton, like the Mathers who succeeded him in power, sank to a vulgar, old-wives'-tale kind of gullibility about chimney noises, monstrous births, and devil-thrown stones in the dark. It was a short step to believing in satanic witches.

Such ignorance did violence to the spirit of the new land, the American earth, its amplitude and opportunities. This bitter ritual of fear and selfish power was no sacrament of water and corn; it did not permit the people to develop the wealth or find fresh hope in this new realm. This vast, generous New World with its magnificent resources called not for narrow dogma but for free enterprise and free men. Boston's rigid insularity could not match the grandeur of the continent or command its treasures. The land could not grow great so long as the magistrates and ecclesiastics were able to hold the minds and bodies of men in bondage. Only free spirits could tackle the wilderness, brave spirits, hopeful spirits. For the time being, the world of freedom, the world of the future, was with those who were driven out or could escape to the frontier, learn its ways, and thereby become Americans.

5

In July, 1635, Williams was again summoned before the magistrates and all the ministers. How, they demanded, if the magistrates were not permitted to "intermeddle" and enforce religious obedience, could the Church avoid running into "heresy, apostasy and tyranny"? Williams's beliefs would destroy both religion and authority. If he did not reconsider, punishment would be imposed at the next General Court. As an added warning, the court refused to grant Salem—which had shown "great contempt of authority" by refusing to dismiss him—additional land needed at Marblehead Neck.

The Salem church called upon "all the Visible Saints" in the other churches "to admonish the Magistrates" for their "heinous sin." This democratic appeal to the constituency did not get far. The magistrates and the preachers, saying the people were "weak, giddy and rash," persuaded the church elders to pocket the Salem communications.

Williams and the Salem elders protested against such highhandedness. Their communications belonged to the whole church, not the officers. The "wishes of the Lord Jesus" were not revealed "to one or all the elders, but to the whole Body met together in His name." The true way of the church was to discuss matters "openly in the sight of God."

The ministers warned that those who "corrupted" the

church would be struck down by the magistrates. Under the strain Williams's health failed. "It pleased the Lord," said Cotton, "to stop his mouth by a sodaine [sudden] illness." It was a crucial moment, when Williams needed to rally his congregation. The magistrates unseated the Salem delegates until the town recanted.

John Endecott, the first to settle under the original charter, came roaring to Boston to protest. He was jailed and at once ate humble pie. His retreat turned the tide in favor of the magistrates. Williams's support seeped away in the sands of timidity and lethargy.

He fought on. Unable to accept "Anti-Christ," he called on his congregation to secede from the spiritual jurisdiction of the Massachusetts churches. But the majority wavered, and Salem slid down the greased ruts of orthodoxy—on down to the gross witchcraft superstition.

Under the stress of controversy, Williams's philosophy developed to embrace a political and economic system ample for the work, dignity, and spirit of man. The authorities, though undeviating, were confused by this bright-winged, stormy eagle whose keen thought and brilliant phrases beat about their heads with such vivid imagery and bold metaphors. Though his logic could not pierce their closed minds, they were perplexed—as men misusing power usually are—as to why a superior intelligence should risk dire punishment when, by conforming, his hands would be heaped with rewards.

With the fading of Salem's support, they grew confident, and Williams had to face the extraordinary court session of October 8, 1635, unaided. In true Inquisition style, his whole past was raked over. His services to the Lord were ignored, but every phrase he had ever uttered that could be construed as critical of the Charter, the magistrates, or the church was hauled forth. Though confronted by fanatics who wielded all the power, he stoutly demanded a free church in a free state. He was answered with niggling biblical quotations.

The court offered him a month more to recant. He declined

this last-minute cat-and-mouse show of grace, which merely sharpened the claws of injustice. Governor John Haynes, who had succeeded Winthrop, handed down the sentence of banishment for Williams's "divers newe and dangerous opinions."

6

Having no mind to be sent from the tyranny of Boston back to the tyranny of Laud, Williams, by agreeing not to go abroad "to draw others to his opinion," secured a stay of banishment till spring because he was ill and Mary was expecting a second child.

But people flocked to his home, and many withdrew from the Salem church. In January the angry magistrates ordered his immediate deportation. "His corrupt imagination," said John Cotton, "provoked the Magistrates rather than to breed a winter's spiritual plague in the Countrey to put upon him a winter's journey out of the Countrey."

Suave Governor Winthrop, though during his tenure he had imposed all the cruel punishments demanded by the men of God, was not without generous human instincts. Secretly he advised Williams to head for Narragansett Bay outside Massachusetts' jurisdiction. Publicly, though, he stated that Williams had persuaded twenty persons to set up a colony there whence "the infection could easily spread to these churches."

When the authorities went to Williams's home to arrest him, he was gone. He had plunged into the wilderness, carrying a little parched corn, as the Indians did, and battling "God's white legions"—the deep snow—fording icy streams and sleeping in wet clothes. "I was sorely tossed for one fourteen weeks in bitter winter season, not knowing what bread or bed did mean." At the winter quarters of Sachem Massasoit, whose friendship he had won at Plymouth, he was given shelter, food, and kindness "more Christian" than the Boston Saints had shown. But those months in "filthy smoke holes" and the cold and misery of that "sorrowful" winter flight from home, wife, and children, bit lifetime deep into his bones and heart and soul.

In early spring, with four of five others, he went to Narragansett Bay. More discontented families arrived. The great migration from the spiritual and political tyranny of Salem and Boston had begun. Three whole towns moved en masse to Connecticut. Other people fled into the New Hampshire and Maine wilderness.

Hardly had Williams and his friends put up houses, cleared the land, and planted crops, than the Plymouth authorities warned them to leave Plymouth territory. Everything had to be abandoned.

They crossed the Seekonk River in canoes to a towering hill at the junction of two small rivers. Land was purchased from Narragansett Sachem Canonicus for a basketful of beads. Williams called the plantation "New Providence" in thanks "for God's mercy . . . in distress." Mary came on with the two children. So was Rhode Island started.

Late though it was, the settlers procured corn, bean, pumpkin, and squash seeds from the Indians. To get tools and supplies, Williams mortgaged his Salem property. The building of a new settlement without resources cost his family years of "miseries, poverties, necessities, wants, debts and hardships." He was deeply touched when Governor Edward Winslow from Plymouth passed through and, observing that even food was lacking, pressed a gold coin into his hands.

7

Persecution in Salem continued. Its most useful families were moving out. But timid persons, especially those with small children, dreaded the wilderness as much as human persecution: the country was "sharp, the forest dense, the winter cold, the summer gnats ferocious, and the nights were hideous with howling wolves." Then the Pequot War, pro-

voked by Massachusetts, burst across the land, halting further
migration for the time being.

A marauding band of Long Island Indians crossed to Block
Island and killed John Oldham—"Mad Jack"—ousted from
Plymouth for his democratic ideas. Though the island was
outside Massachusetts' jurisdiction, John Endecott led an
armed force there and ruthlessly burned homes, cornfields,
and canoes. He demanded the delivery of the marauders, an
annual indemnity of 1,000 farthings of wampum, and twenty
children of head sachems as hostages. When these impossible
terms were refused, he razed a Pequot village on the mainland.

Williams protested against brutalities to innocent people.
Lion Gardiner, acting head of the new Saybrook colony at the
mouth of the Connecticut River, told Endecott severely, "You
come here to raise wasps about our ears, then you will take
wing and fly away."

Endecott's savagery left the whole valley aflame. Saybrook
and new upriver settlements were threatened with annihila-
tion. It was reported that the brother of the Saybrook minister
had been roasted alive; that at Wethersfield nine persons were
slaughtered. Two "maids" carried off had been rescued stark
naked.

Williams relayed to Winthrop these atrocity stories, which
he "hoped" were not true, ironically adding he did so because
the Governor had already made such "good use of poisoned
and lying newes . . . to waken the people." He also tried to
convince Massachusetts that his friends, the Narragansetts and
their good chief, Canonicus, were not involved in any punitive
acts. Only when the Pequots, already allied with the powerful
western Mohawks, made direct appeals to Canonicus for aid,
did the alarmed magistrates, fearing that even Boston might
be put to the torch, beg Williams to try to prevent the alliance.

Without telling Mary of the great danger, Roger at once
set forth alone across the bay in a "poor canoe . . . through a
strong wind with great seas" to Canonicus's lodge.

The Narragansetts were assembled in their ceremonial

robes, listening to the Pequot emissaries. The Pequots warned that if they were destroyed separately, the Narragansetts would then be exterminated. They outlined a hit-and-run strategy to wipe out crops, cattle, and houses until they could drive the weakened, hungry English out of the land forever.

Williams did not believe that his eloquent arguments saved the day, but rather that God had "stirred up the barbarian heart of Canonicus . . . to looke upon me as his son to the last gasp." Thanks to Williams, Canonicus's nephew, Sachem Minatonomu, journeyed to Boston with an impressive retinue to sign a treaty of alliance. Canonicus raised a strong allied force, which he paid for by a special wampum tax on his people.

By his diplomacy and friendship Williams, singlehanded, had restricted the war, gained a native ally, and saved much of New England from destruction. During the months that followed, he was stripped of food and resources by repeated entertainment of Canonicus and his men, but Massachusetts made no effort to reimburse him. Winthrop asked that the decree of banishment be lifted. But the magistrates, though they kept calling on Williams anxiously for more help, refused.

Massachusetts sought to shift the burden of the war it had provoked onto the other colonies, demanding money, supplies, and men. Rhode Island refused to join. Plymouth, though in no danger, reluctantly provided fifty men, with a tart reminder of the many affronts it had suffered from the arrogant Bay colony. Saybrook and Connecticut River settlements had to fight or be destroyed.

Williams sent word how to attack the main Pequot encampment, the Owl's Nest, on a hill in a swamp near the Mystic River, but asked that all women and children be spared.

The allies surprised the sleepers and set the place on fire. Half a thousand braves and their women and children were burned alive, and as many more, who ran out, were slaughtered regardless of age or sex.

"God...," reported Connecticut Captain John Mason, "laughed at his Enemies and the Enemies of the People to Scorn, making them as a fiery Oven.... Thus did the Lord judge among the Heathen, filling the place with dead bodies." As more Pequots were killed or sent off as slaves, such Old Testament hosannas grew more joyous.

"Innocent blood cries at Connecticut," Williams wrote. "The English settlers" had "forgotten their pretences to King and State and all the world."

Throughout, the bloodiest fighting fell on Connecticut men and the Narragansetts, but the Massachusetts troops seized all prisoners and booty. War costs were paid by selling Indian men, women, and children into slavery in Boston and the West Indies.

Fearing perpetual slavery would be riveted on New England, Williams protested bitterly and relayed repeated complaints from Canonicus, who felt his people had been deprived of recouping their heavy outlays. Both urged that enemy prisoners be restored to their families to allay the alarm among friendly tribes at such ruthlessness.

But the Massachusetts Bay folk were too busy persecuting their own people, branding, splitting tongues, cropping ears, to act intelligently toward "heretics and savages." Plymouth and Rhode Island had found the way to live at peace with the Indians, but now New England was condemned to a century of war, some of which might have been avoided. Only Williams's repeated interventions over the years prevented more bloodshed. Had his advice been heeded, friendly King Philip would never have been driven into a war that wiped out much of New England and set back settlement for half a century. Throughout those many conflicts Rhode Island persistently followed a policy of friendship and was rarely harassed.

People kept coming to Rhode Island. By 1643 three more towns had been laid out: Portsmouth, Newport, and Warwick, each of them by people escaping from Massachusetts, led by Anne Hutchinson, William Coddington, and Samuel Gorton.

A new, freer pattern of life was created, a commonwealth of democracy, land equality, and religious tolerance. It was not a way of life that those long obedient to strict religious conformity and political absolutism could easily understand, and some years after Williams fled there, Winthrop wrote asking what he had gained by his new-found "practices."

What had he gained? Williams retorted. Many friends, esteem, independence, and great evidence of "God's love in time of tribulation."

He had gone forth as Abraham from among the Chaldeans, as Lot from among the Sodomites, as the Book of Corinthians had ordered, to escape "the filthiness" of such places.

Williams believed that Winthrop had written, not as a "Pharisee," but as a friendly physician; however, the Massachusetts folk were the sick ones. Winthrop still wore "a poisoned shirt on his back," still followed "false idols . . . unable to abstract" himself "from the dunghill of this earth."

In Providence, Williams had put into practice his advanced ideas of religious, political, and economic freedom, the abolition of all class barriers, concepts a hundred years and more ahead of his contemporaries. He rolled back the medieval mists to become the world's first great apostle of the full-fledged rights of man in *all* human undertakings.

No man could be enslaved. No indentured servants were permitted, and—like Morton's settlement—Providence sheltered refugees and was similarly hated by the elite of the other colonies.

The town meeting, with all having equal voice, reigned supreme. Elections were frequent. Officials could be recalled. Proposed laws could be introduced by any individual. No control was exercised over religious matters. Freedom and diversity, not orthodoxy and compulsion, were the slogans. Thus, as Williams phrased it, was "the Grand Cause of Truth and Freedom of Conscience" put into effect.

Not land monopoly, but "liberty and equality" in both

"land and government" were the goals for all comers, who were admitted as quickly as possible to full political rights.

Thus more than a century before the great French agrarian thinkers, the Physiocrats, more than a century before Thomas Jefferson and Thomas Paine, Williams not only set forth their economic ideas but tried to put them into practice.

His advanced political concepts rejected the theory of the divine right of kings and adopted the theory that the State was a voluntary compact, born of necessity to prevent big fishes from eating little fishes. Government was merely the repository of the State, the laws of Nature, and the social will.

He rejected the ideas of Hobbes and Locke that an original compact of government had been made in earlier times between the elite and the many that had set up an eternal, inviolate system never to be altered. There was no such thing, as Burke later argued, as an irrevocable contract, no sacred, everlastingly fixed law or authority. Government had to be flexible, continuously readjusting to necessary changes, constantly reflecting the wishes of its citizens.

He stated it bluntly: The people "may erect and establish what forme of government seemes to them most meete for their civil condition." Government had to accept the equality of all its subjects and could always be changed at the will of the people. Every magistrate, as he noted in his *Bloody Tenet Yet More Bloody*, exceeded his authority the minute he intermeddled "with that which cannot be given him as coming from the people." Compromise, arbitration, reconciliation, not force, should be the true instruments of government. The power of the State was no greater and should endure no longer than its equal citizens desired.

From this general democratic thesis—in itself a new and daring doctrine in the world—Williams moved on to create in Rhode Island the necessary governmental machinery to make such a free commonwealth possible. He marked out clearly the proper spheres of church and state, of local and federated government, and he recognized that the individual had certain inalienable rights over and beyond all government.

His ideas were broad, not rigidly mechanistic. He saw society as a whole, in every phase of human activity, and man's proper part therein.

This should be a universal pattern. No government should war against another government because of differences in religion or in the nature of the State. Williams was an apostle of the modern nationalism just coming into being, and he held to the doctrine of inviolate national sovereignty, which nations were to come to guard so jealously for themselves but violate for all others. Williams saw beyond such narrow selfishness, that the system of national sovereignty would not work, would bring only war and tribulation, if such violations were countenanced. He saw all relations made strong by respect and tolerance. Like St. Francis, who sought to stop the bloody Crusades, and who believed that the true mission of Christianity was not to kill heretics but to convert them, Williams argued that heretics had a right to their own religion and customs. All people did. God's will, as he repeatedly reminded the Massachusetts authorities, could not be imposed by the sword. That was to destroy God's will, and those who attempted to impose religion merely perished by the sword and destroyed their own religion.

Rhode Island became America's first truly democratic frontier, and its influence spread gradually to leaven all New England, to bring new liberties to the whole area, and on across the country to shape future government and the system of homesteading.

Thus did the seed planted at Plymouth ripen at Providence. Here in Rhode Island, the majority rule established by the Mayflower Compact was widened to include all citizens, and amended to protect the rights of all minorities. Thus defined, free majority rule was made an effective instrument of democratic government, civil liberties, and all basic human rights.

8

Religious tolerance, for which Williams is mostly remembered, was merely one of his goals, one of the desirable end
products of a free social system. Schoolchildren have long been
taught that America's first law of religious freedom was the
Maryland Toleration Act of 1649. But the Maryland statute
merely permitted Anglican churches alongside existing
Catholic churches. In the same act sedition was punishable by
boring the tongue, slitting the nose, branding with a hot iron,
cutting off hands, and nailing the ears to the pillory.

Years before this, Williams laid down and put into practice
twelve basic tenets for religious tolerance—the first and last
word on the subject—and from the start Rhode Island, in
those early years of persecution and book burning, allowed
full freedom of thought and expression. It was one of the few
communities on earth without an established church from the
day of its founding, where any sect could put up a temple, and
tolerance was practiced throughout and was embodied in the
1644 charter. Thus Rhode Island blazed the way for complete
religious freedom in all America.

Quakers and Baptists were being executed in Massachusetts.
In New Hampshire two Quaker girls, tied to the rear of an
oxcart, were whipped naked through the snow from village to
village. Excessive piety had reached its darkest depths of sex
sadism. But in Providence, the abhorred Pennsylvania sect
worshiped freely; there Roger Williams debated with them
publicly in his pulpit and in theirs on the true meaning of
Christianity.

Rhode Island also provided the first New England asylum
for persecuted Jews. A boatload of Brazilian refugees, refused
admittance to New Amsterdam, were invited to Newport.
There they built the first synagogue in the country. With new
industries and trade, they soon transformed the town into one
of the more prosperous ports in the colonies. Presently Con-

necticut also gave asylum to the Jews. Early Colchester was largely settled by them.

The desire for freedom of religion and of thought could not be choked back even in Massachusetts. Anne Hutchinson, a fervent lay preacher, and her brother-in-law, John Wheelwright, roused the conscience of the entire colony and shook the hierarchy. The ferment nearly developed into a true enlightenment. But Winthrop rigged the elections against the new elements, and the two apostles were seized, tried by the General Court, excommunicated by the church, and banished. Wheelwright fled to the New Hampshire wilderness, where, with other refugees, he founded Exeter, which adopted the Mayflower Compact. When Massachusetts' long arm reached out to annex New Hampshire towns, he had to flee to Maine.

Anne Hutchinson, with her husband, children, and her sister Mary Dyer, fled through the forests to Rhode Island, where, with another exile, William Coddington, she founded Pocasset, or Portsmouth. There she established her own church, based on "Antinomianism," which emphasized "grace" rather than "works," personal revelation rather than authority.

John Cotton and other ministers told their congregations horrible falsehoods about the two sisters. Struck by "God's disfavor," they had given "unsavory birth" to "deformed monsters" without heads, instead a "horn like a beast; scales or rough skin, like a fish . . . leggs and claws like a fowl, and in other respects as a woman child." Pulpit demagogy reached its apogee.

At Williams, Cotton hurled more silly epithets: "evill worker . . . windy fancies . . . offensive and disturbant doctrines . . . delivered up to Satan." Williams "cast forth firebrands and arrows and mortall things." More to the point, Cotton said sarcastically that Williams was such a "transcendent light" he "putteth out all the lights of the world besides." That was because other lights were pale, not because Williams snuffed them out as Cotton did.

The Boston leaders really feared that the fire of Williams's ideas would burn up their snug Presbyterian fields. A windmill could be turned so fast that the heated grinding stones would burn it up, and Cotton noted that "a whole country in America" was likely to be set on fire "by the rapid motion of a windmill in the head of one particular man."

Nothing so upset the Massachusetts Saints as the mushrooming of new Rhode Island sects: Brownism, Anabaptism, Antinomianism, Baptism, Seekerism, Familism, Libertinism, Quakerism, "blasphemous sects . . . depthless ditches that blinde guides lead to." Rhode Island was "a mad house."

The first Baptist church in America was founded there in 1637, with Williams's encouragement, by Catherine Scott, sister of Anne Hutchinson, and Ezekiel Holloman. Williams found Baptism more in line with the New Testament and liberty of conscience. The Baptists elected all officers by vote of the entire congregation; each church had full autonomy.

But by midsummer Williams found the Baptists too "narrow" and became a Seeker, the most individualist of all Separatist sects. John Cotton at once branded him "a haberdasher of small questions."

The reverse was true. Williams, with unflagging zeal, was following the Protestant premise of rationalism to logical conclusions. He became the quintessence of Protestant individualism and the glory of personal revelation. He had found what William Ellery Channing rediscovered two centuries later: the idea of free individual conscience and the basic worth of all human beings regardless of rank or estate, whether Jew or gentile, black or white, ideas that, even at the later date, astonished and frightened New England. Williams became the world's first outstanding "Unitarian" and "Perfectionist" two centuries before the marching banners of those ideas were carried in excited processions across New England hills.

Williams was left, finally, with a devout personal belief in the unprovable mystery. He became basically a "Transcendentalist" in the Rhode Island wilderness long before Emerson and the Concord School. He had discovered, not a Calvinist God of wrath and punishment, but the indwelling God of love, in all material and living things. Here, he was retracing the footsteps of Jesus of Nazareth and St. Francis, but he carried their concepts of brotherhood over into all practical affairs. The meanest as well as the highest were equal, not merely before God's throne but on the broad steps of the State House and the temples of justice.

9

The new colony was not without internal problems. Freedom permitted those who hated freedom to flourish. To suppress such people, however unpalatable, Williams saw with more wisdom than we have today, would mean an abandonment of his principles and eventual loss of freedom for all. He met all such critics in the open lists of argument and reason.

In time, new towns, which sprang up as a result of refugees from Massachusetts' persecutions, were not so sympathetic with his ideas of complete freedom or his attempt to set up a federated government. But by patient reasoning, constant conferences, fair compromises—finally by voluntary arbitration —he worked out a going system. He insisted upon home rule: full rights for each town and for those he opposed.

There were also a few greedy and godless men, such as sour William Arnold and his son Benedict. Both had been thrown out of Massachusetts, not for their beliefs but for their crimes, and they had lawlessness deep in their veins, as did a later flamboyant descendant. They destroyed or altered part of the original Indian title of Providence in order to steal Pawtucket.

The Boston magistrates had no compunction in using such unsavory elements to harass Williams and cause trouble among the Indian tribes, and they used the pretended rights of the Arnolds as an excuse to intervene by force in various Rhode Island communities. In 1642 Governor Richard Bellingham of Massachusetts proposed that Plymouth join hands

in wholly suppressing Williams's settlement. The following
year negotiations were started with the other colonies—Plymouth, Connecticut, and New Haven—to form a confederation to encircle Rhode Island.

To offset such schemes, Williams hurried to England to try
to get an independent charter. The Long Parliament, dominated by the Puritans, was now fighting King Charles tooth
and nail, and Williams's old friends from Otes—the Barringtons, Mashams, and others—were now powerful in London
affairs. The High Church party had fallen, and hated Bishop
Laud had been impeached and lodged in the Tower.

Unable to go through Boston, Williams sailed from New
Amsterdam, stopping there long enough to patch up differ-
ences between the Dutch and Indians and prevent a war.
During the voyage he worked on *The Key to the Indian
Languages of America*, an account of the customs, lore, and
languages of New England Indians, and published it on his
arrival in England. One of his first copies was dedicated to
Lady Barrington.

"Nature," Williams declared in his book, "knows no difference between Europeans and Indians." As in Acts, 17, God
has made "one blood of all mankind":

Boast not proud English of thy Birth and Blood
    Thy brother Indian is by birth as Good.

Morally, he felt, the Indians were in many ways superior.
He repeated earlier observations by Thomas Morton that
there were no beggars or fatherless children such as swarmed
the streets of civilized London. He told of Indian skills and
woodcraft, their clever manipulation of boats, how neighbors
worked together to plant the fields, "a very loving sociable way
to dispatch it."

Williams was hailed as "the true missionary of the Indians,"
and his book aroused great interest in the New World peoples
at a time when the birth of freedom for the Separatist sects
had created a new atmosphere of investigation and discussion,
a new joy in the pursuit of knowledge. The country, sodden

so long under the terrorism of Laud, was seething with new ideas and hopes.

But the old order did not die easily. Open civil war had begun between the Crown and the Puritan Parliament, the struggle between the Cavaliers and the Roundheads. Liberator John Hampden had just been killed in one of the first battles. King Charles, who had raised forces in the north, was trying to recapture London and liberate Laud. All coal was cut off from the city, and Williams immediately took over the task of gathering wood for the shivering poor.

He also jumped into the polemical fray with spirited and biting tracts—"blasts from my despised ram's horn"—in support of full religious and political freedom. They were flung off at white heat between his wood-gathering expeditions and his preaching for the Seekers. Brilliant, rich with vivid metaphors yet simple and direct, they presented Williams's whole philosophy of government, society, and religion in terms of the current conflict. He struck out not only at the old tyranny of Laud but at the arbitrary Scotch Presbyterians and the Massachusetts distortions of Congregationalism. One church, he insisted, would never fit every conscience. Religious monopoly, backed by the State and its police, was bound to result "in a world of hypocrites" and "a wracking and tormenting of soules."

The Massachusetts authoritarians fought back. John Winthrop issued another bitter attack on Anne Hutchinson, the "Familists," and the "Libertines." John Cotton defended coercive orthodoxy in *A Letter of Mr. John Cotton to Mr. Williams*. It was "butchery to heal every sore in a member with no other medicine than absission from the body."

Williams retorted that infants were often saved by separation from a diseased mother. New England, he noted, had grown old while Old England was growing younger.

Massachusetts did not restrict itself to polemics. In connivance with "old malicious Arnold," it divided the Indians by alliances against the Narragansetts, and troops moved into

Rhode Island to destroy the homes of the Gortonist extremists at Shawmut. The men were sent in irons to Boston, the women and children left without shelter in the winter wilderness.

By May, 1644, Massachusetts successfully completed its plan for an armed defensive alliance with Plymouth, New Haven, and Connecticut—the United Colonies of New England—to have jurisdiction over interstate quarrels, fugitive servants and criminals, and Indian affairs, and to protect the area against the French, Dutch, and Indians. Except for an early short-lived alliance promoted by Plymouth to suppress Thomas Morton and the Merry Mounters, it was the first effort to unite the colonies. Massachusetts, however, hoped to make it into a "Holy Alliance" it could manipulate to isolate and destroy "Rogues' Island." All trade and travel were cut off with Williams's colony; an iron curtain was rung down.

Williams's answer—and it came in the nick of time—was the Rhode Island charter, secured March 24, 1644, on the eve of Cromwell's first important victory against the King at Marston Manor. The charter at once changed Williams's settlement from a "wilderness no-man's land" into a recognized colonial entity and thereby checked Massachusetts' armed raids and territorial ambitions. Williams had not wished to bring overseas England into New World controversies; he had feared that it might work against his broad concepts of government. But fortunately the new charter embodied all his ideas from beginning to end. As an instrument of free self-rule, it went well beyond Commonwealth government. Rhode Island was granted full power to rule itself by "any forme" of civil government selected "by voluntary consent of all or the greater Part" of the inhabitants, and there was no state jurisdiction over ecclesiastical affairs.

Before returning to the New World, in another broadside pamphlet Williams delivered one more powerful blast at the authoritarians from his despised ram's horn. In it, he focused his whole philosophy of free religion and free government into a white-hot weapon. It was strong meat, and its tidings spread fast among the people and Cromwell's army. Parliament, still dominated by the Presbyterians, though about to be taken over by the Separatists, was so alarmed it ordered his pamphlet burned.

Williams rushed straight into the dragon's mouth. With his brother and his printer, George Dexter, whom he had converted to the Seekers, he landed in Boston without permission, September 17, 1644, and boldly demanded safe-conduct. He backed this up with a letter signed by the prominent leaders of Lords and Commons, condemning his persecution at the hands of the New World prelates and authorities and lauding his efforts with the Indians, "the like whereof we have not seen extant from any part of America."

Some of the magistrates were clamoring that the Gortonists seized in Shawmut, still in jail in Boston, be put to death, but they did not dare touch a person with such powerful influence in the new English government and grudgingly gave consent "this once" for Williams to pass through Massachusetts territory.

He was glad to get out of Boston. The sermons he heard there were "meat only to be digested by an ostrich," the general atmosphere more hateful than ever. The Boston chill was quickly dissipated by the rousing welcome in Providence. A flotilla of decorated canoes escorted him across the Seekonk River, the same crossing he had made ten years earlier when fleeing into exile. People were "delirious with joy" at his success in England, and he was elected "Chief Officer" under the new charter.

For the next thirty years he continued to serve the colony, as governor, to settle controversies and execute new projects.

In 1654, worried by the intolerance of the new Cromwell Protectorate, he wrote Sir Henry Vane in London that Rhode Island was "sweet." "We have long drunk of the cup of as great liberties as any people ever can hear of under the whole heaven." Here we are free "from the iron yolk of wolfish bishops." We have been saved from "the streams of blood of religious conflict" that had flowed in England. We are free also of "the new chains of Presbyterian tyrants and the so-called Godly Magistrates." We have forgotten the meaning of the word tithes, and there are many other special privileges, "ingredients of our sweet cup."

10

Until his death in 1683, Williams fought on steadily, unremittingly, for his ideas of freedom in and out of Rhode Island. He constantly protested to Massachusetts about rank injustice and cruelties. He was quick to denounce the treacherous assassination of betrayed Sachem Minatonomu, who had done so much for Massachusetts. He devoted his whole life to the cause of political and religious freedom.

As persecutions to the north became more bloody, he wrote in behalf of men and women of many sects. But slowly the witchcraft mania—final disintegration of a terrorized regime—was seeping in, creating mass hysteria, steadily building up to its dark bloody climax. Rhode Island answered by providing sanctuary for all supposed "witches" who could escape.

Nothing is more scorching than his letter to John Endecott, who had become governor and had thrown three prominent Rhode Island Baptists into jail. Endecott was "as the Tyrant" who put "an innocent man into a bears skin and caused him as a wild beast to be baited to death." His was "the common cry of Hunters or persecutors everywhere" whether "Turkish, Popish, Protestant, etc. This is the outcry of Pope and Prelates, and of the Scotch Presbyterians, who would fire all the world to be avenged of the sectarian Heretics, the blasphemous Heretics, the seducing Heretics. Ah remember," he warned the governor, "it is dangerous for the potsherds of the earth to fight with their dreadful potter.... The dreadful voice from the King of Kings, and Lord of Lords" rings out: "Endecott, Endecott, why huntest thou Me, Why imprisoneth thou Me, Why...so bloodily whippest, why wouldst thou hang and burn Me?" Rather than "hunt poor devils to torture," Endecott should "cry at the gates of Heaven" for light for his own soul and conscience. He should search, listen, pray, and "tremblingly" inquire as to the "holy pleasure" and "embrace moderation toward the Spirits and Consciences of all mankind." No one could maintain Christ "by the sword . . . and not fight against God at the same time."

Out of such spirit and such ideas was the free commonwealth of Rhode Island created. It kept alive the light of liberty in the early darkness of America. The one sanctuary for men of all faiths, it created and cherished basic American ideals until an awakened New England could rid itself of persecution and belief in witchcraft. That light shone far across the land to help create a free nation. All this we owe to Roger Williams more than to any other man of his day. He was the first original thinker of New England, the greatest, most brilliant, and most generous of all the Puritan immigrants.

He was cast out by the narrow-minded to dream his dream in the wilderness and there to give it life and strength and reality. Not until Emerson was New England to produce an emancipated mind and spirit of such stature. But Williams's concepts were far broader than Emerson's; he was a man of action as well as a thinker. Though a full century and more ahead of his time and of his contemporaries in Europe, he was able to put his ideas into actual operation, to prove that freedom was a workable doctrine, and thereby he made his philosophy and his religion, by word and deed, a living part of the American heritage.

IV. The Fundamental Orders

FOUR MONTHS after Roger Williams fled through the wilderness, Reverend Thomas Hooker led forth the Visible Saints of New Town, or Cambridge, to start a settlement on the Connecticut River. He was a New World Moses, leading the Chosen out from under the magistrates to the promised land of the rich Connecticut Valley, there to found a society of freedom and open a new frontier.

In the early morning light of May 31, 1636, the cavalcade lined up, more than a hundred men, women, and children, with horses, pack animals, oxcarts carrying worldly goods, tools, and house furnishings. Sheep, pigs, goats, fowls, and a hundred and sixty cattle were in the procession. Most people had to go on foot. Mrs. Hooker was ill and had to be carried on a horse litter.

Part of their food en route was provided by game and early berries, but provisions, seeds for planting—wheat, corn, pease, oats—had to be carried. Butter and cheese were taken along. The cattle, which had to be given time to graze, provided milk.

To get their equipment over faint Indian trails, across mountains, ravines, swamps, and through dense thickets, they had to fell trees, remove rocks, and build rafts for streams swollen by melting snow. Alert for attacks by Indians or wild animals, they found their way by compass, aided by information from previous explorers.

Spring was in full sway, the forests bursting with new foliage. Wild flowers were in bloom, the birds singing. Days were warmish, but nights still damp and chilly. Each day began and ended with prayer. During two Sundays, they camped all day to worship.

They reached Windsor on the Connecticut River, where

the Farmington River flowed in, a settlement established in 1634 as a trading post by Captain William Holmes from Plymouth. Two years later, contingents from Dorchester, Massachusetts, under Roger Ludlow, arrived and purchased the Plymouth rights. Ludlow, one of the finest, best-educated leaders ever to reach the New World, was a great admirer of Hooker.

After a joyous reunion, the Hooker party proceeded downstream for some seven miles to Fort Good Hope, put up three years before by the Dutch, who were cultivating twenty-five acres of river bottom.

Already encamped in the meadows north of a large side creek—Little River—were sixty New Town neighbors who had come on ahead the previous year under John Steele. They had survived the terrible winter chiefly because of the Indians, who had brought them food.

Five miles downstream was Wethersfield, where ten men under John Oldham (whose death on Block Island was to bring on the Pequot War) had put up cabins in 1634. Both Windsor and Wethersfield were enlarged during that summer of 1636 by the arrival of the entire congregations of Dorchester and Watertown. William Pynchon of Roxbury, a fur trader, led a large group to Springfield in the upper Connecticut Valley, where the Westfield and Chicopee Rivers flowed in—a magnificent site.

Such was the beginning of the westward movement of colonists that inaugurated the whole conquest of the continent to the far Pacific. These were the first settlers to move definitely inland from the coast and to become really part of the New World empire.

Springfield was in Massachusetts territory, but the down-river settlements were in "no-man's" land, a wilderness, and they planted themselves there without any Crown grant or patent. They duly purchased the land from the Indians, but under English law they had no valid or legal title whatever, so that when they faced their unfamiliar problem, much as did the folk who came on the *Mayflower,* and set up their "one publicke State or Commonwealth" embracing the three communities, they were *de facto* an independent sovereign state. They adopted the Indian name of the place where they settled, Connecticut (Quinatucket), which means "upon the long river," though some claim it means "the river of pines."

New Haven was similarly settled on the Quinnipiac in 1638, without legal title except land purchase from the Indians, and there another distinct autonomous colony was set up that by 1643 included a federated "general court" of Milford, Guilford, Stamford, Branford, and Southold, Long Island.

In all Connecticut, only Saybrook—a third independent colony, at the mouth of the Connecticut River, planted there in 1635—enjoyed formal authority from a company chartered by the Crown and headed by Lord Warwick. He made the specific grant to Lord Saye and Sele and Lord Brooke, a definite deed of conveyance. In 1644 all rights to it were sold to Connecticut by the acting head of the colony, though he had no such powers, but thereafter it came under the jurisdiction of the Connecticut General Court.

Not until 1662 did Governor John Winthrop, Jr., hasten to London to secure a charter because of a threatened cession of the area to New York. The grant he secured, which safeguarded all local and democratic rights, included New Haven, all of Rhode Island as far as Narragansett Bay, and all lands not yet settled as far as the Pacific Ocean. New Haven resisted absorption until 1665, and Rhode Island stubbornly held on to its territory, granted by prior charter. It almost led to war, but Roger Williams averted this by patient and firm negotiations.

But in 1635 the Connecticut River settlers were braving the little-known frontier. To face the untried wilderness with their wives and children, to leave Massachusetts so soon after the founding of the Bay Colonies, abandoning their new homes and freshly cleared fields that had cost them so much toil, betokened powerful motives and almost passionate determination.

The driving spirit of the four-pronged migration was Thomas Hooker, quiet, thoughtful, unassuming, but with such personal magnetism and eloquence that in a few years he had won the fervent loyalty of the ablest men of the colonies, numbers of whom went with him to settle Connecticut. He was an ardent Calvinist who "fastened the nail of terror deep" into the hearts of sinners. He had the knack of making pungent phrases and bright, startling metaphors. In his personal relations he was warm and kindly.

As a good Calvinist, and as required, he had sat with the other ministers who had passed judgment on Roger Williams's "heresies," but there is more than a hint that he was uneasy about the persecution and out of sympathy with the arbitrary methods of the local hierarchy. He believed strongly in free discussion and persuasion, not violence, force, and cruelty. He had already suffered from persecution in England and, even before Williams's banishment, found himself irked by Cotton, but though elbowroom for two such dominant personalities was not great, he had managed to avoid controversy, and he had sidestepped trouble with the magistrates, though there had been some protests by New Town and neighbor communities.

By this time, Hooker had learned caution from the bitter results of his own early independence and rebellion, which had obliged him to flee clandestinely to the Low Countries, finally to New England; now he planned, in his quiet way, to escape from Massachusetts with his entire flock.

Without stressing any religious or political issues, reasonably, persistently, he kept insisting to the magistrates, "Let my People go." Various pretexts were urged. New Town claimed it lacked sufficient land for its cattle and found fault with the generous additional tracts the magistrates offered. It was a patriotic duty, Hooker said, to occupy the Connecticut Valley before the Dutch appropriated it, and he added simply but earnestly that in any case his people had "a yearning to go."

Already sizable contingents had gone off without permission, and the magistrates, though several stonily opposed any migration to the end, finally decided that it would be better to control the movement, which could not be successfully checked, rather than lose all hold on the people. After much delay, with great reluctance, they authorized the New Town congregation and three others to go forth, provided they agreed to continue under Massachusetts law and authority. A special governing commission was set up for them.

And so, quietly, lawfully, Hooker and his congregation folded their tents and departed. It soon became evident, once they were outside the territorial jurisdiction of the Bay Colonies, that they had no intention of remaining under Massachusetts sovereignty. Though Hooker did not have the breadth of Roger Williams and little of his philosophical grandeur, beneath his espousal of rigid church doctrine and his conciliatory tact smoldered a real devotion to democracy, a belief in the collective will of the people.

2

Thomas Hooker was born in 1586 at Marfield, Leicester, one of a cluster of tiny villages in that lovely corner of England which worshiped jointly at the stately old gray St. Peter's on Tilton hilltop, with its "four bells and four moss-grown burial grounds." After the devastating Wars of the Roses, the four villages had left only forty-three thatched houses and the old Rose and Crown Inn that later became Cromwell's headquarters.

Hooker's father had come to Marfield as overseer of the Derby estate, and Thomas went to school in a market town twenty-five miles east. He won a scholarship to Emmanuel College, but it was so meager he had to register as a sizar (a student who earns his way) and wait on tables. Among his fellow students were John Cotton and John Wilson, the two iron-minded pastors who later took charge of the Boston church.

Hooker received his A.B. in 1608, the year the Scrooby congregation fled to Holland. In 1611, when he took his M.A. degree, King James dissolved the first Parliament, and religious controversy grew more bitter. Hooker, always troubled by religious meanings, once remarked, "I can compare to any man living for fears." He avoided disputation and lingered on at Cambridge as catechist and lecturer. His systematic essays on experimental religion proved popular without upsetting the Conservative faction. Though often turgid, his thought was logically organized, and his pungent phrasemaking delighted his hearers.

In 1616 he took a post in Surrey, sixteen miles from London's Parliament House, in a little chapel maintained by Francis Drake, at whose home he lived. Mrs. Drake was a remorseful hypochondriac, convinced she had committed unpardonable sin, but Hooker's religious consolations worked wonders, and she became so cheerful she soon died in "a fit of sudden extreme ravishing unsupportable joy beyond the strength of mortality to retain." Hooker married her maid, Susanna Pym, sister of John Pym, the great Parliamentary leader who later opposed King Charles.

Hooker moved on to the gray Gothic church of Chelmsford, Essex, a busy center thirty miles east of London. He preached market days and Sunday afternoons without ritual. Such "lecturers," popular with the masses but obnoxious to the High Church Party, were soon forbidden to discuss questions of the faith, and were bidden to explain only the Catechism, the Creed, and the Ten Commandments.

Hooker ignored these bare-bones restrictions, and auditors, "hungry for light," flocked from far and wide, even persons of quality. The Earl of Warwick's soul was pierced by the "powerful word of God in the mouth of this faithful Hooker ... a true conversion." When doing his Master's work, Cotton

Mather later remarked, Hooker "could put a king in his pocket."

Bishop Laud sent Reverend Samuel Collins to bring Hooker to heel. The young preacher's learning, Collins reported, surpassed that of any minister he had known. Hooker's "genius was haunting all the pulpits in the country," and his followers were so "clamorous" that if the High Commission Court wished for "future peace" let it "connive at Mr. Hooker's departure" rather than bring him up for "admonition and punishment." He should be persuaded to leave the diocese "quietly" and take a private teaching position.

But prevailing bigotry made such pliant procedure impossible. Hooker was dismissed and bonded for fifty pounds to appear before the Bishop. The ministry was split down the middle.

Before a vast audience Hooker delivered a memorable farewell jeremiad. Heatedly he warned that England was risking withdrawal of the Lord's favor. "We play mock holiday with God, the Gospell we make it our pack-horse; God is going, His Glory is departing. . . . England hath seen His best days, and now evill days are befalling us." Even the Turks and infidels would have "a cooler summer parlor in Hell." Hooker thoroughly burned his bridges.

Retiring to Little Meadow, he earned a bread-crust existence by teaching school in his home till the blow should fall, but his life in the tiny hamlet was enriched by association with the liberal Reverend John Eliot, soon to go to the New World and become "the Indian Apostle."

The Laud party did not forget. In July, 1630, Hooker was ordered to appear before the High Commission Court. It was an evil moment. Nonconformist Minister Alexander Leighton had just been "pilloried, whipped, branded, slit in the nostrils, his ears cut off by successive hackings." Hooker remarked that it would not be bad to suffer an hour's hanging, but "to lie in a ditch like a broken vessel and suffer many deaths before dying" was too much to ask "distressed souls" to endure.

Friends paid his bond to the court; the Earl of Warwick took in his wife and children, and he slipped away to the Netherlands, the constables nipping at his heels. But under Laud's implacable pressure, freedom was vanishing from the Holland churches also. Hooker decided to go to America.

He slipped back into England to make arrangements with his close friend, Reverend Richard Stone. Constables knocked on the door, but Stone coolly told them Hooker had just left for the other end of town.

Hooker, Cotton, and Stone, concealing their identity, took the same boat for America. On their arrival in 1633 the colonists quipped that they were now well provided for: "Cotton for clothing; Hooker for fishing; and Stone for building."

With proper consecration ceremonies, on October 11, 1633, the New Town, or New Cambridge, church was organized—headed by "grave, goodly and judicious Hooker" assisted by the "rhetorical" Stone. Mostly it was made up of Essex friends. Both men had domestic burdens. Susanna had become an invalid, and Stone's wife, as Hooker phrased it, "smoked out her days in the darkness of melancholia." Because of his power to soothe troubled souls and his generosity to the poor, Hooker became known as the "Son of Consolation," and because of his oratorical onslaughts on sin, the "Son of Thunder."

3

Hartford, where Hooker's party settled, was a fair place. The broad placid river—alive with jumping shad, sturgeon, and salmon—rolled past the encampment on Little River, where the women prepared supper over the fires. Small, undulating hillocks, planted with Indian corn, hemp, and squash, rose from the wide fertile "Black Lands," as the Indians called the river meadows.

The contours had been formed ages before by powerful glaciers that had left "shale, sandstone, and conglomerate" on an upturned sheet of lava where earlier vegetation had pressed its record in stone leaves and gigantic lizards had left the permanent engraving of their claws.

In the forested hills to the west, pines, cedars, and hemlocks crowded great spreading oaks and maples. Chestnuts, walnuts, and basswood, ash, beech, and whitewood were plentiful. Above, towered giant elm trees. The undergrowth was a tangle of wild grapes, raspberry and blackberry vines, and in swampier spots grew currant bushes. The settlers found bayberries and dewberries, whortleberries and strawberries, wild cherries and plums.

The newcomers were intruders. This Eden was claimed by three thousand Indians, by the Dutch, and by Plymouth colony. Plymouth had made no settlement except at Windsor upstream, but the Dutch had bought the whole area from the Pequots, paying with a piece of duffel twenty-seven ells long, six axes, eighteen knives, one sword blade, one pair of shears, some toys, and a musket, and their sturdy Fort Good Hope stood within stone's throw of the encamped settlers.

The Suckiage, or "Black Earth," Indians, who had their tepees in fair Hartford meadows, were led by proud, clever Sachem Sequassen. He had never bowed to Pequot overlordship and, not conceding the right of the Pequots to dispose of Hartford land, considered the Dutch unlawful interlopers. Eager for protection against the aggressive Pequots and also the Mohawks, he welcomed the Massachusetts settlers and was predisposed to listen to the Reverend Mr. Stone's offer to buy land. In return for the usual assortment of cutlery and cloth, Sequassen readily granted title to land six miles back from the river as far as the bounds of Windsor and Wethersfield, with all "meadows, pastures, woods, underwood, stones, quarries, brooks, ponds, rivers, profitts, commodities and appurtenances whatsoever."

The Dutch, only thirty strong, including women and children, were in no position to oppose the transaction, and the Hooker-Steele party staked out the new town north of Little River.

The first map—that of 1640—shows Meeting House Yard (State House Square) with church, burying ground, and site for the town hall, facing the "Road from the Palisades" (Main Street), which ran north from Little River along high ground to Centinel Hill, where it forked to the "Cow Pasture" commons and to "The Neck" and North Meadows. From the back of the square a road slanted to the mouth of Little Beaver Creek in Little Meadow, where presently a "Landing" was built to accommodate a ferry crossing "The Great River."

Inland, well west from "Dutchman's Land," two extra-wide thoroughfares flanked Little River as far as the mill, then joined and became "The Road to the Country," running south, and, farther out, "The Road to the Great Swamp." Crudely widened Indian trails (turnpikes a century later) led toward Wethersfield and Windsor.

It was a generous, stately design that brought order to the confused topography of hills and twisting streams and provided for future growth and grandeur.

The central area was parceled out in two-acre plots and farm tracts granted—size and value corresponding to each individual's contribution in worldly goods or services, or to family needs and claims to personal dignity. Each grant had to be improved within twelve months, a dwelling built according to specifications, fields cleared and planted. Each house had to have a ladder or notched tree trunk to within two feet of the eaves as an outside fire escape.

A small church was put up. Two years later it became Hooker's barn when a large combined Meeting House, Town Hall, and Arsenal was erected.

The first houses went up promptly, with a clangor of broad-axes and saws. Fields were cleared and sowed. Meat and fish were salted down in attic and basement. Bins overflowed with walnuts, chestnuts, butternuts, hazelnuts, and acorns. Wild game provided meat and pelts for clothing and trade.

Food plants and edible roots grew wild: leeks, onions, garlic, turnips, pease, radishes. In Wethersfield, the onion thrived so well that it became the staple crop for three centuries and still is. The plantings were pushed to within sight of Fort Good Hope so the Dutchmen could not look that way "without tears in their eyes."

Some medicinal herbs were already known, and the Indians taught the settlers the use of many more; the housewives' cupboards were full of "simples," or home remedies, for all ailments. From the Indians, the settlers also learned the best ingredients, such as oak bark, hemlock, and sumac for tanning leather.

Most trading was in kind; Indian wampum, made legal tender, was the chief medium of exchange. By 1643 the town market was set up by law on Wednesdays; two years later biennial fairs were authorized. An extensive river trade developed; presently ocean vessels ranged from Newfoundland to Delaware and Virginia, later to the West Indies. John Whiting, famed early trader, was given a seven-year monopoly on whale fishing out of Hartford. In due time boats rounded Cape Horn, hunting seals and whales, and moved on into the rich China trade.

There was sporadic friction with the Dutch, occasional "broken pates." Hartford complained they sold the Indians guns and powder, harbored runaway servants, and celebrated forbidden marriages of eloping couples. The Hollanders were forced to give up all fields north of Little River, but were never molested in their main "bowerie" south of the creek until ten years later, when war broke out between the Netherlands and England. The fort was seized, and the Dutch were forced to go back to New Amsterdam.

4

The earliest Connecticut town meeting was held in 1635, and the first General Court of the three river towns, April 6, 1636, a month before Hooker arrived. Springfield, settled as part of the Connecticut River migration, had already adopted the Mayflower Compact and held aloof, perhaps because its

Roxbury founder, fur trader William Pynchon, preferred remote control from Boston to close control by his near neighbors.

The early Hartford town meetings provide a perfect picture of town planning and the gradual growth of free government and institutions so typical of most later frontier settlements. Except for obligatory church, town-meeting, and Training-Band attendance, there was little compulsion, though wages and some prices were fixed.

A government of "Townsmen" (selectmen) was set up; constables, surveyors, "Chimney-Viewers," and from time to time special committees and arbitrators, were appointed. The townsmen, empowered to order "the common occasions of the Town," also supervised morals, manners, and church attendance. But admission of new inhabitants, taxes, land grants, and highway alterations had to be decided by full town meeting.

Early ordinances related to taxes, public employment of men and cattle, Indian trade, upkeep of roads and fences. Children were forbidden to swing on public gates. The "Fence-Viewers," paid a few pence an acre, obliged owners to repair fences; they also looked after stray swine and cattle, which were impounded near the cow pasture. The "Surveyors" looked after boundary lines and highways, but anybody could rent the town surveying chain for two pence a day, provided he repaired it if it broke. The "Chimney-Viewers" were important, for early "catted" chimneys of wood and lath, lined with clay, were fire hazards.

In 1639 John Steele was made town clerk. A "Town Husband," or treasurer, was appointed, and a court set up to handle civil claims. In 1640 Thomas Woodford became "Town Crier" and also rang the church bell installed that year. As sexton and gravedigger he received up to three shillings, according to whether the grave was "the lesser sort," "the middle sort," or "the highest sort."

In 1642, thirty pounds a year was voted to maintain the

town school, and the next year, the town voted to pay also for "the schooling of the poor."

Each male citizen from sixteen to sixty was required to participate in biennial Training Day exercises and in Watching and Warding. Day and night vigil from sentry boxes high in elm trees was maintained at four points: on Centinel Hill, on what became known as Charter Oak Hill, and at either end of Palisade Street. A guard with fixed arms and at least two charges of powder and shot attended every church service and public gathering.

The Training Band was composed of one corps of pikemen (the tallest men) with two corps of musketeers on the flanks. The pikeman's post was considered superior, and there was sharp rivalry between the two branches. The Hartford fathers found it necessary to order that "Gentlemen of the Pikes and Gentlemen of the Musketeers should go hand in hand in love like dear Brothers, and neither should envy the other . . . and . . . God would give blessing to their undertakings."

The muskets were matchlocks with bandoliers or wooden boxes for powder and ball. A rest, or forked support for the barrel when being fired, was tied to the wrist and, on the march, served as a cane. The pikes were ten feet long, i.e., "half-pikes," tipped with metal spears. Swords, pistols, and daggers were carried. All wore "corslets" and padded cotton coats against Indian arrows.

Hardly was the Hartford Training Band organized than it had to set forth on the terrible Pequot War. The Reverend Mr. Hooker preached a farewell sermon on the riverbank, and the Reverend Mr. Stone went along as chaplain.

The Training Band members came back as veterans, and those not already proprietors were given quarter-acre plots, in Soldiers' Field, carved out of the Cow Pasture, the first instance of postwar rewards to ordinary soldiers, not merely to officers. Captain Mason received vast acreages in western Connecticut and elsewhere. Among the Soldiers' Field veterans was Thomas Barnes, fresh from England. A few years later he helped found Farmington. A son founded Bristol. They were ancestors of men who built a great industrial dynasty.

5

On January 14, 1639, about two hundred freemen from Windsor, Wethersfield, and Hartford assembled at Hartford Meeting House to frame an over-all government. It was not an easy moment. Since few crops could be put in during the war, the last twelvemonth they had suffered a famine so terrible that "even the richest" had gone hungry.

They did not come to the meeting unprepared. The previous spring Hooker had preached to them on the need for joint government and the form it should take. He told them, according to Deuteronomy 1:13, "Take thou wise men, and understanding, and known among your tribes, and I shall make them rulers over you." He laid down startling new doctrine:

The foundation of authority is laid first in the free choice of the people.

The choice of public magistrates belongs unto the people by God's allowance. . . .

The people have the power to appoint officers and magistrates; it is in their power also to set the bounds and limitations of power and place unto which they call them.

The lesson is: to persuade us, as God hath given us liberty to take it.

Reasons: Because by a free choice, the foundation of authority is laid firstly on the free consent of the people.

Because: by a free choice, the hearts of the people will be more inclined to the love of the persons chosen and more ready to yield obedience.

Though Hooker continued to consult by correspondence with the Boston Bay leaders, his democratic doctrine was frontal defiance of the Massachusetts system and the governing commission set up for Connecticut by the magistrates.

Here was patent proof of the deeper reasons that had led Hooker to take his flock beyond their reach. In reply to Winthrop's opinion that it was "safer" for "the few" to govern "unbeholden to the people," Hooker wrote back that "in matters of greater consequence, which concern the common good, a general council chosen by *all*, I conceive, under favor, most suitable to rule and most safe for the relief of the whole."

His bold idea was carried out. In accord with his democratic concepts, Eleven Fundamental Orders were drawn up, probably penned by Roger Ludlow, and presented to the special constitutional assemblage of the river towns in 1639.

"Where a people are gathered together, the word of God requires that to mayntayne the peace and union of such a people there should be an orderly and decent government established according to God to order and dispose of the affayres of the people."

The need is stated, next comes the compact:

[We] doe therefore associate and conjoyne ourselves to be as one Publicke State or Comonwealth; and doe, for ourselves and our Successors and such as shall be adjoyned to us att any time hereafter enter into Combination and Confederation together to mayntayne and preserve the liberty and purity of the gospel of our Lord Jesus . . . as also in Civell Affayres to be guided and governed according to such Lawes, Rules, Orders and decrees as shall be made, ordered and decreed.

Article I provided for two annual meetings of the General Court or Legislature in April and September. All citizens were to elect seven representatives, of whom the governor would be one, for one-year terms, and no governor could serve twice in succession.

Succeeding articles took up the manner of holding free elections, the nominating of candidates, and their qualifications.

Article V set forth the duties and work of the court. Article VI obliged the governor to issue proper notice of regular or special meetings, which he was empowered to call with the consent of the majority of the court. The citizens themselves could also call a special meeting, which, if properly announced, would be legal.

Articles VII and VIII prescribed the number and qualifications of town representatives and the manner of electing them. By Article IX they were to assemble before the legislature met to certify that its members had been properly elected, and to make out an agenda.

A majority of town representatives (according to Article X), four magistrates, and the presiding officer had to be present for a legislative session to be lawful. The legislative powers were defined.

Article XI provided that the share of taxes to be borne by each town should be fixed by a committee with an equal number of members from each town.

No separate judiciary was provided for, but in a short time special claims courts were set up, grand jurors were nominated, and presently trial by free popular jury was instituted for the first time in America.

The new document defined precisely the powers of all officials, and the people could act at any time, regardless of governor and magistrates. Here were the principle and instruments of popular initiative, in operation in Rhode Island also, which, nearly three centuries later under Woodrow Wilson, became a part of American political practices. The definition of powers was in itself an attempt to safeguard the rights of the people, indicating that Hooker was well aware of the tendency of all governments to usurp more and more authority and proliferate into overpowering monsters even if democratically elected. Thus, simply, in straightforward language, the adopted constitution vested all fundamental powers in the people, acting under God's commandments. It widened the bases of the "Great Fundamentals" of Plymouth by providing direct rather than indirect representative government.

It ignored Massachusetts authority entirely, and the settlers continued to ignore it when, a year later, the Massachusetts court belatedly laid down regulations for the river towns. But what was even more significant, the Connecticut document was the first on record that made no mention of the King or British authority. It invoked neither his protection nor British sovereignty. It was wholly an American document. Unlike the Mayflower Compact, it recognized no superior national power; neither did it recognize any superior colonial authority or any outside sovereignty whatsoever except God. Thus the Eleven Fundamental Orders of Hartford were America's first declaration of independence, the first formal expression of the dual principles laid down more than a century later for all the colonies in the 1776 Declaration: that there must be liberation from overseas rule and that "governments derive their just powers from the consent of the governed."

Massachusetts was irked, and stories circulated in Boston of wild radicalism, unrest, poverty, and multiple disasters on the Connecticut River. Hooker, considering this a deliberate slander abetted by the Bay authorities, wrote sharp letters to Winthrop complaining that such defamation was a studied, malicious attempt to stop settlers from coming out. No community in the wilderness, he said, had shown more rapid progress. Under Hartford's free institutions the people were peaceful and harmonious; they had prospered and had a large accumulation of worldly goods. All were living happily in relative comfort.

These people who had struck inland boldly from the coast for the first time came to real grips with the American soil, even more than did the folk who went to Rhode Island. They were makers of their own world, wholly so. As such, they assumed the responsibilities and duties of their condition. They became "Americans." They were the first truly "independent" Americans.

In Hartford and in Providence were laid the enduring cornerstones of democracy and representative government. The two great architects of civil liberties and legal constitutional framework for the later American republic were Roger Williams and Thomas Hooker. More than anyone else, they were the fathers of American freedom. They provided the basic concepts, the phrases, the living documents, and the organizations and institutions that spread across New England and provided the basis for all the important institutions of independence.

V. There's Iron in the Bogs

WHEN THE townsfolk of New Haven, Connecticut, met June 4, 1639, in Robert Newman's "mighty Barn" to form a government, they adopted as their motto:

> Wisdom hath builded her house
> She hath hewn out her seven pillars.

Among the outstanding "freemen" present was Stephen Goodyear, who had been awarded the largest plot on the Green, where he built a fine house and, next door, an ordinary, or inn, run by John Harriman, with exclusive right to sell liquor.

Goodyear also secured the concession to set up a town brewery. He probably had an interest in the Mill River gristmill and in Governor Eaton's brick kilns in North Haven and at Grape Vine Point on the Quinnipiac River. Goodyear was engaged in other enterprises and was always quick to back any undertaking, mercantile or civic, proposed by the community.

A successful London "Merchant Taylor," he had inherited numerous "messauges and tenements" near "Paul's Chain" from his father, Zacherie Goodyear, who had been a prosperous vintner. Stephen had belonged to the well-to-do parish of St. Stephen's, where Reverend John Davenport held forth— the most eloquent, popular preacher in London—until Laud's displeasure drove him to the Netherlands.

When Davenport arranged with his lifelong friend, Theophilus Eaton, a prominent merchant and diplomat, to found a New World colony, Goodyear sold his London properties and joined the undertaking.

Eaton had been highly honored by the Crown and the Merchant Adventurers. Among his prized possessions was an engraved silver ewer they had bestowed on him for his successful negotiations with the Baltic States, but he was now suffering from malevolent tax collectors because his brother, Reverend Samuel Eaton, had been thrown into prison for his Separatist ideas.

Goodyear went with the first Davenport-Eaton group on the "good ship *Hector*" in 1636. It was well outfitted, for the company was made up of men of high standing, education, and means, including many well-to-do tradesmen and fine artisans.

The Boston authorities gave them every inducement to settle in Massachusetts, but at heart completely Separatist, the Davenport congregation was eager to set up its own free church and community.

From Pequot War veterans, they heard magical tales of the beauty of Quinnipiac River and Harbor, and Goodyear went with an expedition to have a look. They found the wide meadows under two dramatic red cliffs fair beyond their desires. Seven persons, including six-year-old Michael Wigglesworth, were left to winter in river caverns. One man died, and Michael suffered rheumatic pains all his life but lived to a vast age and became the leading poet of the colonies. His *Day of Doom*, a best-seller published in 1662, was a jog-trot ballad of ferocious Calvinist Last Judgment, which generously assigned unbaptized infants to the "easiest room in hell."

The Davenport-Eaton party left Boston in a large pinnace early in April, 1637. They rode into Quinnipiac Harbor and up West Inlet, where they dropped on their knees under a great oak while Davenport delivered a sermon on "Temptations in the Wilderness."

Land was bought from the Indians with the usual cutlery and cloth, and Surveyor John Brockett, a nobleman who had given up his castle and inheritance to follow a "Puritan maid" to the New World, staked out the town. He laid out a nine-block quadrangle around a large Meeting House Square from which three creeks forked. A wedge-shaped row of double properties angled down to the harbor front. At once, William

Andrews, the town carpenter, began putting up the meeting house and watchtower and building bridges over the creeks and the Quinnipiac. Soon there were ferries also.

Beyond East Creek—which two centuries later became part of the great Farmington Canal and, twenty years after that, the sunken bed for railroads—stretched Oyster Field, coated with six feet of oyster shells, piled there by the Indians over centuries. Oysters became part of the regular diet of the new-comers, and in years to come, oyster battles were fought in Wild West style. Peddlers rushed them in gallon kegs to the Ohio. Oystering is a major industry that still flourishes.

Brockett acted as physician and supplied materials for the Training Band, and Goodyear frequently worked with him as agent for the New Haven court to settle land disputes. When the Indians protested that cattle and pigs were destroying their cornfields, everybody was ordered forth to build fences around the natives' patches: as the Court put it, "So their squaws and children may not cry."

2

Soon after the settlement was started, Goodyear returned to England to bring out more colonists. He secured a license to transport 250 on the *St. John*, among them his friend Thomas Gregson, a well-to-do trader. With Goodyear, he soon engaged in many New Haven enterprises and served as town "truckmaster," with an exclusive monopoly on Indian trade, a post created to prevent the sale of arms and liquor.

He and Goodyear purchased considerable property in and out of New Haven, some in trust for the town, including part of Milford and other lands where adjacent New Haven settlements were laid out.

From the Earl of Shelby, Goodyear privately purchased Shelter Island, which he held for ten years, then resold for 1,600 pounds of "good, merchantable sugar." Also from Shelby, in association with Governor Eaton and Governor Haynes of Connecticut, Gregson, and others, Goodyear purchased all of Long Island, "not otherwise disposed of," for £110. It was repurchased from the Indians, and various settlements were started. New Haven colonized Yencott, the village of Southold.

Gregson and Goodyear set up harbor-front warehouses and acquired ships. They were associated in some trading enterprises with two able shipbuilders and owners, George Lamberton and Richard Mabron. Presently Isaac Allerton, originally of Plymouth, a great trader, moved over from New Amsterdam, built a splendid white-oak mansion, with warehouse opposite, on Oyster Field, and began sending his ships to the West Indies.

With Gregson, Mabron, Lamberton, Eaton, and others, Goodyear put money, goods, and labor into the "Great Shippe *Fellowshippe*," the first good-sized vessel built in New Haven, chiefly the work of Jasper Crane of nearby Branford. Apparently it was not too satisfactory, for it was "walt-sided." Prices were soaring in England, and this was a chance to reap quick profit at a time when New Haven was in bad straits.

The vessel was loaded with a fourth of the colony's wealth: a thousand feet of planking laboriously cut and sawed by nearly all New Haveners, pease, meat, hides, beaver pelts, and $25,000 worth of silver plate.

The freezing January day when the boat was scheduled to leave, they had to saw through three miles of ice to get it out to sea. It was never heard of again.

Seventy worthy New Haven "Christians" were lost, including Skipper Gregson, Captain Nathaniel Turner, head of the Training Band, Lamberton, and Goodyear's wife.

One June day eighteen months later, just before sunset, the cry went up along East Creek and through the town, "The great ship!" Everybody rushed joyously down Fleet Street to the harbor front.

There off Rocky Point reeled a great square-rigger, every sail set. Under its flying colors, a solitary figure pointed out to sea dramatically with upraised sword. The vessel was on fire;

smoke poured from the decks, and as it swept into the harbor, the top mast broke off in a tangle of spars and shrouds, and the hull plunged under the water in dense smoke and spray. No trace of it was left.

What ship it was, whence it came, where it was bound, whether it was merely a "Phantom Ship," as it came to be called, no one has ever found out. Possibly it was a ship in distress, abandoned by all its crew, but the strange vessel, real or fancied, carried all its secrets to the bottom of New Haven harbor. Certainly it was not the Great Shippe *Fellowshippe*, but undoubtedly, explained the Reverend Mr. Davenport, the disaster was God's sign of what had happened to that unfortunate vessel—"fatal . . . perfidious bark, built in the eclipse and rigged with curses dark."

In spite of the setback, which filled New Haven with gloom for years, Goodyear prospered. Through his warehouses flowed pease, flour, biscuit, malt, livestock, horses, dairy products, beef, pork, hides, leather and shoes, furs and skins, shingles and clapboard, pipe staves, fish, whale products, and wampum. Incoming vessels brought sugar and molasses, wine and rum, tools, window glass, tea, cotton goods, and silk.

Shortly after the disaster of the lost ship, Goodyear married Gregson's widow. The children of the two families thus united attended school across the Green at the home of young Ezekiel Cheever, who received thirty pounds a year for teaching the Scriptures, Greek and Hebrew. Cheever became the leading educator of New England, later heading the famous Boston Latin School, where he was still actively teaching when he died at ninety-odd years. His text *Latin Accidence*, written and published during his early days at New Haven, ran to eighteen editions and was used in the schools of all America continuously for two hundred years.

3

Goodyear took a great interest in education. From Davenport's letters and writings, early court decisions, and church records, one may piece together that the settlers came to establish a "Utopian Trinity" of Church, State, and College. They desired a community in which all lovers of God would be equal and have equal voice, where they could prosper by work and goodness, where all could "enjoy all privileges and bear all burdens." Davenport dreamed of a great, enlightened institution of learning—"a free schole"—and as soon as possible tried to get one started.

Goodyear was very active on the project and served with Eaton and Davenport on a town committee to that end. The town set aside land for it, thus initiating the system of land support for schools that was to be put into practice all over New England, most extensively in Vermont, and which was to include land grants by the federal government in the Northwest Territory and beyond.

By 1655, largely through Goodyear's persistent efforts, private subscriptions of three hundred pounds were secured, and the town guaranteed sixty pounds annually for the president's salary. Milford pitched in with a hundred pounds in donations and a sixty-pounds-a-year guarantee. Goodyear offered his own home on the Green for a college hall. Eaton promised twenty pounds' worth of books to start a library.

This total did not seem adequate, and the aid of Connecticut Colony was sought to make the college a joint undertaking. With such tangible support from New Haven Colony already pledged, the Connecticut General Court guaranteed forty pounds annually and books. Governor John Hopkins died in 1657 and left five hundred pounds' worth of property in England and the rest of his estate, after lifetime use by his wife, to the project.

Thus was set a pattern for later educational undertakings throughout the country, including the founding of western state colleges by joint government and private initiative.

The New Haven college got under way in 1661, but so few pupils, and these of such unsatisfactory caliber, attended, that after two years, the enterprise was abandoned. Not until sixty

years later did New Haven get its college, when the general
Connecticut institution, founded in 1701, moved there from
Saybrook in 1716. Elihu Yale, the grandson of Governor
Eaton's wife and former governor of Madras, who had become
the wealthiest man in England, sent over from London a
picture of the King, a library, and a modest donation to
complete the first college building on the town land facing the
Green. And so the institution became Yale University and its
students "Sons of Eli." Ironically, in her day, Anne Yale had
been excommunicated by Davenport and the elders for not
believing in child baptism.

Goodyear's advice was sought on most civic undertakings.
In 1643, when negotiations were under way to form the
United Colonies "for the exalting of Christ's end and the
advancing of the Publique Good in all the plantations," Goodyear, Davenport, and several others were named to advise the
delegates to Boston on the proper course of action.

He was often trouble shooter for the colony. When Stamford, founded by New Haven and a part of its General Court,
threatened to secede unless voting privileges were widened to
include non-church members, he journeyed to that "Quaker-
sympathizing" community, quieted a riotous assemblage cou-
rageously, and persuaded the people to present their grievances
to the General Court in an orderly fashion.

New Haven claimed land in Delaware, but its early settlement there had had serious trouble with the Swedes. Goodyear was sent and successfully negotiated an agreement. He
offered to throw the bulk of his personal resources behind the
Delaware undertaking if enough other New Haveners would
help out, but after a few years the Dutch took over and drove
the New Haveners out entirely.

4

The constitution adopted unanimously at Newman's barn
established the Bible as the law of the land and restricted suffrage to freemen who were church members. Twelve men

were elected who, in turn, were to select the "Seven Pillars."

After some years, it was found that biblical law needed specific defining to answer practical needs, and Governor Eaton, whom the Indians came to call "the Great Big Study Man" because of his scholarly habits, was appointed to draw up a code. This was printed in London in 1657 at a guinea a copy, but was distributed in New Haven, where every householder was required to own it, for only a shilling.

Adultery, sexual perversion, and treason, some fifteen allied offenses (compared to more than two hundred in England two centuries later) were punishable by death; drunkenness and Sabbath-breaking were serious offenses. But the code was far from the harsh Blue Laws ordinarily associated with Connecticut; indeed, these never existed and were merely the apocryphal invention of a latter-day disgruntled Tory. Many features of the Eaton code would be considered liberal even today. Certainly the divorce law was more civilized than that of present-day New York.

The General Court, which came to be elected annually directly by all freemen, with ballots of black and white beans, combined executive, legislative, and judicial functions.

Goodyear frequently served as lawyer before it, and presently he became a deputy, then deputy governor. The administration of the laws, in which he played a large part, was enlightened. The proper safeguards of testimony, evidence, and self-defense were carefully observed. One offense always dealt with severely was that of bringing nuisance suits. Except for several well-proved cases of sexual perversion and a murder, maximum penalties were rarely imposed. Only one instance of branding on the hand occurred, in Southold, Long Island, and the authorities there were sternly taken to task. Stocks and whipping post were seldom used more than once or twice a year, usually for constant offenders, charged with drunkenness, or for the most flagrant cases of adultery or rape.

A number of "sedition" trials, over which Goodyear or Eaton presided, were held against "Quakerish sympathizers" or those wishing to broaden the suffrage. The proceedings were calm and fair, without vindictiveness. In several instances the accused "confessed" and were given light fines, with a year's grace in which to pay, plus an admonition to go home, think things over, and "get right with God." In most instances the fines were later reduced or remitted.

Indians and indentured servants frequently came into court and were accorded justice even against notable leaders of the colony. One Indian, beaten on the wharf by his employer, was awarded medical costs and heavy damages. Any servant, on proper proof that his master had ill treated him or failed to give him proper instruction, food, or clothing, was either freed or bound over to a new master. Indentured servants who burned the barns or homes of their masters or stole from them were usually given banishment, which the proud New Haveners considered a punishment harsher than death. All in all, compared with early Boston, New Haven was an enlightened, civilized place. Were the law administered as equitably today, this would not be such a bad world.

In 1653, Goodyear had the unpleasant task of presiding at the trial of one of his servants, old Betty Goodman, on witchcraft charges. In his home, it was testified that Betty, not liking the conversation, "cast a fierce look" at him and flounced out, whereupon he fell "into a swound." Apparently neither Goodyear nor his wife took much stock in the charges. Mrs. Goodyear flatly contradicted most of the testimony. But for several days the court listened patiently to the old wives' tales. Another man had also fallen into a fit when Betty visited. In another house, good meat had suddenly become maggoty. Two neurotic teen-age girls looked through her high window and saw her lying on her bed nearly naked—shameful conduct possible only in a witch even on such a hot day. The girls swore that some unseen creature had performed unnatural sexual acts with her.

The court finally told Betty gravely that she had heard the charges and that they were on record; now she should go home and henceforth keep her nose out of her neighbors' business. The verdict, if scarcely satisfying the prurient, vengeful desires of the accusers, respected the legal process and was typical of Goodyear's tactful skill.

Five years later, Betty was brought back on the same charges, with similar results. A kindhearted Branford boatbuilder took her into his home and kept her until she died.

Now and then, humor peeks through the solemn legal record. A young man, fined for kissing a girl, retorted that whatever the governor and his "fine court" thought or did, he intended to kiss a pretty maid every chance he got. There is no record of punishment for contempt.

So, step by step, Goodyear helped raise the New Haven mansion and its seven pillars.

5

Within fifteen years, with modest tools and resources, where everything had to be done by the hands of the people, the progress in New Haven was remarkable. By then handsome houses encircled the large Green. The Reverend Mr. Davenport's fine Queen Street house was built in the form of a cross. Eaton's place, on what came to be called Elm Street, was "the finest in all New England," E-shaped, with nineteen "chimneys," or fireplaces. Isaac Allerton's Oyster Field home had fourteen chimneys and four porches. River and harbor landings had been built, bridges thrown across all streams. Ferries traversed the harbor and served various points on the Quinnipiac.

There were numbers of stores, carpenter and blacksmith shops, a tailor, weavers, shoemakers, bakers, grist- and sawmills, shipyards, coopers, meat shops, two doctors, a barber, a school, a livery stable, a brewery, an inn, a cartwright, and a ropemaker.

The town was reaching out to North Haven, where Eaton, with the help of one of the Yale boys, had put up a brick kiln. Another kiln had been erected on the meadows of Grapevine

Point near the Quinnipiac and Mill Rivers, where clay-chinked cabins with sedge roofs had been built by the workers. Large herds of cattle grazed in the meadows. They supplied the tanneries on Morocco Lane and the meat and leather goods shipped abroad.

New Haven hides, leather, and meat were carefully inspected and packed. Early faulty wares, rejected by Virginia, had occasioned lawsuits between shippers and shoemakers. Now all hides had to be stamped "N. G.," meaning "Good Neats Leather," or "N. F.," "Faulty Leather." No inferior goods could be sold abroad, and only locally if clearly labeled "Deceitful Ware"—for the "Rules of Righteousness," said the General Court, were not merely for New Haven but "reached to far places."

The new project afoot that year of 1655 was to start an iron foundry and blast furnace in New Haven—the first in Connecticut. Iron had been discovered in the North Haven bogs and, though difficult to work, it would provide enough ore to get the plant well started. To set up such a foundry on the fringe of the wilderness so soon after settling betokened the determination of the newcomers to create an enduring society, independent of the mother country overseas, to take hold of the resources they had, and to shape this new world to their own needs.

As usual, Goodyear was full-shoulder behind the project, along with Davenport and Eaton. Interested also was John Winthrop, Jr., of New London, son of Massachusetts' first governor, a friend of Roger Williams and John Davenport. Winthrop, who had put up and operated a foundry near Boston, had both the means and the knowledge to contribute to the New Haven enterprise. No man in the colonies knew more about such things.

He had first come to Connecticut as governor of Old Saybrook, settled under a grant to Lord Saye and Sele and Lord Brooke at the mouth of the Connecticut River. Later he bought Fishers Island and, in 1646, founded New London.

Over the years he had discovered many New England deposits of iron, copper, lead, tin, and cobalt. For a time he set out a circle of iron pots to refine cobalt near East Haddam—a place that became known as "Winthrop's Ring." He was also renowned for his knowledge of astronomy and eclipses, chemistry, drugs, and medicine. The Reverend Mr. Davenport sometimes wrote to him for prescriptions for his wife.

Winthrop was now visiting in New Haven to work out the iron project. He was still young, tall, well built, with enormous sloping shoulders, a luxuriant mane of black hair, and unusually large dark eyes.

Eaton, Davenport, Goodyear, and shipbuilder Jasper Crane talked over the matter with him, where best to locate the foundry and organize the company. The North Haven bog iron was well inland, the Quinnipiac might freeze, its water supply was uncertain. They hit upon Furnace Pond, at the boundary of East Haven and Branford, both on the shore. Ore could be barged up to the head of the tidewater, or in a pinch be brought across the hills by oxcart. The company was organized February 13, 1656, by Winthrop, Goodyear, and Crane, with contributions from others.

Everybody was enthusiastic and wanted to push the project forward. Iron products, imported across the ocean from England, were costly; poor farmers were hard put to it for even simple tools. Having to buy expensive imported goods made it difficult to accumulate reserves for a rainy day or capital to start new enterprises. New Haven pitched in with 140 days of free labor to build the necessary dam, each citizen working or hiring a substitute.

The undertakers were freed from all taxes on the enterprise and on their personal estates, and the foundry was granted twelve acres from the commons on condition that operations continued for three years. Both New Haven and Branford allowed it to take water, wood, ironstone, ore, and shells for lime from the public lands.

Actual construction and operation were put in the hands of

John Cooper, an ironsmith who had come on the *Hector*. He was a Jack-of-all-trades, farmer, lawyer, holder of town offices —keeper of the pound for strayed animals, chimney sweep, fence-inspector, and town crier. He received one penny per "cry" for calling out lost articles and strayed animals at fairs and public gatherings, and twopence an acre for inspecting fences.

The local people were anxious to induce Winthrop to leave New London and settle permanently in New Haven. A man of such great talents would not only help make the foundry a success; he would be of enormous benefit to the struggling colony. He was offered Gregson's fine house on Queen Street, facing East Creek, either as a gift or rent-free. The place was next door to Davenport's imposing residence and to Thomas Nash, a skilled metalworker, who perhaps made the first clock in America.

Winthrop declined the house as a gift but bought it with goats from his Fishers Island farm. Mrs. Elizabeth Davenport got it ready for him and his family, having it scrubbed and the rooms well warmed. The well was cleaned out and a new pump installed, supplies laid in—twenty loads of wood, thirty bushels of wheat, twelve pounds of candles—and she secured for them a "clean, thrifty maid servant."

But Winthrop was soon elected governor of Connecticut and had to move to Hartford. Later, he sold his foundry interest to Boston people, which did not sit well with the New Haveners, who for a time considered voiding the sale.

The bloomery, or iron foundry, was soon spewing out yellow smoke. It attracted a new type of worker to East Haven and Branford, rough, brawling men whose uninhibited ways shocked the New Haveners.

The ore from the bogs was taken by oxcart to the Quinnipiac and loaded onto barges, which were poled down the river and across the harbor past the new shipyard, where one of the ferries crossed, and under Rocky Palisades and Beacon Hill, topped by an Indian graveyard, then on into the open

Sound. By strenuous efforts the barges were pushed several miles up the Farm River, which looped lazily through salt meadows thick with geese, ducks, and other fowl.

The iron ore was worked with limestone derived from shells and oak charcoal. The poured iron was hammered with sledges to drive out cinders and impurities, a "shingling" method that reduced the iron to rectangular slabs, or "blooms." The shop planned to turn out iron pots and pans, firedogs, movable trammels for fireplaces, grates, shovels, tools, wedges, clamps, chains, and specially shaped iron for local shipbuilders.

Goodyear, who had put more into the undertaking than anybody else, devoted much of his time to it. Other and better sources of iron ore had to be tapped. With provisions and wampum worth 9,000 guilder, he bought the thirty-ton sloop *Zwoll* in New Amsterdam to bring ore from the Dutch colony and points along the coast.

On making delivery of the *Zwoll*, the Dutch manned it with armed men and seized the Dutch ship *St. Benirio*, anchored in New Haven harbor, because it was trading without a license from the Dutch East India Company, which had a monopoly on all Netherlands ocean commerce. In the eyes of Dutch officialdom, the *St. Benirio* was no better than a pirate ship engaged in illegal traffic. At the time of its seizure in New Haven, the three owners, who were on shore, escaped. Dutch Governor Peter Stuyvesant demanded that they be delivered over to him.

The New Haveners considered the seizure in their territorial waters not only a violation of sovereignty and New Haven law but a treacherous, highhanded act. The three Dutch owners were made citizens, and New Haven refused to give them up. Governor Eaton wrote angrily that the Dutch colony had grossly violated New Haven's hospitality, its laws, and territorial jurisdiction. The interchanges became so heated that Eaton threatened joint armed action by the United Colonies and broke off correspondence.

Deputy Governor Goodyear took up the interchange.

Though more tactful, he was no less pointed. New Haven wished to live in loving friendship with New Amsterdam, but if paid back in different coin, its people, he doubted not, would give a good account of themselves sword in hand. In the meantime, he suggested that the Governor send on the *Zwoll* with fifty or a hundred "skipples" of salt and other merchandise he wanted. It came.

For the time being, Goodyear sent the *Zwoll* into West Indies trade, one of the first American vessels ever to venture into that area.

Another difficulty at the foundry was the unsatisfactory nature of its hearthstones. A Milford merchant offered to supply new ones from the Isle of Wight, but Davenport said better stones could be obtained more cheaply from Quarry Hill, near London. Goodyear, planning to visit England on business, said he would secure them.

He never returned to New Haven, for he was stricken ill in London and died there. But by his varied business and trading activities, he had helped New Haven along the road to industrialization and importance as a future metal and gunmaking center. There, over the years, were developed many new skills, some still unique, for the carriage, wagon, automobile, and airplane industries. Goodyear was the father of New Haven industry, and his descendants played magnificent roles in the industrial growth of America. His work laid the foundations for the enterprise of inventors like Abel Buell, the early brass foundry and clockworks of Isaac Doolittle, the mass production initiated for the first time in American industry by Eli Whitney. Goodyear helped build both the industry and the free institutions of New Haven. He and the Goodyears who came after him made a great contribution to the strength and progress of the colonies and the country, to the shaping of the American heritage.

VI. New Towns on the March

A FEW MONTHS before Goodyear arrived on the good ship *Hector* to help found New Haven, Thomas Barnes arrived in Hartford from overseas in time to enlist in the Pequot War. With other veterans, he received part of an acre in the new Soldiers' Field beyond Centinel Hill.

About 1645 he relinquished his Hartford property to become one of the original eighty-four proprietors of Tunxis, or Farmington, in a rich little valley west of the Talcott Ridge.

By Indian treaties and General Court grants, Farmington came to include what are today Waterbury, Watertown, Kensington, Wolcott, Terryville, Plymouth, Bristol, Burlington, Southington, New Britain, Berlin, Plainville, and Avon, and became known as "the Mother of Towns." This vast area was hurriedly granted because it was feared the Crown intended to usurp all unoccupied lands without title. For a time Farmington was the largest, most populous community in the state.

The settlement was laid out along Main Street, which ran up and down along the hillside, well above the river flood area. A few lanes, mostly old Indian trails, led to hunting grounds, ponds, or river fords. It had no central green, and its churchyard was a tiny triangle squeezed between two forked valleys.

Barnes was allotted a fine house plot on the crest of a commanding hill, and ten acres sloping west to the Pequabuck River meadows. Next door lived Samuel Hooker, the minister, son of the famous divine of Hartford.

Like his neighbors, Barnes probably put up a provisional log cabin but later built a substantial two-story dwelling with full-sized basement and massive stone foundations.

Below the big south bay window, a pleasant field fell away to the creek from Richard Bronson's mill on a pond tucked in the hills. The north windows looked out upon the thin redstone markers of the burying yard, land Thomas had given to the town. Below the front yard, on the other side of the street, stretched the apple and plum orchard he had set out, dropping away to the Pequabuck meadows—all of it rich black soil. On the opposite bank he had acquired more acres. Beyond, the village commons and the horse pasture encircled a high glacial gravel mound known as Round Hill.

On the high east slope back of Barnes lived John Scovell, who later married Sarah, Barnes's oldest daughter, and moved to Waterbury on its founding in 1672. Their descendants became great metal and brass industrialists. Also, high on the hill, lived the Cowleses (some of whom became "Coles" in order to avoid confusion), who were storekeepers and inn-keepers.

Well on the north side of town was John Steele, first arrival in Hartford, who, as he had in Hartford, served as Farmington town clerk until his death. William Lewis, his successor, also at the north end, married Mary Cheever, daughter of Ezekiel Cheever, the renowned New Haven and Boston schoolmaster. Nearby lived the Standleys, sturdy smiths and carpenters, whose descendants were to found a great steel industry in New Britain.

Though Barnes, like some of his neighbors, did not know how to write, the community respected his honesty and common sense, and he was kept busy appraising property and probating wills. He became a large landholder, getting an additional fifty acres as a Pequot War veteran and, as proprietor, some two thousand outlying Farmington acres, a large domain even in wilderness days. It provided the basis for the eventual rise of several financial and industrial dynasties.

Early in 1662 tragedy hit the Barnes family. Thomas's wife was jailed in Hartford as a "witch." This accusation was chiefly the handiwork of a spiteful, hysterical girl of neighbor Cowles's family, who later got John and Mary Carrington—able, intrepid spirits in Wethersfield—hanged as witches.

Fortunately, the early witchcraft poison spread only briefly to a few Connecticut towns. The testimony of accusers often reveals prurient concern with sex perversions, a distortion typical of most fanatical repressions, perhaps a pathological manifestation of self-accusation. Stories of perversion were tagged onto the most haggard witches, and there was intense preoccupation with physical details of intimate anatomy, a sort of Satanic hoofs-and-horns symbolism. Odd markings and colorations around the nipples were sure signs of guilt.

On March 5, 1662, Mary Barnes was convicted of "entertaining familiarity with Satan" and given the death sentence. "Goodman Barnes" was billed for her jail keep, twenty-one shillings plus fees.

Her mental aberrations, if any, may have stemmed from marital uncertainties for, a few weeks after she was sentenced to be hanged, Thomas Barnes entered into a marriage contract to wed nineteen-year-old Mary Andrews, a neighbor's daughter. In the crabbedly written document, signed with an "X," Barnes agreed to give his new "tandar wife" his house and orchard and all "appurtynances," during "the time of her naturall lyfe," and six acres, to be entirely hers, at the fork of the Farmington and Pequot Rivers "called the allebow" (elbow). In case of prior death—he was forty—he was to leave his "tandar wife" and any children a "comfortaball maynte-nance," and she was to have "hallf the moofables ... or hous holld goods." The children were to be brought up by the "Rules of the gospull."

Barnes further agreed to "putt out" all his children by his first wife, except nine-year-old Benjamin, but, if the bride found it "comfortaball," he could also keep his daughter Hannah at home.

Barnes's grown children, after the tragic witchcraft business and his remarriage, married and moved away; and Thomas, too, must have been uneasy in Farmington. By ceding thirty acres in Farmington center, he secured a preliminary grant in the unsurveyed western hill country on the upper Pequabuck in a section called "Pole Land," later "Poland," whose forests

furnished the coopers and tanners their necessary supplies. But
Mary Andrews gave him two more children, and he never got
away.

When he died in 1689, only his youngest son, Ebenezer,
aged thirteen, was left at the homestead to carry on the farm
for his mother. The entire property—house, orchard, fields,
and all tools and "quickstocke" (livestock)—on his mother's
death would go to one of his brothers, but he had inherited
four acres on Rattlesnake Hill and large grants in Southington
and on the upper Pequabuck, where he hoped to settle when
he came of age.

2

Ebenezer Barnes was twenty-three when he married
eighteen-year-old Deborah Orvis, daughter of the village
tanner, who gave him seven children before she died. By then
he was forty-three, the western lands were still unsurveyed,
and he was still tied down in Farmington.

He then married twenty-three-year-old Mabel Hancox,
daughter of the village butcher. She was only three years older
than his oldest boy by Deborah, and she, too, proceeded to
give him children with clocklike regularity until he became
the father of fifteen.

The western lands were surveyed in 1721, and in due time
allotted to the heirs of the original Farmington proprietors.
By 1728, the way was cleared for Ebenezer to take possession.
He was then over fifty—well along in years to face the frontier
hardships of clearing land, getting in crops, putting up a house.

But the moment seemed propitious. Waterbury, to the
south in the Naugatuck Valley, settled by Farmington folk
after the discovery of lead deposits, was now flourishing
because of its many mill streams. The main traveled route
from there to Farmington and Hartford, the capital, was the
ancient Tunxis trace across Ebenezer's Pequabuck property.
He planned to build his home there as a tavern for travelers.

After complicated land transactions, trading off the inheritances and properties of former wives Deborah and Mabel, he enlarged Thomas's 1663 grant and consolidated three hundred acres on either side of the river where it rushed over ledges and could be dammed for future mills.

On a spring day in 1728, he set out with oxen and tools to tame "the Great Forest" wilderness as the Indians called it. Probably several of his grown sons, who had not yet left home, went along.

They forded the Pequabuck, crossed swamps by the Indian trail, followed higher rolling country, and at the southern end of a densely forested ridge on high ground above the river, Barnes drew rein and drove in his staff and heaped stones about it as the site for the house. Close by in 1850 would rise the first brick shop of the Bristol Brass Company, of which his descendants would become directors, as of most of the great industries that came to center in the town that arose.

Barnes built well. For the chimney he laid up a massive footing, heavy stones tied in with sixteen-inch timbers. The whole house and the broad oak flooring were pegged. Tables, benches, cabinets were built, and household belongings were brought from Farmington. Winter supplies were laid in—corn, fish, and meat.

That summer and the following year, four other settlers bought land on "King's Road," as the Indian trace was re-named. Another built a small cabin upstream at "Goose Corner." The third year, another settler bought land south of the river. So was founded the tiny settlement on the Pequa-buck around Ebenezer Barnes's tavern. But not until twelve years later did any considerable number of settlers begin coming.

The New Cambridge settlement marked a new type of colonization, a change of methods and frontier techniques that was to set the tone for the whole development of the west.

3

The first Connecticut settlements, along the coast and the Connecticut River, were laid out simultaneously in clusters. After the river towns, Springfield, Windsor, Wethersfield, and Hartford, came Old Saybrook, at the mouth of the river—"a lords and ladies" settlement, which had a hard time in spite of many indentured servants and ample resources. Soon the Davenport-Eaton expedition arrived at the Quinnipiac in three contingents, two of which settled nearby Milford and Guilford one year after New Haven.

The Pequot War took the English far and wide through the colony, and their eyes lit on many handsome spots. Captain Roger Ludlow of Hartford, pursuing Indians after the Mystic Swamp fight, gazed upon beautiful Black Rock Harbor, on the southwest shore, and two years later got together a group in Windsor, joined by some Massachusetts people, to found Fairfield. That same year, 1639, Bridgeport and Stratford were laid out alongside.

From these initial four clusters—the upriver towns, Saybook, New Haven, and Fairfield—a few more adjacent villages were soon set up, usually by belated newcomers arriving after land allotments had already been made, who could gain full-fledged civil rights only at the pleasure of the "old comers-out."

Settlers failing to get in on the ground floor at once looked for nearby acreage where they would automatically become freemen or proprietors. Often they were joined by capable men of the initial colony who saw a chance to exercise leadership or to get better land. Thus out of Hartford, within ten years, Farmington was founded, by a contingent of veterans, but also eminent Hartfordites such as John Steele and John Hart, the Wadsworths, Newmans, and the son of Thomas Hooker.

Ludlow, builder of the Bridgeport-Fairfield area, founded Norwalk in 1649. New Haven was active immediately. Second "comers-out," after settling Milford and Guilford, soon filled in Branford, West Haven, East Haven, and North Haven, and, before long, Wallingford, well inland. In 1640 New Haven founded Southold, Long Island, and that same year, Nathaniel Turner took over Stamford lands on which were settled Wethersfield families. Two years later, Derby was started as a trading post, with Skelton and Ansonia alongside, and shortly became an active shipbuilding and trading center.

The Connecticut River, like the coast, was a magnet for quick settlement. Almost at once, traffic between Hartford and Springfield led to the building of the Enfield warehouse north of Windsor, where goods had to be portaged around rapids, and a settlement quickly crystallized there. Settlers from Springfield, Massachusetts, soon pushed a few miles north to found Hadley, then Northampton and Hatfield, also west along the large tributary to Westfield.

Rocky Hill was a southward river-port extension of Wethersfield. Middletown was settled in 1650, with a grandiose amplitude of streets and open spaces, and for a time became the largest, busiest town in Connecticut. A trading post was set up at East Haddam, and Old Saybrook pushed up to Deep River and soon peopled New London on the Thames.

4

After this initial activity came a lull. Before a more general attack on the frontier could be made, people had to slough off European ideas and habits and grapple with the new realities. They had to become Americans before they could make America. They had to acquire the know-how of wilderness settlement; laying out, building, and organizing towns, recording deeds. They had to learn to raise fowl, livestock, and new crops. They had to accumulate capital for each new move.

It took time to get together enough surplus of cows, horses, sheep, and swine—even seeds for planting—to carry on in a new community. It took time to raise a family that felt pinched for lack of land. There was a definite rhythm, dependent upon industrious habits and improved well-being, but largely obeying Nature's own rhythm. As more and more settlements were founded, as experience—also a form of capital—was built up, the tempo quickened, and the human river became wider and stronger.

Many Indian wars slowed down the timetable, especially in Massachusetts and farther north. It took a century to find the people, animals, and equipment to settle the better part of Connecticut. Even then, western Massachusetts, thanks to Boston's restrictive policies, wanton provocation of the Indians, and its own peculiar topography, was still mostly wilderness. Only the fringes of New Hampshire and Maine were inhabited, and Vermont, except for a few trappers, was still wilderness.

Not for two centuries after Plymouth's founding did the movement across the Appalachians finally gather momentum. The leading surveyors of the Northwest Territory were Connecticut men, with a map of New England towns in their retinas, and the founders were mostly from Connecticut, western Massachusetts, and upper New York, the latter mostly New England folk taking to the trail again. The New England cultural heritage carried on well beyond the Mississippi. "Connecticut villages," with central park, schoolhouse, church, and town hall, appeared along the Ohio, in Wisconsin, in the Minnesota woods.

But this came as the culmination of the New England process. In New England, after a lapse of approximately twenty years following the first clusters of settlements, a new wave of people—mostly "Americans" now—struck out for new places. Many towns were founded in the sixties. Bloomfield was laid out and settled in 1660; Norwichtown about the same time; Meriden, in 1664; North Stonington, 1668; Waterbury and Woodbury, in 1672.

In Massachusetts, the only early inland towns were Sudbury and Concord (Musketaquid) the latter founded, named, and run by an ancestor of Ralph Waldo Emerson, Reverend Peter Bulkeley, who had been driven from England by Laud. Concord was soon famous for imitating Laud by expelling Anne Hutchinson. Far inland was only Springfield and its cluster of villages, tied in more closely with Connecticut than with Boston.

Between the coast and the rich Connecticut River country, a wide strip of poor land, including much of Worcester and parts of two other counties, where hostile Indians roamed, deterred settlement, so coastal areas from Cape Cod and the islands north to St. George in Maine were thickly settled before people tried to go inland. When they did, because of the "barrens" they had to jump far west, so movement was slow. Only the fairly fertile meadows of Brookfield, Lancaster, and Groton were settled in the sixties. The only "far west" settlements in that period were carried out by the Pynchons and their neighbors, who pushed north along the river to Deerfield and Northfield.

By 1675, when the terrible struggle known as King Philip's War erupted in fire and blood across the land, there were 120,000 people in New England, 16,000 of whom could bear arms. Nearly all the settlements in Vermont, New Hampshire, Maine, and western Massachusetts were reduced to ashes, and those regions did not recover for half a century or more. In Maine only six coast settlements survived. Sixteen Massachusetts towns went up in flames, and terror struck at Dedham and Plymouth on the coast. Even in friendly Rhode Island, four towns were burned; even Providence was attacked. Connecticut suffered little. The Indians were not subdued for nearly two years. King Philip was shot down in Assowansett Swamp, August 12, 1676, and his wife and nine-year-old son were sold into slavery in the West Indies.

Western Massachusetts, after that, was practically dormant for decades. The surviving settlements languished; new ones were not laid out. The plague of war and uncertainty had shaken men's security and confidence, and settlement there and farther north scarcely got under way again until the Peace of Utrecht in 1713 diminished the danger of French and Indian inroads.

In Connecticut, however, new settlement continued and by 1680 had even gained volume. Massachusetts people came down and settled Preston and Groton. Roxbury citizens pushed down to northeast Woodstock, into John Eliot's beloved and beautiful Nipmuk missionary region.

Captain Sabin, another friend of the Indians, built a wilderness fortress house in Pomfret in 1689 and was joined by other Massachusetts people, a few from Norwichtown. Soon after were founded Plainfield, Windham, and Lebanon. But land titles and jurisdictions were so confused that gun-toting and feuding went on for years.

Out of Bridgeport and Norwalk in the southeast in 1684, Danbury was founded. New Milford, Newtown, and Hebron came along after the turn of the century.

By then a speculative, get-rich-quick fever had slid under the guard of Puritan humility and piety. It was the era of John Law's wild "bubble," and speculation became the order of the day.

Although it was almost a hundred years after the first Connecticut settlements, much of the state was still wilderness. Western Massachusetts was mostly blank. But in both areas nearly all land had been staked out—with large grants to veterans, particularly officers, to political favorites, to proprietary towns. What land the colonial governments had left was no longer given away but was being sold to obtain money for schools.

The new clamor for expansion and opportunity ran head on into this artificial land shortage. Soon lands were being sold by the Massachusetts and Connecticut General Court to speculators or auctioned off to individual buyers. It was on this basis that marginal Worcester County, long spurned by settlers, began to fill up—towns like Ware in 1729. Similar bonanza sales took settlers in a big jump far west to the upper Housatonic in Berkshire County, where they met a countertide of Dutch settlers from New York. Sheffield was laid out in 1733, and other towns followed.

Many settlers came in from more crowded Connecticut. Alford, Sanderfield, Lenox, Otis, Williamstown, Pittsfield, and various Vermont towns were settled by Connecticut people. A freer breed, used to more liberty, they paid little heed to the reactionary seaboard authorities. It was they who formed the backbone of the more militant independence movement against England, and later, the core of Shays's rebellion of veterans and farmers.

There was a land rush everywhere. In less than thirty years the speculative frenzy promoted about fifty new towns in Massachusetts. Maine and New Hampshire were parceled out to veterans and heirs of veterans of the Indian wars, but mostly it was a land boom, not bona-fide veterans' settlement. Even so, devastated Maine recovered only slowly. By 1750 a few settlers had pushed into Vermont.

The same speculative fever gripped Connecticut, with sales of lots in the boom style of later western "kiting" towns, where deeds that looked more like lithographs converted unpeopled gullies into railroad tracks and buffalo dung and skulls into magnificent imaginary palaces. The new town sites in Connecticut were also extravagantly commended by the speculators.

Litchfield, bought from the General Court in 1722 as a northwest trading post, still obeyed in part the older formula. Though its people came from three different towns, they moved in en bloc as congregations. It soon became an important farming and industrial center.

From there people doubled back, meeting others out from Hartford and Windsor to the "bought" lands in the Torrington hills, the deep black forests of Harwinton, and the Pequabuck village of New Cambridge. Soon "kiting" towns were laid out along the lower Housatonic and the lots auctioned off all over Connecticut.

Sharon and Goshen were auctioned off in New Haven, the latter in 1738, to people from New Haven, Wallingford, Farmington, New Cambridge, Litchfield, Durham, and Sudbury. It quickly became a dairy center. Cheese making by the Nortons became famous country-wide, especially in the south. Later they took the art to Wisconsin and, once the lumber companies had stripped away its forests, provided that state with its major industry. Another Norton in Goshen made pottery, which was also nationally known, and carried this art to Vermont.

The speculative boom represented the taking-hold of the rougher hill country—less accessible, less productive marginal lands. But new land was not the only incentive. Religious disputes continued to split communities. Trading posts sprang up early and late: Windsor, Haddam, Derby, Litchfield. The need for pitch and turpentine for shipbuilding and supplies sent folk to the Simsbury pine forests as early as 1643, to Canton in 1740. Lumbering built up Union Lands in 1727.

Iron deposits were always a magnet. North Haven was settled almost immediately after the discovery of bog iron and good clay for brickmaking, an industry that has never died there. East Haven expanded with the building of its foundry.

Kent was auctioned off in Windsor in 1738, chiefly to people from Colchester, Fairfield, and Norwalk. Iron deposits caused a stampede and kept blast furnaces going for more than a century. Silver created Roxbury Station in 1750, but the ore proved to be a fine siderite—rich iron—which was dug out at the rate of ten tons a day for half a century. Garnet deposits brought other people.

The greatest iron discovery was in Salisbury, in the remote northwest corner of the colony, which became the leading iron center for the Thirteen Colonies, with great blast furnaces flaming beside a high mountain lake. For years, it was a wide-open "western" town with "the longest bar east of Albany." The first church was raised enthusiastically in 1749 with the encouragement of "16 gals rhum, half one hundred eight of shuger and two-pounds of all-spice." There in Salisbury Puritanism went down before the new industrialism.

The Salisbury mines and foundries brought on a land rush to nearby Cornwall, whose lands were auctioned off to eager buyers in Fairfield and settled by people from Plainfield, Colchester, Norwalk, Toland, and Midbury, Massachusetts.

By the time of the Revolution, the American colonies, in spite of British restrictions, were actually producing as much iron as England.

Copper, another powerful magnet, led to the rapid expansion of Granby after 1705, where for a time, smelting was carried on secretly because of British restrictions. Copper in Bristol later led to the populating of the south side of Burlington, mostly with Irish.

"Black lead" drew people to Waterbury and Plymouth, the future brass and clock centers. Cobalt, used for glazing chinaware, discovered near East Haddam by John Winthrop, eventually led to the founding of Cobalt. Gold drew people to Hamden, outside of New Haven.

Feldspar pulled settlers across the river from Middletown as early as 1690, and they named the place Portland after the famous quarry town in England. When brownstone fronts became popular in New York, Portland flourished.

During this period of rampant speculation, migration, mining, and new industries, Connecticut's population doubled in less than thirty years, reaching 70,000 by 1760, not including Indians and Negroes. By then it had become imperative to build many new roads and bridges.

5

Settlement out of Farmington obeyed the rhythm of population and capital accumulation of the earlier settlements. Farmington people first took hold of the localities easiest to handle with the techniques they had, such as Southington, a broad, treeless plain open to the plow, though its thin soil was the poorest in the area. All the many villages around Farmington were settled long before New Cambridge, which lay in a tight little valley ill-adapted to farming.

No surveying was done there for nearly a hundred years. By the time it was undertaken, the original proprietors were dead and their heirs were either well established or had moved away, so New Cambridge was laid out in response to the speculative fever as a suburban appendage of Farmington. The stiff quadrangle of right-angled streets, gridiron style, scorned topography; none of the thoroughfares designated in the survey except West Street could be used. Nor was there any provision for a green, churchyard, village commons, or burying ground—a lack of foresight that has given the town a clumsy arrangement from that day to this.

Thus New Cambridge, started by Ebenezer Barnes, unlike the earlier settlements, typified the individualistic rather than the group settlement. Previously people had migrated in a body from the same community or congregation and helped each other build shelters and clear fields for crops to get through winter snows. But Ebenezer went alone into the wilderness, and the settlers who followed came from dispersed localities—Hartford, Lebanon, Hebron, Middletown, Meriden, Waterbury, Wallingford, Litchfield, Colchester, some from Massachusetts and Rhode Island, buying title to individual holdings, not receiving them as an allotment.

Another important difference: New Cambridge was peopled by the sons and grandsons of immigrants, hence by people already "Americans" of a sort, not transplanted Europeans. They gave the place a savor considerably different from that of early New Haven, Old Saybrook, Plymouth, or Boston. Unlike early seaboard inhabitants, they did not cling so strongly to Old World ideas and culture. The King, the established church, were more remote from their awareness. Already they had had fruitful experience of the American earth and had inherited techniques of frontier farming, handicrafts, how to deal with Indians and carry on isolated community life in the American style. These were all matters requiring courage, alertness, and adaptability. These more individualistic, self-reliant people, used to frontier realities, thereby created an enduring pattern for western settlement for the next century and a half. A considerable number of the first Wyoming Valley settlers, the forerunners of the later great exodus to the Northwest Territory, came from New Cambridge.

For the most part, these newcomers to places like New Cambridge, ready to accept every change and challenge and face every physical obstacle, were "rude and hard." They were energetic, practical, more independent, and, being so individualistic, more tolerant. Tightly knit congregations or political groups demand a certain abdication of individual prerogative and individual thinking; hence they are tolerant only by force of circumstance. The New Cambridge settlers were not "congregationalized," not tribally exclusive, and thus were obliged to work out their own community ways of doing things. Although the hard toil of frontier conditions in general narrowed down intellectual vision and caused many civilized manners and customs to wither away, this agile "Americanism" produced soldierly virtues of loyalty, courage, and stoicism, tempered with greater initiative and self-reliance than soldiers are allowed to possess. This, too, gave a flavor to the new individualistic community decidedly different from that of Boston or Salem.

Though settled by individuals and their families from every point of the compass in "western style," later a few close-knit groups arrived, particularly family clans such as the Gaylords and their in-laws, who swarmed out of Wallingford, bought land right and left, and for a time were numerically a third of the settlement.

Religious groups sought freer air. To high Chippin Hill in the northeast of town came a hard core of High-Church sympathizers, uncomfortable in Wallingford because of the resurgence of Calvinistic revivalism.

Much later, Baptists came to Red Stone Hill, southeast, and to Fall Mountain, southwest, locations chosen because services could be held in any one of three villages according to the temper of the neighbors. These Baptists were hard-working artisans, wood-turners, combmakers, smiths, and iron-workers. Most of the later clock manufacturers were Baptists.

Still later, Irish Catholics came to work the copper mine and to Red Stone Hill. But by the time of the arrival of non-congregational sects, religious and political tolerance had become well-established, and this, too, was to give all western settlement a broader basis, an easier camaraderie and mutual helpfulness.

Not long after the settlement started, Ebenezer Barnes added two large wings to his house; some of his children were getting married. Two sons built on "pitches," or lots, he owned near "Goose Corner."

Around Barnes's tavern, with its punchbowl and decanter sign, were erected many outbuildings: stable, potashery, buttery, summer kitchen, the shed where maple syrup was "sugared off," meat house and smokehouse, the big woodshed. Little by little the huge stones—"episodic glacials"—were pulled into fences to enclose fields and orchards, where grass-cone beehives provided honey. Little by little expensive imported glass replaced the greased-paper windows.

On the far side of the bridge beside the tavern, James Plum, grandson of a famous New London tavern keeper, put in a dam and gristmill, then a sawmill. Soon a fulling mill and tannery appeared. Artisans, woodworkers, blacksmiths, wheel-wrights set up in business. Before long there were two other tanneries and little shops making pewter and tinware.

6

Ebenezer Barnes's last trip to Indian Quarry Hill Meeting House was in 1756, to watch the Training Band, in which his favorite son was an officer. He was over eighty, a great patriarch, outliving all his brothers and sisters and some of his children. He had more than forty grandchildren and great-grandchildren.

By that year the deep yearning of every community was beginning to be realized, one ignored in the original survey: the central hilltop, where five streets now converged, was beginning to take on the contours of a civic center—two churches, the school, a long row of Sabbath Houses south of the church, the ring of substantial private dwellings, and "Aunt Deb's garden." There was no official green, but the wide churchyard was ample for drilling.

The Training Band day that Ebenezer attended was the usual gala occasion when all the men turned out in breeches and jackets and tall, wide hats, the women in bonnets and long, full skirts. Special gingerbread cakes were baked for the children.

There was a grim note this particular year. Many New Cambridge men were off in the French and Indian War. Some would never come back.

The drums rolled, the fifes screeched, and the militia—every man from sixteen to sixty—lined up in a double row with pikes and muskets before the church to listen to a short sermon by Reverend Samuel Newell. The officers wore blue-tailed coats with cotton-tuft epaulets, red sashes, white trousers, and high boots, and carried long swords.

After the sermon, a red-hot poker was thrust into two big mugs of brandy flip, which were passed from hand to hand. Following the maneuvers and lunch, there was target practice, and games were played: stool ball, wrestling, stave contests, broad jumping. Girls joined in the running games.

So it was that a century after Plymouth, as on the first Thanksgiving, the citizens drilled and prepared to defend a free way of life. Thus was a new community born in the Great Forest from the half-dozen houses around Ebenezer Barnes's tavern.

More than a decade went by, then a steady trickle of settlers spread over hill and dale; finally came the church society, then the organization of the village, the creation of a political and spiritual center—a complete pattern of faith, education, industry, and defense, all resting on the free homes and the free will of the people.

It was a simple society, mostly a one-book society. Like the nomadic Arabs with their Koran, the New Cambridge people leaned mostly on the Bible. There were not many ideas as such —there was no call for higher culture—faith and work were more needed. The folk were a trifle ingrown; not until the whole land was laced together could horizons widen. But they laid the basic foundations for the good life, freedom and education for all men. Such was the pattern of the New England frontier. It was the pattern for a great part of America.

VII. Schools for Everybody

THE ACHIEVEMENT of religious tolerance, in New Cambridge as elsewhere, was achieved only at the cost of some conflict. Its schools were built by community effort, following the models in previous settlements but facing new local problems. Thus the building of early churches and schools in New Cambridge throws special light on the religious and educational system of New England and the new West.

In 1742 Ebenezer Barnes, then sixty-five, though still hale and active, found the long Sunday trips through snow and ice to Farmington Meeting House a chore. He had a scrivener draw up a round-robin petition to the Hartford General Court, asking permission to hold winter services in New Cambridge. There were twenty-one signers.

A surge of new settlers arrived about then, and gatherings soon grew too large for private homes. Two years later, another petition was forwarded asking that they be set apart as an all-year congregation, with a church and a permanent minister. This, too, was granted, and the church membership soon found itself a sort of governing body, which had to attend to numerous other things, such as setting up a burying ground, a pound for strayed animals, a Training Band, and a school. It was typical of the way many early settlements split off to become, of necessity, self-governing communities.

A new survey was ordered to locate the exact center of the village. People were pleased when it turned out to be a staddel, or young sapling, on the crest of Indian Quarry Hill, so their church would sit nearer heaven and overlook their homes. The General Court listened to the two-man delegation from New Cambridge and approved the site. There, presently, Ebenezer's son and his neighbors set the lintel to enclose the stones heaped about the staddel, and all toiled together putting up the first church.

But they quarreled over the choice of a minister. The majority favored a blunt, fervent Calvinist in keeping with current revivalism. The High-Church sympathizers of Chippin Hill, craving tradition, less emotional authority, and a comfortable ritual that made no trying demands, had little stomach for the harsher Calvinist dicta.

But the Puritans found the sterner doctrine more in keeping with the stones and thin soil—the daily struggle to survive. Strangely enough, in this severe, intolerant, despondent creed, they saw, as more cultured people could not, the glowing light of truth and liberty. It expressed basic independence from England, full identification with the new soil. In their narrowness, crude, near-repellent, and ignorant though it was, they were partly right, for the Chippin Hill people still yearned for Mother England and the old culture that had no real roots in this new land. The older enlightenment and learning from overseas were superior, since the culture of America, scarcely in the making, was still gross and homespun, but the more refined High-Church people were not in the mainstream of the future. They belonged to the past, to a faraway realm, not to the place in which they lived. Their nostalgic world withered away and died unnourished, and in the end they breathed their last as Tories—"traitors" to independence, like all diehards of history, unable to avert their doom.

When the majority at the time of building the first church chose a rigid Calvinist preacher, the Chippin Hill group seceded, refusing to pay taxes to support him or the church. Ironically, these stubborn conformists to a more ancient way of life became the fierce rebels and were dragged to jail in Hartford.

For several years, the controversy was bitter, then was compromised. The Anglicans were allowed to build their own church across the street on the same hill, and their taxes were refunded to pay a minister of their own choice. Thus New Cambridge belatedly learned the lesson of religious tolerance —something more universal and more American than any particular creed.

2

Besides building a meeting house and hiring a minister, the new Church "Society," in addition to other community duties, arranged to build two schools, one on Indian Quarry Hill opposite the Congregational Church, the other on Chippin Hill. This building of two schools at the very start required some discussion, and it represented tolerance toward the Anglicans. But it was also almost a necessity. The steep, icy hills were treacherous in winter, almost impassable in miry spring, dangerous when the little streams flowing into the Pequabuck were flooded.

Eventually New Cambridge schools on the hills and along the Pequabuck and its side brooks numbered twelve. Though nominally under the general supervision of the "Society"— that is, they were Congregational Church schools until long after the Revolution—actually they were run by neighborhood communities or districts. Each had its own tax collector, maintained its own building, selected its own teachers, secured books and materials.

Thus grew naturally out of the topsy-turvy topography of New Cambridge, before adequate roads or conveyances, a democratic frontier system of local self-government for schools that was typical of most of New England and was to be carried west.

As the population of each little nucleus of settlement spread itself out from the original plantation [wrote Welford Addis in his 1894-95 report of the Federal Bureau of Education], it early became convenient ... to allow neighboring families at a distance to form themselves into a school district. ... This system, so necessary in a growing agricultural system ... was adopted after years of use as the State System by the [Massachusetts] Act of 1789. ... Thus originated the school district community.

Well before this belated official recognition of a century-old reality, the system had been carried into Vermont, Maine, and New Hampshire and had been spread across the Alleghenies by the first daring settlers, who took with them, not merely tools, herds, and guns, but laws and institutions. They carried with them the Mayflower Compact, the Eleven Fundamental Orders, the Rhode Island Charter and laws, the church "Saciety" schools, the town meetings and democratic associations.

"Since the world began," Reverend Henry Ward Beecher told an educational society in 1859, there had been "nothing so remarkable as the formation of society along our western border." Other migrations in the past had taken little more than their flocks and personal habits. "But our ... people, scarcely less nomadic than the tented Arab ... pour abroad long the western wilderness in swarming millions, countless, with wealth of flocks and herds, and with a breadth and depth of civilization such as never emigrated before. They drive schools along with them, as shepherds drive their flocks. They have herds of churches, academies, lyceums; and their religious and educational institutions go lowing along the western plains as Jacob's herds lowed along the Syrian hills." A great part of this was New England, plus all it learned on the march.

An Ohio Commission of Education report (1889), reviewing the past progress of state education, noted that in areas settled from seaboard colonies where education was restricted to "the favored class," popular education was almost completely neglected, but in southeast and northeast Ohio, settled from New England, "people brought along in their immigrant wagons, the ideas of educational facilities at home, the little log schoolhouse rose with the church and the home." By "little public schools or private arrangement, the children were kept above the 'barbarism of ignorance.'"

Many western seminary schools and higher institutions were founded and long supported by New England. The early Illinois College near Jacksonville was started "under God" by several Yale graduates on a self-help basis, with a main brick edifice, farm fields, and workshops. Besides getting an education, students were able to earn their keep and some cleared as much as $150 a year.

3

Another abiding New England educational feature came to have a "western" flavor: the support of schools by public lands, coupled with state (later federal) aid. The New Cambridge "Saciety," on ordering its first two schoolhouses built, at once petitioned the General Court for school-tax refunds and its share of educational moneys derived from the sale or lease of public lands.

In the more fluid period of migration, the early stable wealth was land, and the New England governments—local, colonial, state—turned to land for school support. Other communities followed the early example of New Haven, which set aside its land for a college within ten years after settlement. Gradually the Massachusetts and Connecticut General Courts, in all grants or sales, reserved lands for the school, the church, and the minister's house. Vermont—President Ezra Stiles of Yale noted in 1780—had appropriated a tract in every township to support a state college. Here was the prototype of the western land-college system.

The Thirteen Colonies turned over all western lands to the Confederation, but Connecticut retained a big area spotted in the Northwest Territory that was utilized wholly for education. Money from it provided early Connecticut with one of the finest school systems in the country, and income from there continued to flow in until 1950, or for more than a century and a half.

For years this area was administered by James Hillhouse, "the Great Sachem" of New Haven, backer of Buell and Whitney in making coins, textiles, and guns, promoter of turnpike roads, stagecoach lines, banks, and the Farmington Canal. Up until his death, he was forever riding along the western roads in his one-seat buggy, through heat and snow, collecting the Connecticut "tax" for Connecticut schools.

The 1785 Ordinance provided that a section of land be set aside in each township for support of a school. When Illinois was admitted to the Union, Congress granted Section Sixteen in each township for schools and gave other grants for educational purposes.

Another "western" habit, the "traveling school," originated in frontier stretches of New England, particularly in Maine, to provide education to small settlements unable to carry the burden of a school and teacher.

Other things also came out of New England, helpful for western schools. The exodus of young men hurrying to the frontier left an excess of women, and young ladies increasingly took the place of men teachers. A "high standard of female education" resulted—a large body of women better educated than the men who were feverishly seeking opportunity and wealth.

An early volunteer educational society—according to the report of the Board of National Popular Education, published in Hartford, Connecticut—posed the question, "While young men are rushing to the new portions of the country . . . cannot means be furnished by which these benevolent women may *do good*—to instruct the rising race and assist in laying deep, and strong, and sure, the foundations of society?" The means were found. The young women traveled west to log-cabin or sod-hut schoolhouses. They (the young women) had to be replaced frequently.

All through New England there was a spontaneous and generous effort to help the struggling western settlements, not only with education but with religion. Besides the scramble for lands, there was a zealous endeavor to control the souls of men, an intense rivalry among the denominations, particularly Congregationalists, Presbyterians, Baptists, and Methodists, that, on occasion, became acrimonious and perhaps not wholly ethical.

The Massachusetts and Connecticut "Missionary Societies," with whom famous geographer Jedidiah Morse of New Haven was intimately associated, paid many ministers to go west as traveling preachers to set up schools and churches. Reverend Timothy Flint of Massachusetts, hired by the Connecticut Board, also became a notable chronicler of life on the Mississippi.

When he got across the mountains to Ohio, he rubbed his eyes. It was a "Yankee State"—the same towns and buildings and, also, he noted, "the same disposition to dogmatize, to settle not only their own faith but that of their neighbors, and dispute fiercely for the slightest shade of difference of religious opinion." Partly the New England migration there had been the work of the Ohio Company of Manassah Cutler and Winthrop Sargent, which had facilitated the movement of thousands of Revolutionary War veterans across the mountains.

Scores of societies were organized throughout New England to provide better opportunities for people in the West, an early Point Four program for "undeveloped and retarded areas." One public appeal declared: "The power ... there is in the accumulation of small sums gathered from the whole mass of the community—single drops that accumulate and gather force and swell to rivers—[is] ... the power of the individual in Beneficence." Thus "the march of dimes" gathered for western schools and churches inaugurated a characteristic democratic method of keeping the good things of society alive and growing.

When the slavery issue developed, New England became even more militant in its efforts to influence the West and started the Emigrant Aid Society to help populate contested areas with antislavery people from New England. In 1854 Edward Everett Hale published a handbook to popularize the society. It was, he said, "incorporated to protect emigrants ... *to organize emigration to the West and bring it into a system.*" The Society sought to protect the emigrant against fraud in traveling, buying land, and getting settled. It organized those departing into large companies and provided them shelter and food "at the lowest prices" until they were settled. By concentrating large numbers of like-minded people from New England, the new settlers would at once be able to exercise "those social influences which radiate from the church, the school and the press."

New Cambridge on the Pequabuck provided an example for, and later took part in, these various undertakings. And thus, the churches and schools of New England went lowing across the land like Jacob's herds.

VIII. Sons of Liberty

NORWICHTOWN, which became Norwich, on the Yantic River above its junction with the Shetucket, at the head of navigation on the broad Thames River flowing down to New London, had been shunned for half a century because of its barren, stony soil, infested with rattlesnakes, where only goats could survive.

An early "Pied Piper," playing a fiddle, is said to have lured some of the reptiles from the stones, and a few hilltops were fertile. The Indians found the soil good for beans—one eminence was named Bean Hill—and these became the community's chief specialty. Later, Norwich people, moving to western Connecticut near Danbury and to Nova Scotia for better lands, took along their knowledge of bean cultivation; in fact Danbury soon became known as "Bean Town."

In 1750 energetic young John Durkee from Windham bought a farm on Bean Hill, opened a tavern, and engaged in river trading, which was just beginning to develop. Perched on abrupt rocks rising from the river, Norwich looked more like a citadel than a town. Its steep streets, even after cobbles were laid, could hardly be traversed on icy days. There was a tiny, irregular-shaped green high up, with a plain little meeting house, a small courthouse, and two taverns, one owned by Eleazar Lord. Nearby in his home, Daniel Lathrop had started the first apothecary shop in the colony and waxed rich importing drugs. Out of such beginnings, eventually great drug factories rose in Connecticut. The Huntingtons—a notable family in Connecticut annals and later in the Far West—owned the great house in the north lane, originally built by John Bradford, son of Plymouth's early governor.

Soon after Durkee, hundreds of Acadians arrived, driven out of Nova Scotia—ironically enough at the very moment when many Norwich people, giving up the disheartening struggle with the rocks and snakes, were emigrating to Nova Scotia—

enough of them to found four towns. Later, many of the Acadians were run out of Norwich by vigilante methods and deported back to Canada. But some prospered, and their children married into good Yankee families. Durkee's own daughter, his only child, married one of them.

John Durkee was born December 11, 1728, in the frontier village of Windham—"the place of frogs"—in northeast Connecticut. He was the second child of Deacon William Durkee and Susanna Sabin, a relative of the famous Captain John Sabin who had founded nearby Pomfret in 1698. Both families probably hailed from Rehoboth and Roxbury in Massachusetts.

This had been a favorite spot of John Eliot, minister of Roxbury, "the Indian Apostle" who had preached to the Indians here more than half a century earlier. For Eliot it had been an "Eden," a "New Canaan," an "Acadia," but when Durkee was growing up, it was torn by bitter land-title feuds, "Wild West style"—long years of violence.

Durkee was twenty-two when he arrived in Norwichtown to farm and trade. Three years later, he married Martha Wood, but in 1756 he had to go off to the Indian wars. The Connecticut General Court appointed him second lieutenant in Joshua Abell's company of the Second Connecticut Regiment, organized to accompany the forces of the inept Earl of Loudon against Canada.

The following year, Durkee became captain of the Ninth Company in the Third Regiment, stationed near Lake George. He was ordered to scout for enemy stragglers after the battle at Wood Creek. His experiences—he and his men going single-file through the dense forests, ambuscades, hand-to-hand knife fighting, scalping—read like pages from Fenimore Cooper.

The following year he was under the command of Eliphalet Dyer of Windham. The regimental quartermaster was Zebulon Butler. After the wars, both Dyer and Butler were with Durkee in various exploits.

Promoted to major in the spring of 1762, Durkee went with

the First Regiment, one of 2,300 Connecticut men, to assist the Earl of Albermarle's expedition against Havana. When Durkee and his men arrived there on July 28, he found a great armada of 44 warships and 150 transports, with 14,000 landing troops, besides sailors. The British had already seized Cabaña Heights, but yellow fever had struck down more than half the force. Scores were dying daily.

The wall of El Morro, the castle at the harbor entrance, was blown up, and the fresh Connecticut troops were hurled through the breach. The assault cost 2,000 lives.

The troops fought step by step through the suburbs, seized high points, and began pouring 6,000 shells and grenades a day into the city. It soon capitulated. Besides other booty, fifteen million silver and gold dollars were captured, and three and a half million were distributed as prize money to the surviving British soldiers.

Not many Connecticut men ever got back. Yellow fever raged during the entire voyage home that November.

2

Prior to the Havana campaign, Durkee had gone into partnership with his fellow officers, Joshua Abell, who had a successful iron foundry near Fitchville, and Elisha Lord, son of the innkeeper. They bought a sixty-ton sloop, one of the first vessels ever built in Norwich, which they named the *Three Friends* and put into the profitable West Indies trade.

Durkee's Bean Hill tavern soon became the rendezvous of people chafing against British rule and trade restrictions. More every day, the "three friends" were beginning to feel the pinch of British taxes and arbitrary British regulations on manufacturing and commerce. Like Benedict Arnold in New Haven, it has been hinted that Durkee found ways to evade the customshouse, and maintained a band of stouthearted fellows who wielded sapling staves in the dark of the moon against too nosy Royal officials or sneaky informers. He became known as "the bold man of Bean Hill."

The county Superior Court, which alternately sat in New London and Norwich, tried many violations of the arbitrary regulations. One interesting case, early in 1764, was that of Abel Buell, a young silversmith from a well-known Killingworth family, charged with counterfeiting the King's money. Legend has it that Durkee visited Abel in Norwich jail and offered to arrange for his escape; in any case, he probably sat in on the trial in the local courthouse. The harsh sentence of bodily mutilation and life imprisonment given Abel was typical of the growing severity of New England courts, a throwback to earlier cruelties and a sure symptom of the defiance brewing in the colonies.

The year 1764 was a dramatic one. Winthrop secured a surprisingly liberal charter for all Connecticut, but New Haven, till then independent and not consulted, refused to give up its sovereignty, partly from pride, partly from dislike of the Hartford jury system and abolition of church membership as a requirement for voters. Guilford stanchly met the Connecticut militia arms in hand, refusing to bow to the authority of the charter. But when the Crown itself blithely ignored the charter and ceded Connecticut Valley to New York, a quick compromise was reached by creating a dual capital, both New Haven and Hartford holding six-month sessions, and the two colonies thus united drew together for common defense.

But what was stirring up the wildest emotions that year of 1764 was the effort of His Majesty's Minister, Lord North, to push a Stamp Tax through Parliament. The alarmed Connecticut Assembly issued a hundred copies of a booklet telling why it opposed the tax, and these were passed from hand to hand throughout the colony. It hustled Jared Ingersoll, a New Haven lawyer, off to London to try to block its passage.

In London, during the debates on the Stamp Act, two famous members of Parliament, John Wilkes and Isaac Barré, raised their voices valiantly in behalf of the colonies and were sent to the Tower for their boldness. In Barré's flaming speech he said that the New World "Sons of Liberty" would never bow to British coercion or be less than free men and equals.

The phrase took hold. The group of protesters meeting in Durkee's Bean Hill tavern at once organized themselves as the "Sons of Liberty." The organization spread lightning-fast through the Thirteen Colonies and spearheaded the militant battle for independence during the next ten years and more.

In formal meeting, the Norwich people passed resolutions denouncing Crown restrictions, asserting that the colonies had a right to engage in manufacturing and trade wherever they pleased. They adopted the slogan "Liberty and Property!" England had stirred to life a sentiment and a force it could never quell.

In spite of protests, the Stamp Act was passed. The colonies seethed with wild resistance. As historian George Bancroft described it, on all sides crudely printed handbills were hawked about the streets, "by daylight, moonlight and torch-light," with "quaint proverbs, scornful satires, jests with biting edge, pamphlets all flowing with indignant remonstrances or wailing with the cry of expiring freedom." In town after town the offending bill was put into a coffin and ceremoniously and derisively buried, usually with the local dignitaries marching in the funeral cortege, or else was burned in a bonfire before the "Liberty Pole."

The Liberty Pole, either a particular tree on the village green or else a specially cut tall trunk stripped of boughs, became the rallying point of independence and of protest everywhere throughout New England and New York. On it were tacked bulletins, calls to meetings, propaganda, verses of protest. Around it gathered the growing forces of freedom.

When Stamp Tax agents were appointed to put the bill into operation, more direct action was taken. The Boston agent, Andrew Oliver, was hanged in effigy, then the figure was carried through the streets by a great crowd and burned in front of his house.

The hint was plain enough. He resigned, as under similar

circumstances did every agent in the colonies. Aroused feeling in Boston led, ten days later, to the burning of the Vice Admiralty Court, the looting of the homes of the Comptroller of the Currency and of Chief Justice Thomas Hutchinson, Oliver's brother-in-law and perhaps the biggest landholder in Massachusetts.

3

In Connecticut the Sons of Liberty, led by Durkee, ordered everybody, under pain of reprisals, to refuse to buy stamps. Town after town voted to use no stamps in any transaction. Town clerks were forbidden to file deeds or record property sales. Courts were closed down for all civil suits.

Not only did Connecticut's London representative, Jared Ingersoll, fail to stop Stamp Act passage; he accepted an appointment as the Crown Stamp Tax Agent—"a barefaced betrayal of trust."

New Haven and other places, by town-meeting vote, called upon him to resign. The Norwich and New London Sons of Liberty, the core of the movement, held angry demonstrations about the Liberty Pole and burned Ingersoll in effigy. Demonstrations followed in Lebanon and Windham.

Direct warnings were sent to him. He was reminded that his initials corresponded to those of Judas Iscariot, that unless he resigned, he would go down like "chopped hay" along with every person who enforced or obeyed the act.

Not daring to bring any stamps in from New York, Ingersoll planned first to get the backing of the General Court at its September meeting in Hartford. The Assembly was bitter against the act, but Ingersoll had great influence, and the legislators might not be brave enough to stand up publicly against Royal authority. Durkee decided Ingersoll had to be stopped, and sent out a call for the Sons of Liberty to assemble on horseback with eight days' rations. They were to wear a red band across the chest and carry a white staff. Militia officers were ordered to appear in their uniforms.

The group from New London followed the shore to North Lyme, where others under Captain Zebulon Butler joined up, and rode on toward New Haven to try to catch Ingersoll at his home or countinghouse.

Durkee led the main body out of Norwich. They entered villages four abreast, white staves lifted, headed by two men all in red with laced hats, and three trumpeters raising echoes across hilltop greens from church to courthouse. They passed through Windham and Lebanon, gathering recruits. In all they were a thousand strong.

One group raced toward the Connecticut River at Haddam, the other at Hartford. The southern force galloped into Middletown early in the morning. They learned that Ingersoll had left New Haven the previous night in the company of Governor Thomas Fitch and an assemblyman. He had slept at Bishop's Stonehouse Tavern and had already ridden north.

They caught him and the assemblyman near Wethersfield and escorted them into town, riding in formation, white staves lifted, trumpets shrilling. The other group, coming south from Hartford, joined up. Durkee sent the assemblyman about his business and called on Ingersoll to resign.

He refused, saying if the General Court did not wish him to serve he would not do so, but he would resign only to the authorities who had appointed him.

Angry shouts arose, and Durkee had Ingersoll taken to the tavern. He refused to dismount, saying he was either going on to Hartford or back home to New Haven.

"You shall not go two rods from this spot till you have resigned," they told him, seizing his horse's bridle.

Ingersoll asked what his fate would be. Durkee said it would be difficult to pacify his men. Ingersoll said he could die now just as well as some other time. "Then we shall take you prisoner to Windham till you change your mind," Durkee warned him.

Ingersoll answered pleasantly that he was very fond of Windham and would like very much to visit there for a while.

He finally went inside the tavern, but kept near the window where he could wave to assemblymen passing by on their way to Hartford. Durkee ordered him to quit "enraging the people."

The crowd outside was milling around, shouting menacingly. Groups rushed inside, fierce and threatening, and it was difficult for Durkee to get them to withdraw.

Steadfastly Ingersoll refused to give up his post. "I must wait to learn the sense of the government," he persisted.

"Here is the sense of the government," answered Durkee. "No man shall exercise your office."

"What good will it do you if I resign? The government will appoint someone else. Is it fair for two counties to dictate to all Connecticut?"

"It does not signify to parley," replied Durkee curtly, losing patience. "A great many people are waiting, and you have no other choice but to resign."

After three hours, when tempers were frayed and angry shouts rose to string him up, he capitulated and wrote out a resignation.

It failed to satisfy Durkee and the others, so they wrote their own version, which included the proviso that he was never again to act in his present official capacity. Ingersoll signed without further argument.

The infuriated crowd, fearing a behind-doors deal, insisted that Ingersoll stand up before them and swear to it loudly and reiterate his promise never to serve again. For good measure, on being pointedly urged, he gave three cheers for "Liberty and Property" and threw his hat into the air.

After a not unpleasant dinner with Durkee and other officials, Ingersoll was taken on to Hartford in formal procession. He was riding a white horse and said bitterly, with forced wit, "Death on a pale horse and Hell following."

The cavalcade halted before Government House, where the Assembly was in session and where a great assemblage of citizens had gathered to protest against the enforcement of the act. There, mounted on a table in front of the tavern, Durkee reread Ingersoll's resignation. Once more Ingersoll had to repeat his promise loudly. Resolutions were adopted by voice vote to be put before the Assembly at once.

The Sons of Liberty rode solemnly about Government House three times, white staves lifted, trumpets blaring, then dispersed across the hills to their homes.

Governor Fitch took Ingersoll's side, and the lawyer thereupon went back on his promise, declaring it had been extracted from him by illegal coercion. But he could sell no stamps, and Fitch was treated like a smallpox case. He was defeated for re-election, and Durkee was sent to the Assembly.

Resistance to the Stamp Act rallied all the colonies to a common cause. Muffled bells tolled. Drums beat lugubriously. Fast days were celebrated. Guns were fired. Flags were kept at half-mast. The nephew of Benjamin Franklin, Benjamin Mecom, editor of the New Haven *Connecticut Gazette*, brought out his paper in mourning, with the streamer: "The Bells Toll No-Vem-Ber in the most melancholy fashion."

As a result of the initiative of fiery John Otis of Boston, delegates from nine colonies celebrated an official Anti-Stamp Act Congress in New York and sent a protest to King and Parliament. The merchants of Boston, New York, Philadelphia, and other cities agreed to import no more British goods. Trade came almost to a standstill, and British exporters began to go bankrupt. By March the following year England had to repeal the hated tax.

Toward the end of 1766 London made a few other concessions by reducing or eliminating a few duties in the burdensome trade laws, but imposed a more onerous proviso: henceforth all trade to and from Europe and the colonies would have to pass through British ports. In one way or another, the mother country intended to have its pound of flesh.

The fabric of trade was not quickly mended. Concerns like Durkee's had a hard time. Joshua Abell pulled out, and it was continued as "Durkee and Lord," which took over the in-

ventory, shop, all "appurtenances," and the *Three Friends*, at
sea on a voyage to Antigua.

In 1767 Lord died, "greatly insolvent." To meet obligations,
Durkee had to mortgage his home, land, and other properties.
The following year, the Townshend Acts imposed duties on
many new items, set up additional Vice Admiralty courts, and
imposed new agencies directly responsible to the Crown, not
to the colonial governments. Once more, trade ground to a
halt as town after town boycotted British goods. New non-
importation agreements were signed, and steps taken to promote domestic industry and employment. But Durkee's business could not weather the difficulties. He had to turn to
something different.

Before going to Havana he had bought half a share in the
Susquehanna Land Company, organized in Windham by his
former commander and fellow deputy in the Assembly,
Eliphalet Dyer, and by Vine Elderkin, both outstanding
jurists and wealthy men. The company proposed to settle
Wyoming Valley in Pennsylvania, a region claimed by Connecticut under its sea-to-sea charter that gave it "sovereignty"
over all uninhabited areas as far as the Pacific, or "Southwest
Sea."

There were difficulties. England frowned on frontier settle-
ment, considering western resources to be the property of the
Crown and the Royal Navy, and fearing that dispersion of the
colonial population would weaken control. Also, Wyoming
Valley was claimed by the Penn family and by the powerful
Six Nations Indian Confederation.

One by one, obstacles were cleared away. The Connecticut
General Court readily gave consent. Reluctant sanction was
obtained in London by company emissaries, and some thousands of pounds were paid to the Indian sachems. There
remained only the Penns. Their grant bore a later date, but
they prepared to defend it.

The Indians, in spite of the payments, had wiped out an
early Connecticut settlement in the valley, precipitating a long

Indian war that flared for several years from Georgia to Maine, but the frontier was now at peace again, and the company planned to go ahead in earnest. Five or six townships were mapped out, each to contain forty settlers, who would receive four hundred acres free. The "First Forty," to be led by Dyer and Elderkin's son, would have the choice of the best township and would receive two hundred pounds for supplies. The company also voted fifty pounds for a road "to said Susquehanna River," the stream that ran through the valley. Major Durkee was to follow a few months later with two hundred more settlers.

When it was learned that the Pennamites planned to give out all Wyoming Valley in big manorial estates, a hurry-up call was sent for the First Forty to leave Connecticut before the end of January, 1769.

They braved winter storms and deep drifts in the high mountains and finally topped the great Moosic Ridge and gazed down upon the magnificent white valley—the "Promised Land," the "New Canaan of their dreams." Smoke curled up from a few log huts and Indian tepees.

The Pennamites were already in full possession of the valley. They had staked out the best land and had built a strong fort.

Undaunted, the Connecticut men followed the Susquehanna down from its junction with the Lackawanna to Mill Creek, below the Penn fort. They were met with leveled rifles.

"In the name of the Commonwealth of Pennsylvania," Sheriff John Jennings arrested Dyer, Elderkin, and another leader, and herded the rest out of the valley, back over the mountains.

The leaders were taken sixty miles through the snow to the little log-cabin jail in Easton, on the lower Delaware. After four days, by deeding over land, they obtained bail and rejoined their followers on the Minisinks farther up the Delaware. Stubbornly, for the third time, everybody recrossed the icy mountains to the valley. They managed to throw up temporary log cabins.

"Those rash and incomprehensible people of New England," sputtered the governor of Pennsylvania.

Backed by additional Pennamite forces, Jennings burst into the cabins, arrested everybody, and set fire to everything.

Half the prisoners escaped on the way to Easton, but twenty were lodged in jail.

4

Durkee set out from Connecticut in April with about two hundred settlers. He led his forces across the Connecticut River and through Wallingford, where they picked up contingents from New Cambridge, Waterbury, and New Haven. Passing through Danbury, they crossed the Hudson at Poughkeepsie and went through the Quaker settlements in Dutchess County, New York, then followed the Delaware down to the Minisinks, where they found the remnants of the First Forty.

All climbed over the rough mountain ranges, ridge after ridge. Spring was well advanced, little snow now, though they had to cross many swollen streams. They reached the junction of the Susquehanna and Lackawanna, and Durkee led them boldly past the Pennamite fort to the burned cabins on Mill River. Jennings lacked sufficient men this time to oppose them. They hastened to plant two hundred acres and build houses. All the new dwellings faced a quadrangle, with only loopholes at the back. Some months later a high pointed-stick palisade was constructed. So was Fort Durkee erected.

The two forts glowered at each other only half a mile apart. Lone stragglers, caught by either side, were badly beaten. Getting reinforcements, the Pennamites staged a surprise attack. Durkee was taken to Philadelphia in chains, and the Connecticut settlers were driven out again, their homes burned, their livestock seized.

The company rushed Captain Zebulon Butler to the scene. The Connecticut settlers were scattered, but he secured the help of the Paxton Rangers of adjacent Lancaster County, who had been fighting the Penns for years in behalf of squatter's rights against the big manors. They swept into the valley and took back Fort Durkee at a gallop.

Durkee, by then released from jail, gathered the Connecticut men on the lower Delaware, secured supplies and weapons, and hurried back to the valley to join Butler in besieging the Pennamite fort. It was fired on with a captured cannon, assaults were made and thrown back, but finally the Pennamite stores were set on fire, and the defenders surrendered and were expelled from the valley.

Quickly Durkee laid out two towns: Wilkes-Barre, in honor of the British statesmen who had stood up for justice to America, and "Forty Fort" across the river, soon renamed Kingston, the choice of the First Forty.

Early in June, allotments were made by lottery, numbers in one hat, names in another. In accord with usual Connecticut procedure, a town lot, outlying meadows for farming, and rougher land for grazing were allotted. The communities were replicas of Connecticut settlements, meeting house, school, the usual green.

But hardly were crops going in and houses going up than the Pennamites crept back over an unguarded northeast trail. After clubbing Kingston settlers, they crossed the river and seized Fort Durkee, trampling women and children. Butler was badly wounded, and he and Durkee were taken in irons to Philadelphia. Once more the settlers were driven out, their houses and barns burned, their livestock stolen. Men, women, and children toiled over the mountains in early autumn cold. Many perished in the mountains and the swamps.

In spite of everything, they went back. There were other battles, but they rolled in, not by hundreds but by thousands, and the valley became Westmoreland County, Connecticut.

5

All efforts by the Susquehanna Company to get Durkee released were unavailing. For two years he lay in a filthy dungeon and came out broken in health.

The Norwich Sons of Liberty gave him a roaring welcome. They were again fighting British coercion. Durkee was caught up in the gale of defiance.

The focus of resistance was now Boston, where the new merchant class was hard hit. Massachusetts, once the center of oppression, thanks to the stirring efforts of Samuel Adams, James Otis, wealthy John Hancock, and others, had become the cradle of liberty.

Adams had strong backing. The emerging shipowners, industrialists, and traders were in no mood to have their freedom and business extinguished by Crown restrictions. They enjoyed popular support because of high taxes and abuses by the soldiery and overseas bureaucrats who arrogantly pushed the most respectable colonials off the sidewalks. Everywhere people were defiantly erecting more Liberty Poles on the greens. They were replaced as fast as the redcoats tore them down.

In answer to a call from Samuel Adams, Massachusetts towns began setting up "Committees of Correspondence," spearheaded by the ardent Sons of Liberty, to keep an eye on Tories, boycott British goods, keep other towns informed of developments, and help them if necessary. Propaganda was circulated.

Durkee was put in charge of organizing similar committees in Connecticut and arranging correspondence with other colonies. He traveled widely about the state and also made two quick visits to Wyoming Valley as "President of the Settlers" to lay out several more towns.

In all the Connecticut towns he visited, he saw new developments, a widespread effort by the colony to supply its own needs. England could no longer prevent the colonies from inventing, producing, and manufacturing. His Bean Hill neighbor, Edmund Darrow, was making the first cut nails in America out of barrel hoops. Richard Collier was making warming pans. Combs were being made. Similar enterprise was being displayed nearly everywhere. Norwalk had started paper mills and was making clocks, watches, and shingle nails.

Western towns were making hats. Berlin and New Cambridge were producing tinware. Mansfield had a silk factory. Glastonbury, New Haven, and other places were making gunpowder. Brassware, metal type, silverware were now being turned out in New Haven. Benedict Arnold advertised in the New Haven paper for bids on a large order of gun barrels.

The Boston Tea Party! Durkee got the full details from Thomas Harland, a London clockmaker fresh from England, who had started a shop near the Norwich Green to make "spring, musical and plain clocks." Harland had arrived in Boston on the tea ship. At Griffin's wharf, 8,000 people had crowded the shore, while Sons of Liberty men, garbed as Mohawk Indians, whooped it up as they hurled every one of the 342 cases of tea overboard.

England retaliated drastically. Benjamin Franklin, colonial agent in London, was insulted by a high official and dismissed as colonial postmaster. Parliament, thoroughly angered, shouted down calmer spirits of conciliation such as Edmund Burke and, in spite of the dismal failure of Stamp Act enforcement, closed Boston port to all trade except military supplies until the city compensated for the destroyed tea and damage to Royal property. Governor Thomas Hutchinson prorogued the Assembly.

All New England was infuriated. Protest meetings were called at the Liberty Poles, and resolutions were passed to send supplies to the beleaguered port, where the redcoats patrolled the idle wharves.

Parliament also rushed through a bill suspending Massachusetts' charter and making all officials, even down to sheriffs and justices of the peace, Crown appointees. Juries could no longer be elected, no town meetings held except by the governor's permission—to discuss only what he designated. Thus did England, seeking to prevent New World industry and control all its trade, wipe out a century and a half of democratic growth in an attempt to destroy the deep-rooted free institutions of the colonies.

A third Parliamentary act quartered troops on householders. A fourth legalized the transfer to England for trial of all those arrested in connection with "riots."

The storm of protest grew so disorderly that Hutchinson, no longer able to face Sons of Liberty demonstrations or listen to the "alarm bells pealing night and day," departed suddenly for England, leaving the newly arrived Commander, General Thomas Gage, as acting governor. With each punitive stupidity, this heavy-handed militarist became more deeply mired in difficulties. Each challenge made him more stubborn and aroused the people more.

6

Every town and village began drilling, getting arms together, accumulating supplies. Connecticut reorganized its militia, putting General Israel Putnam in charge. Durkee was head of the Norwich contingents.

There, as elsewhere, supplies were collected to succor Boston. Gunpowder was made. Family pewter was melted down for bullets. The lead sash weights were yanked out of the Huntington house. Women formed anti-tea-drinking societies, joined sewing and knitting bees, wove cloth for the uniforms that might soon be needed.

News came of the battles of Lexington and Concord. Putnam left his plow in the field and rushed north. From Concord he sent back word that every man "fit and willing" should hurry to the scene of action. Messengers galloped forth, quirt and spur, assembling the villages by beating drums. Volunteers streamed toward Boston.

Durkee's unit left Norwich May 23 and participated in the Battle of Bunker Hill on June 17. Owing to Putnam's promotion and the departure of Benedict Arnold to Ticonderoga, Durkee was left in full command. In July his force was incorporated into the Continental Army as the Twentieth Regiment, and he received a colonel's commission, later confirmed by General Washington himself.

After the British evacuation of Boston, the Twentieth was sent to New York. For the next few years, because of his courage and steadiness, Durkee was given the unique and dangerous task of holding the rear to the last minute against British advances. Since it was mostly a period of retreats, his daring and skill more than once saved the revolutionary forces from being wiped out.

The disastrous Battle of Long Island would have annihilated the badly outflanked American army had it not been for Washington's brilliant retreat across the East River to Manhattan. Durkee's Twentieth was sent at once to New Jersey to Fort Lee, opposite Harlem Heights, to cover Washington's evacuation of New York, then to hold the rear while the main body moved to the west side of the Hackensack. Durkee stuck to his post to the last possible moment—so long in fact that 1,000 barrels of flour, 300 tents, and all mounted cannon had to be abandoned, and his men had to scurry out leaving their mess kettles on the fire, but it permitted the bulk of the army to retire in order.

Cornwallis drove the American army out of Newark, and Durkee's regiment covered its retreat to the Delaware River. After fighting in the Battle of Trenton, December 26, 1776, his outfit guarded the crossing and was the last to row across the Delaware that night in a driving sleet and snow storm through cakes of floating ice. Within a week they were fighting in the Battle of Princeton. They wintered in Morristown.

Durkee rushed to Connecticut to raise more troops, for desertions had been high, but in September he was ordered to rejoin Washington in Pennsylvania, where his men took part in the Battle of Germantown, October 4, and in other affrays, suffering considerable losses. They shared the terrible Valley Forge winter. In the spring they fought in the Battle of Monmouth.

Durkee was put in charge of the Fourth Brigade and wintered at White Plains. In the spring of 1779, he was back in action on the west bank of the Hudson, where he moved against the Six Nations, which had joined the British, committing many serious depredations. The previous year, a great horde of Indians and Tories had descended on almost defenseless Wyoming Valley, bringing fresh horrors to that bloodsoaked paradise. Six hundred Connecticut people were scalped and more than three thousand driven from their homes, which were pillaged and burned. All the women and children who tried to struggle through the Great Swamp perished. A few escaped down the river. Most of the remainder toiled across the mountains, their children tugging at their skirts, scarcely daring to pause to look back at their burning homes. Frequently they had to hide in the bushes to avoid roving Indians; they ate roots, berries, and bark in order to survive.

During the next winter, Durkee held outposts near Morristown but spent the succeeding two winters on the Hudson opposite West Point. Before the second winter was over, he had to return to Norwich on sick leave.

His fighting days were over. In his early years, he had helped push back the French and Indians from the northern frontier. He had followed the track of his own trading vessel to storm the heights of Havana. He had led the first westward push of Connecticut people across the Appalachians. The First Forty and the Durkee group rode out on the long trail, blazing the way that in another quarter-century would see the whole Northwest Territory opened up.

But more than anybody else in Connecticut, the "Bold Man of Bean Hill" had recruited the militant forces for liberty and independence.

He was honored with the most splendid military funeral in Norwich's history. But his real reward, which he never lived to see, was the final liberation of a people, the creation of a nation. But the vision must have been there, the Promised Land on the far horizon, as he lay dying on that Pisgah in eastern Connecticut above the rolling Yantic River. The slogan of his militant Bean Hill followers, "Liberty and Property," is still the slogan of the entire country.

IX. Clocks of Independence

IN 1747 three brothers named Roberts rode from Middletown, where their family had resided for three generations, into New Cambridge, past high Compounce Lake and across the bridge near the Barnes tavern and the grist and lumber mills.

The oldest, Jabish, a tanner, bought four acres on the Pequabuck, just west of the mills, and soon became famous for his fine leathers. Jacob, the youngest, bought twenty-one acres and began farming. Elias, then only nineteen, purchased a beautiful tract on the brook at the foot of Chippin Hill. He culled out the good timber for a cabin, burned the scrub staddles for potash, sowed rye and "Injun corn" between the stumps, and put up a house for his wife Susanna, and two small children. She was the eleventh child of Gideon Ives of Wallingford and Waterbury, known as "the Mighty Hunter" because of his legendary prowess at exterminating "bears, deer, wolves and wildcats" in the Great Forest of the Pequabuck.

Elias was a mechanic and woodworker. After a few years he purchased a house and blacksmith shop on Wolcott Street on the slope running up toward Fall Mountain. Over the years he became one of New Cambridge's more prosperous citizens.

It occurred to him that clockmaking might be profitable; most people had only sundials, or "sand-robbers," as they called hourglasses. He visited nearby clockmakers in Wethersfield and Hartford and, with the help of his second son, Gideon, then in his teens, cut out the necessary wooden wheels, pinions, arbors, barrels, and pillars.

It was precise work that Gideon liked and for which he had unusual talent. As time went on the boy became a fine woodturner. He and his father made furniture, cabinets, and carved chests. Sometimes Gideon also worked at Jabish's tannery, scraping and curing hides. He went to school on the Indian Hill Green.

His mother Susanna died, and his father, then over forty, grew restless and wished to strike out afresh. The Susquehanna Company, seeking settlers for Wyoming Valley in Pennsylvania, had spread Aladdin's-lamp tales of the beauty and riches of the western paradise. The four hundred acres offered free to the first settlers willing to pioneer were an empire compared to Connecticut-size farms, and Elias made up his mind to be one of the "First Forty" to go out, for they were offered extra privileges and some financial assistance.

The call came in January, 1769. Elias rode off with neighbors from New Cambridge and two Yale boys (descendants of Anne Yale Eaton of New Haven) from nearby Wolcott, to join up with the Dyer and Elderkin party at Hartford, and he made the long, hard trip through wind, sleet, and snow across the icy mountains.

Elias witnessed the arrest of their leaders by the armed Pennamites and with the others climbed back over the mountains to the Minisinks. On the return to the valley, Elias saw their cabins burned. He was one of those lodged in Easton jail.

2

Gideon Roberts, just turned twenty-one, and his uncle Jabish, along with eight neighbors, set out from New Cambridge in April, riding south over the mountains past Cedar Swamp. Before descending into the deep Naugatuck Valley, he shifted his rifle and fiddle—he was very fond of music— and looked back at the settlement he might never see again, at the gray church on the hill where he had taken part in Training-Band exercises, and at the new school near the Barnes tavern where he had taught the previous year.

Gideon joined the main Durkee forces from Norwich at Wallingford, where he put up with his mother's family, the Iveses. They crossed the Hudson at Poughkeepsie and in lower

New York found hospitality at friendly Quaker settlements. For a century in New England, the Quakers had been considered "evil heretics." But Gideon found them kindly and hospitable.

Immediately on arriving in Wyoming Valley, Gideon left Jabish building Fort Durkee and rode south to Easton to find out how his father had fared.

Elias and other prisoners, out on bail, were camped on the riverbank, waiting trial on June 12. The case was continued to September, and they were then fined sixty pounds each. Eleven were unable to pay. Elias was among those who went back to the tiny log-cabin jail.

Lacking funds to feed them, the local sheriff turned his back, and the prisoners walked out. Elias and Gideon crossed into New Jersey, out of reach of the Pennsylvania authorities, and at the Minisinks rejoined other refugees, among them Jabish, driven out of Wyoming once more by a new raid of the Pennamites.

Weeks went by. Days grew shorter. Snow swirled. Those icy nights by the campfire, Gideon helped keep spirits up with his fiddle and songs. The three Roberts' finally left for the New York Quaker settlements.

It was spring before they got back to the valley, bright now with flowers and new foliage. By then Durkee and Butler were again in full control. Wilkes-Barre and Kingston, the latter township chosen by the First Forty, had been laid out. In the drawing Elias obtained a town lot, hill field, and mountain tract in Kingston. Jabish expected to take up land in Plymouth township to be laid out to the south. Gideon wanted his tract in the northwest hill township of New Providence, which reminded him of the soft, rolling hills of Connecticut. Gideon and Jabish helped Elias put up a cabin, get crops in, and build Forty Fort.

But the Pennamites, stealing over an unguarded northeast trail, fell on them. That was when Durkee was taken in chains to Philadelphia the second time, and the settlers, losing everything, took the long hard trail over the mountains once more, homeless, not knowing their fate or where to go.

The Connecticut people gathered their energies for a new fight for the valley. Elias insisted on going back, but Gideon and Jabish, knowing it would be many years before peace would permit the valley to be built up, decided to return to New Cambridge for good. With the first flakes of a snowstorm hissing into the campfire, Gideon signed over his four hundred New Providence acres to Elias, and they parted—father and son—not knowing if they would ever see each other again.

3

Gideon was happy to be back with his two brothers and his sister Phebe, who had blossomed into young womanhood, and, above all, to get down to work. For relaxation he devoted himself to his music and acted as chorister for church singing.

A new church had been built during his absence in the Wyoming Valley. Unlike its drab predecessor, it was painted bright spruce yellow with white trim and white doors and a Spanish-brown roof—as though the people's faith, now that the hardships of early settlement were over, had also brightened. It seemed a symbol of the passing of some of the darker fanaticism of early Calvinism, and people appeared to have a new confidence.

The big cloud was the growing bitterness toward England—repressions, taxes, quartering of troops were arousing universal resentment and resistance. The Boston Massacre, which had occurred when Gideon was at the New York Quaker settlements, had outraged the Thirteen Colonies. All over the land militia units were organized. Men went into training to protect their rights. They began making guns, saltpeter, powder, bullets.

As elsewhere, the New Cambridge Training Band drilled several times a week. Gideon and his brother Seth were petty officers. The village bought a strip of land in front of the church—a green for the drills. Gideon was among those who contributed to the funds for its purchase.

Early in 1774 the Boston Port Bill aroused New Cambridge, as it did all New England. At the Farmington Meeting House, Gideon found more than a thousand protesters massed before the huge bonfire and the forty-five-foot Liberty Pole, with its "star-decked Liberty cap." Streamers bore mottoes: "Peace, Liberty and Safety . . . No Taxation without Representation."

The head of the Training Band read the "infamous" Port Bill that sought "to starve the good people of Boston into submission," then cast it into the bonfire. The spurt of flame from those bits of curling paper in a hundred New England towns ran from the seacoast to the Berkshires, from Cornwall to Providence, through all the colonies to Georgia.

Volunteer Minute Men, willing to march at an instant's notice, were called for. Those who signed up wore uniforms under their work clothes, ready to take off when the call came. A resolution was passed to boycott British goods, and a committee was set up to enforce it. Soon Tories were being "excommunicated." It was agreed to gather weapons, ball, and powder, and solicit food and clothing for beleaguered Boston. Hezekiah Gridley of New Cambridge, a leading artisan and businessman, developer of the local copper and iron mines, turned his big West Street house into a "Continental" warehouse, and Amos Barnes, of Red Stone Hill, son of Ebenezer Barnes, took charge of collecting the supplies.

Ships and fishing boats lay idle in Boston harbor, the landings empty and silent except for the tread of redcoats. All New England villages draped their churches in black. Special fast days were called, and at such times every community was silent except for prayers and the drums that beat solemnly, all day, all night; the bells that tolled slowly, heavily, all day, all night, as for an endless funeral.

4

The Connecticut General Assembly, one of the few colonial bodies that stood up stanchly for resistance against English aggressions, offered a ten-pound bounty for each half-hundred-weight of saltpeter or niter, which, pulverized with sulphur and charcoal, became gunpowder. Gideon and his brother Seth began making it at Seth's place on South Street. It was not easy work. Big casks had to be filled with earth, others with wood ashes. Water strained through the dirt was mixed with liquid lye from the ashes, boiled, and allowed to cool; this brought the saltpeter to the surface.

In April, 1775, Paul Revere rode, and Minute Men fought the redcoats from behind every tree and stone wall in Lexington and Concord. The New Cambridge contingent arrived too late for Bunker Hill but took their place in the long siege of Boston. The battle for a new free way of life had begun.

Gideon remained behind, training more recruits, but was soon in the service along with his brothers and cousins. His company was stationed in Hartford in a hill camp above Meeting House Green and the famous Heart and Crown Inn, not far from the *Connecticut Courant* offices, in readiness to repel the expected invasion of the coast.

By this time a fortnightly postrider service—perhaps the first pony express to the west—had been set up between Hartford and Wyoming Valley, so he heard more frequently from his father, also from his older brother, who had gone out.

The valley had little protection, for nearly every able-bodied man had gone off to join the Continental Army. The remaining settlers, the old and young, frantically strengthened their forts, fearing that the Tories and Indians might massacre them. A terrible smallpox epidemic was raging; the country "pesthouse" was crowded with victims.

In December, 1776, Gideon became an ensign. He saw his fellow townsman, Moses Dunbar, a Chippin Hill Tory, "hanged up by the neck between the heavens and earth" for treason. Gideon's outfit was ordered south, and on September 27, he hastened to marry Falla Hopkins, an orphan girl, descended from prominent founders of Plymouth, Boston, and Hartford, a family that was to produce many notable officers, statesmen, and industrialists.

When he got back to Falla again, six months later, she was with child, so he took her to New Cambridge. When they passed under the tall elms of Farmington, they found the place full of Yale students, moved inland because food was scarce in New Haven after British raids on Connecticut supply centers.

In New Cambridge, from the lips of Katherine Gaylord, who had escaped from Wyoming Valley with three tiny children and had walked all the way home through the wilderness, he learned of the massacre by Indians and Tories, all the killing and scalping on July 3, 1778. His father Elias had been killed. Every home in the valley, except those marked with white Tory crosses had been burned, everything wiped out.

Back at the front, Gideon went through hard fighting and suffered through a bitter New Jersey winter. Taken prisoner, he was crammed—according to family records, though his name does not appear on prisoner lists—with more than a thousand others under chained hatches on one of the rotting prison ships at the East River Wallabout. They were fed putrid, maggoty meat and wormy bread. Many had festering wounds. Smallpox, yellow fever, typhus, spotted fever, dysentery raged, and scores died daily. The weighted bodies were tossed into the river; the whole area stank of death.

Gideon escaped and walked back to New Cambridge.

5

Peace was at hand. Lord Cornwallis surrendered his entire army at Yorktown, and after a few minor skirmishes elsewhere, the war was over. The Treaty of Paris, signed provisionally in November, 1782, and confirmed the following year, brought full independence to the Thirteen Colonies and dominion as far west as the Mississippi River.

Those first years after the long struggle were not easy. Inflation was terrible. Veterans, caught with worthless Continental money—"shinplasters"—accumulated debts, and unpaid mortgages, had to sell their claims for eight cents on the dollar, while speculators, pulling strings with the new government, were able to cash them in at par for good new money. Officers got large sums to settle up promised postwar pay, but ordinary soldiers shivered through winter after winter, unable to buy clothing to replace their tattered uniforms.

In Massachusetts the Tories had largely regained control of the government and were playing high and handsome with speculators and privileged elements, so that independence and peace saw many old British abuses perpetuated and aggravated by the new independence regime. Presently all western Massachusetts, even several coast counties, in good Sons of Liberty style, swept behind Daniel Shays's revolt to close down all courts till reforms could be enacted that would free debtors from prison and save homes and farms from foreclosure. Many were Steuben's veterans, with pine cockades in their triangular hats. Shays was a Revolutionary War officer, presented with a sword by La Fayette for bravery, which he had had to sell in order to eat.

The revolt was crushed, though not easily, and Shays, condemned to death *in absentia*, went to the new Schoharie wheat country in New York. Thousands of others fled from western Massachusetts to the frontier, homesteading along the Great Lakes and the Ohio.

Things were better in Connecticut, already more developed industrially than most of Massachusetts, and the forces of freedom kept better control of state and local governments. The economic situation was not so severe, and greater optimism prevailed. The outlook was indeed breath-taking. The new nation stretched from Canada to Florida, from the Atlantic to the Mississippi, and Crown restrictions against western migration were abolished. On foot, on horseback, in Conestoga wagons, men, women, and children pushed across the mountains with their animals and tools. Flatboats and keelboats, loaded high with furniture and supplies, drifted along the mighty rivers and followed the winding thread up through great forests. It was a tremendous tide of discovery and settlement.

All over Massachusetts and Connecticut new industries sprang up to supply clothing, food, tools, and means of transportation, both at home and on the expanding frontier. There was a shortage of everything. The colonies, with most overseas trade cut off, had to make goods themselves or go without. They were free to do so now. What the frontier required, previously supplied by England, soon was being supplied increasingly by the northern seaboard states. New Cambridge and New Haven began making wagons for the long treks into the wilderness. The little foundries of Springfield, Leicester, New Haven, Waterbury, and along the Naugatuck Valley hammered out more and more gunbarrels, spades and hoes, adzes and axes. Saws were manufactured. Power textile mills, both wool and cotton, sprang up in New Haven, Waterbury, Manchester, Hartford, and Fall River, Massachusetts. Shoe factories were started, new machinery developed. More inventions came from every corner, even tiny hamlets. New opportunities knocked at every door. Without independence, the development of the United States would have been slowed up for a century or more, and the greater part of the continent permanently occupied by other powers.

Gideon felt the new urge and started making tall wooden clocks—the old grandfather clock. His tools were a jackknife, saws, bow drills, foot lathe, files, and rasps. The plates were cut from oak; cherry served for the wheels. The teeth were set off with dividers, cut with a jackknife and fine saw, then filed and smoothed. The necessary wire was hammered out by hand by a neighbor across the street. Sheet-iron cans with sand, later filled with lead, supplied the weights. The end of the "wag," or pendulum, carried lead in a trim brass shell. The dial, paper glued on wood—designed by Falla—was neat and severe, whereas early faces had been ornate and overfanciful. Gideon's product was superior to all previous handmade New England clocks. The ensemble, housed in a long, polished, pine case, sold for fifty dollars.

The day came when he finished his first three clocks and loaded them on his horse, two sticking out of his saddlebags, the third crosswise behind on the saddle. He set out over the south trail across the mountain to Wolcott and Waterbury to sell them—the route he had taken long ago to Wyoming Valley. Over the next few years, the boy Chauncey Jerome, who was to become the largest mass producer of clocks in the world, frequently saw Gideon ride by with his awkward load. Jerome considered Gideon one of the best craftsmen of his day. "He made a good article."

But fine timepieces were still a luxury that only the well-to-do could afford. The tax-assessment lists of the various New England towns of the day show only a few leading citizens in each community owning a clock. But every day, in eager new America, time was becoming money. Clocks were needed to pace the whir and stamp of new machinery, the comings and goings at new factories. The challenge Gideon faced was to make a cheaper and better clock that would be within reach of every man's purse. The demand was there, the market growing fast as America grew.

He was kept busy working and peddling, but found time for Sunday-night musical reunions at his home, which are mentioned in his daughter Candace's diary. He also found time for church and civic duties. He gathered money for the families of veterans and the poor—the "salt fund"—which he managed and distributed, got a steeple and bell put up in the church, collected school taxes, assessed property, inspected roads.

In 1785 he was on the committee to set up a town government. Hearings were held under the great oak tree where early parleys had been held with the Indians or in Asa Bartholomew's nearby tavern on the village line. The charter was adopted and officials elected at the Congregational Meeting House on Indian Quarry Hill, now renamed Federal Hill, where, earlier, Gideon had trained recruits. New Cambridge became Bristol, an incorporated town, with the usual assortment of selectmen, grand jurors, justices of the peace, highway surveyors, key-keepers of the animal pound, fence-viewers, leather- and weight-sealers, meat inspectors.

In 1794 Gideon helped start the public library. Now that independence had come, people were interested in history, philosophy, religion, good government, husbandry, and current affairs—all the great ideas and practical concerns that moved mankind. The library subscribed to the new literary review of New York and America's first encyclopedia.

Before long Elias and his other sons were helping Gideon in his clock shop, an abandoned tin shop he had moved and attached to the corner of his house. He used other apprentices: John Rich, who soon became a clockmaker in his own right, and half a dozen boys of his mother's family, the Iveses. They took part in his Sunday-night musical gatherings, and several became the greatest clock inventors and among the most important producers in the industry. More than anyone else, they started and developed the mass production of metal clocks.

Gideon dammed a small brook at the rear of his property—which now comprised thirty acres—to run his sawmill and equipment. Presently he was making interchangeable parts with power tools, a method also followed by Eli Terry in nearby Plymouth. Here was the start of mass production in America, soon discovered also by Eli Whitney in New Haven while making cotton gins, and developed on a large industrial scale in the making of guns. Presently in the clock world it would be taken up by Chauncey Jerome and provide the basis for his astounding success in building up the biggest clock factory in the world. Gradually the use of uniform inter-

changeable parts took hold of the New Haven carriage industry—the main carriage center of the country—and presently it
was adopted by nearly all industry throughout the country.
Here was laid the basis of all America's later low-cost production that made all goods available to everybody and so
dramatically improved the American standard of living that
it stood far above the level of the rest of the world.

As Gideon's output increased, oxcarts loaded with fine
woods and metals strained across the hills and along the
Pequabuck. Turnpikes were built, and stagecoaches began
running through Bristol. A new hotel went up on Farmington
Avenue to accommodate travelers, a place soon famous for its
oyster stews.

Before long, Gideon was selling job lots of clocks to local
traders, such as Stephen and Thomas Barnes, descendants of
Ebenezer, and to George Mitchell, son of a Scotch textile
man. George Mitchell was building up a country-wide peddling business to distribute Bristol tinware—there were now
two-score factories in the area—and clocks, buttons, cider,
alcohol, mirrors, woodwork, furniture, utensils, leather goods,
and other products of the region.

The peddlers were a picturesque lot, salty with travel and
the shrewd wit of trading. The first ones carried their wares in
fifty-pound tin trunks on their backs, or by horse, deep into
the South and along the Ohio to the Mississippi. Bronson
Alcott tried that, going as far as Virginia, where he dis-
gustedly sold his whole outfit for five dollars. "No wonder,"
said one wit, "he went to Massachusetts and became a Transcendentalist."

As roads improved and turnpikes were built, the peddlers
used wagons. Sometimes they traded their wares for linen rags
for paper factories or wood ashes for the potasheries. Many
ended the season in New York, where they sold their wagons
and teams and came back by boat up the Connecticut River.

The Yankee peddler became a national institution. He
floated down the rivers or carried his jingling load over the ruts

past the fresh tree stumps of the latest clearing in the wilderness. Among the products carried were ball bearings made from oak and hickory, a product that foreshadowed Bristol's later industry, which was to lead the entire world. The southern yokel who broke a tooth on one, mistaking it for a nutmeg, is said to have started the legend of Yankee astuteness that persists to this day.

The peddler was often a key factor in the western migration of New England folk, for his keen eye sorted out the best lands, and he brought the tidings back. Sometimes he traded his wares for big acreage, for imported goods sold relatively higher than land and a pane of glass might be worth a whole acre. He went into land speculation, breaking up tracts, starting towns, or trading for eastern farms. Big profits could be made.

Major Walter Wilkey of Maine told a humorous story of how he traded with "Squire Soaper," a peddler from his home state, giving his fine 250-acre farm in Mooseboro for 300 acres in Illinois, "producing 400 bushels an acre," and several house lots in the "thriving city of Edensburgh." He took his whole family out to Illinois.

Edensburgh City turned out to have one shack labeled a hotel. "Soaper," who had bought the whole township for "a few Yankee notions, wooden bowls, pewter spoons and the like," had spent only three and a half days there, staking out College Square and imaginary streets, such as Washington, Grand, Pear, Broadway, State, Wall, and Market. But such shenanigans lured thousands of New Englanders west, where they had to make the best of a bad deal. Those who stuck it out often became prosperous and important.

6

Before long, Gideon was able to open his own clock agency in the South, at Richmond, Virginia, in charge of his brother Seth and his son Elias. The southern business grew so much that three more sons went south to make cases and to sell. He was sending down more than a thousand clockworks a year. His daughter Candace, his fourth child, became a talented painter of tinware and clock dials and cases, and her diary, telling of her work, of the Bristol Training-Band days, Proxin', or election days, church services at the Baptist or Congregational Church, the fine balls at the taverns, the sewing and quilting bees, berrying parties, apple-butter making, provides an intimate record of the busy but exuberant first years of the new century of the new nation.

Even before going into mass production and opening his Richmond agency, Gideon kept on with his personal selling trips. He liked best to go down among the New York Quakers, and in the end became a Quaker, adopting their speech and dress, their wide Penn hats and their faith. His "quaintness" puzzled and upset his fellow townsmen, doubly so because he was one of the most well-to-do citizens, the first in town to own a carriage, a man of whom they were proud. But the old legends about the "terrible" Quakers had never fully died, and though, reluctantly, they had tolerated Baptists and had given permission to the Episcopalians to build a new church, as yet they were not overly accustomed to the new denominations.

Gideon's conversion conformed to his sturdy individualism and independence, his deep-flowing spirit, his kindness to the poor, his helpful deeds for his town and his church, his loyalty to his craftsmanship, his music and his fine books, all his courage and persistent seeking—feelings perhaps deepened by the tragedy of early death that struck down many loved ones; his beloved Candace, at the age of twenty-one, died in one of the dreadful epidemics of those days that swept off whole families. Quakerism and its "Quietism" probably expressed all his love of service and peace, his faith in reason and understanding.

The Quakers, among other worthy actions, had brought to the New World sturdy European cherry trees hardy enough to resist the diseases that were wiping out the native American varieties. Gideon needed cherrywood urgently for his clock-making, but there were few cherry trees in the Pequabuck area. He brought home Quaker seedlings, which he planted on Fall Mountain, above his home. They reared their tall branches high above the town. Many are still growing there.

Gideon Roberts's fight for Independence, his industrious artistry, his manufacturing and business talents, his trading far across the land, the men he trained, who all went on to greater things—these persistent, loyal efforts shaped the Bristol of the years to come and made it the clock capital of the world. From his efforts and the methods he devised, from the new inventions that sprang from his little shop near the Pequabuck, came eventually the timers on every household appliance, every precision machine, every automatic modern weapon. So the spirit of Gideon Roberts lives on in the little city on the hills and in the commonwealth and the nation of today.

X. Shoemaker Statesman

I HAVE FOR several years past for my own Amusement spent some of my leisure hours in the study of Mathematics," wrote Roger Sherman of New Milford, Connecticut, for the Boston edition of his first almanac, published in 1750 in "the Twenty Third Year of the Reign of our Most Gracious Sovereign King George II."

He had "taken much Care to perform the calculations truly," but if some of his information about solar movements, lunar eclipses, and other astral phenomena differed from that of other authors, he begged the reader "not to condemn ... until Observations have determined which is wrong."

Sherman started publishing his almanacs the year after he married Elizabeth Hartwell of Stoughton, Massachusetts—the town where he was brought up—and he continued them for eleven years. The last, in 1761, included a pathetic mention of her death.

He put in "everything" useful that could be contained in the "contracted limits" of sixteen pages: tables of church days, historic anniversaries, General Court days, Quaker meetings, "Free-Men's" Town Meetings, British rulers from Egbert to George II. A "Brief Chronology," which explained the "Old Stile" Julian and the "New Stile" Gregorian calendars, gave notable events from 4000 B.C. The distances by road from New York and Boston to "Quebeck" and Charleston were included.

He salted the pages with epigrams: "Learn when to speak and when to keep silent. Fools often speak and shew their want of wit." He followed this maxim most of his life. Information was interspersed with quotations from Pope, Addison and Milton, Dryden and Young, and from Sherman's own verse: poems on Eternal Judgment and against vice and drunkenness, that "Vile Incontinence" that took away "Reason and Sence," produced a "Mind possest," and turned

Man into "a Beast . . . studding the Face with vicious Heraldry."

For the 1750 New York edition, prepared in haste, he allowed the printer, Henry de Foreest of Wall Street, to put in fillers. De Foreest's quipping lines related the weather to the infidelities of a husband with a maid, and the mistress "making the house too hot for either."

Horrified, Sherman published a letter of protest in the *New York Gazette* about the printer's "Prognostiferous Observations."

Sherman's weather forecasts were breezy and colloquial:

Jan 17–19. "Cloudy and a Snow Storm without a Perhaps."

May 10–25. "Cloudy and perhaps a cold storm within the compass of these days. Let's everyone mind our own ways."

Once his almanac predicted rain for a day that turned out to be bright and sunny, but Sherman dutifully took his cape along to his New Haven court. A young lawyer spoke facetiously about his mistaken prediction. In the afternoon it poured, and Sherman was the only one who did not get wet.

2

Roger Sherman was born in New Town, Massachusetts, April 19, 1721, one of seven children. From his father, he learned the shoemaker's trade and journeyed from home to home. He always kept a book open before him while he worked.

After his father's death in 1741, Roger had to sell off property at less than probate appraisal, which left him in debt to every member of the family, and he also had to shoulder the support of his mother and the younger children. Two years later, he put the family on the stagecoach and pushed a wheelbarrow a hundred and fifty miles to New Milford, Connecticut, where his older brother had settled.

Noisy brooks and waterfalls tumbled through small glens in the low, rolling, wooded hills. The village hugged the bank of the beautiful Housatonic. Over the western ridge beside splendid Lake Candlewood were the tepees of several Indian villages.

Sherman opened a cobbler shop on the green (where later the town hall was built) but two years later qualified as a surveyor before the General Court, which so improved his income that he was able to purchase twenty-two acres of "swampy land" from his brother.

After marrying in 1749, he bought a house on Park Lane near the center, and eighty-seven and a half acres of land. He turned his cobbler's shop into a general merchandise store to trade boots, brooms, and hardware for sugar and tea. Some years later, he opened branches in Middletown and New Haven, becoming one of America's first chain-store merchants.

But he continued his surveying, prepared his almanacs, and studied law. Admitted to the bar early in 1754, within a twelvemonth he was handling more than a hundred cases a year. Asked if all had been decided justly, he retorted that the main thing was: "They were decided and made an end of."

Restless after the death of his wife and his brother, wishing a change of scene and a larger theater for his talents, he took his four surviving children to New Haven, then Connecticut's largest town, where he occupied a house he owned next door to his Chapel Street store across from the Yale campus.

At the corner was Beer's brick tavern, which also sold merchandise and books. Up the street was Isaac Doolittle's famous brass shop, started in 1742, to make andirons, tongs, shovel handles, doorknobs, and other brass objects. Doolittle also imported and repaired silver watches, made jewelry, engraved stone seals, and manufactured wooden clocks and some of the first brass-wheel clocks in America. He also manufactured America's first commercial press.

Sherman was at once admitted as "freeman" and was placed on the school committee. A few years later he was elected deputy to the Hartford General Court. He became New Haven County Justice of the Peace and Judge of the Superior Court.

When the colonial government became bicameral, Sherman was sent to the Upper House, or Governor's Council, continuously for twenty-three years. In 1768, he and two other jurists were appointed to index and publish Connecticut laws.

Yale University had just completed its beautiful new chapel, with its 125-foot bell tower, thanks to the initiative of President Thomas Clap. But the institution was having a rocky financial time when it asked Roger Sherman to serve as treasurer. Over the years, he frequently advanced the college money out of his own pocket. In time, he was able to secure better support from the colonial assembly and steady pay for the president and professors.

On a visit to Woburn, Massachusetts, to see his brother Josiah, whom he had put through New Jersey College and who was now a minister, he met and presently married twenty-one-year-old Rebecca Prescott on May 12, 1763. He was then forty-two. Rebecca's father was a noted jurist and merchant, ancestor of William H. Prescott, the half-blind historian of Spain, Mexico, and Peru. Rebecca gave Roger six more daughters and two more sons.

3

By the time Sherman became judge, the hated Stamp Act had come into force, and he promptly adjourned court. No civil cases were handled until the act had been repealed. Shortly he fined Benedict Arnold, the drugstore man, fifty shillings for having had an informer on his smuggling activities stripped and flogged on the New Haven Green.

His stand on public issues was forthright. When England proposed establishing a British episcopate over all the colonies, he came out strongly in behalf of religious liberty. "Will the numerous colonies who came here for ... freedom from ecclesiastical oppression, and by whose toil a great increase of dominion and commerce hath arisen to the mother country, bear to find themselves divested of the equality and liberty they have so long enjoyed, and brought under the power of a particular denomination that will monopolize all important places of trust . . . ?"

He wrote to the Connecticut agent in London that "no assembly on the continent" would ever "concede that Parliament has the right to tax the colonies," and in 1770 he headed a gathering of New Haven merchants to continue the embargo on British goods.

Excitement mounted, and when the call went out for the first Continental Congress in Philadelphia, Sherman was sent as delegate.

He was a rugged, awkward, peasant type with powerful shoulders, straight, thick neck, and close-cropped hair that accentuated his big, block-shaped cranium. His rough-hewn lantern-jawed face was creased by a very wide thin mouth, and he had a big nose and piercing dark eyes sunk in deep, bony sockets. Blunt and sure in thought and utterance, he gave the impression of ponderous force.

His fellow delegate, Silas Deane, who became a notable diplomat, did not appreciate Sherman's rugged, honest qualities. To his wife he wrote, after a New York dinner en route, that Sherman was "as badly calculated to appear in such Company as a chestnut burr is for an eye-stone," Sherman's blunt remarks, "odd questions," and "odd, countrified cadence" caused "some shrewd countenances . . . and not a few oaths" among those present. The shoemaker would be better off back in New Haven. Deane was furious when his colleague refused to pull out of New York on a Sabbath evening—"so we shall have a scorching sun to drive 40 miles in tomorrow."

In Washington, Sherman put up at Sarah Chesman's boardinghouse, paying thirty shillings a week and twelve shillings for his servant. Here boarded other Congress members, including John Adams and Jared Ingersoll, the "Stamp Tax Tory," now an Admiralty Judge. Adams noted: Sherman "is an old Puritan, as honest as an angel and as firm in the cause of American Independence as Mount Atlas."

Congress convened September 5, with fifty-six delegates, under the presidency of Peyton Randolph of Virginia. Soon Paul Revere galloped in dramatically from Massachusetts with the bold Suffolk Resolves, which immediately drew the lines between those moving for independence and more cautious spirits. The Resolves declared the coercive acts unconstitutional and hence not to be obeyed, and they urged the Massachusetts people to set up their own government agencies to collect taxes and withhold them from the Royal authorities, to arm, form a militia, and impose the strongest possible economic sanctions against England. After much debate, the Resolves were endorsed in full.

There was a superabundance of talk, Sherman wrote Governor Trumbull. "Unanimity being in our view of the last importance, everyone must be heard, even on ... subjects ... not of the last importance." Sherman himself was an offender; he spoke often and long, "heavily and clumsily," John Adams noted, "rigid as linen or buckram; awkward as a ... sophomore." Hogarth's genius could have invented nothing "more opposite to grace." He clenched his left hand "into a fist" and grasped the wrist with his right. But he had "a clear head and sound judgment."

The Congress drew up grievances against England, denouncing all Parliamentary Acts since 1763. It voted to discontinue the slave traffic and to sever all trade with England. A "Continental Association" was formed, to be made effective through local elected committees, to stop all consumption of British products and to boycott all offenders and otherwise punish them.

But the most positive and constructive work of the Congress was the Declaration of Human Rights, a dignified but determined document drawn up by Roger Sherman and Eliphalet Dyer. It set forth the basic rights of the colonies to "life, liberty, and property." Speaking in behalf of its adoption, Sherman stressed that the local legislatures had exclusive power to make laws for the respective colonies "in all cases of taxation and internal policy." They are, he declared, "not bound by the King or Crown by the Act of Settlement, but by their consent to it." They accepted British Common Law, not by imposition but by wisdom and choice. There is, he repeated, "no other legislature over the colonies but the representative assemblies."

He returned home to buy military supplies for the Connecticut Assembly, which mostly he stored in his New Haven business quarters. He helped organize the New Haven Foot Guards, with Benedict Arnold named captain, to supplement the regular Training Band under Indian fighter Major General David Wooster. Arnold armed his men quickly and uniformed them in scarlet coats, with buff collars and cuffs, brocaded hats, white breeches and leggings.

When news of Lexington and Concord reached New Haven by fast postrider, Sherman presided over a special town meeting at the Middle Brick Church on the green. Unfortunately a feud had grown up between Wooster and Arnold, and each military unit was trying to prove itself more patriotic by conducting rival undisciplined raids on Tories, their homes and businesses. This rivalry split the meeting, and since a large faction of pro-Royalists was present, the departure of the militia to aid Massachusetts was delayed.

Arnold was determined—sanction or no sanction—to march his men to the front immediately, but the Town Inspection Committee, which favored Wooster, refused to give Arnold's company needed powder and supplies from the Powder House, the town arsenal.

At once Arnold rallied his company, surrounded a session of the town fathers, and gave them five minutes to turn over the Powder House keys to him, or he would break in. No one, he told them, except "God Almighty," was going to prevent him from marching his men to aid Boston that very day. He got the keys.

The Second Continental Congress, which Sherman also attended, drew up the "Olive Branch Petition" to the King, ignoring Parliament, whose jurisdiction was denied. But little else smacked of reconciliation, and under the presidency of fighting John Hancock of Boston, sought by the British for complicity in the Boston Tea Party, it voted to put the colonies in a "state of ofence." We are "resolved to dye Freemen rather than rot like slaves."

The Massachusetts and Connecticut troops besieging Boston were made a Continental Army, with George Washington, of Virginia, commander in chief. Sherman, who was on most committees for the conduct of the war, would have preferred a New England general but voted for Washington.

On June 11, 1776, Sherman was named with Jefferson, Adams, Franklin, and Livingston to draft a Declaration of Independence. Its basis, in good part, was the previous session's Declaration of Rights, drawn up by himself and Dyer. It was submitted June 28 and, after debate, adopted July 2, New York abstaining. A few changes were made and, on July 4, it was signed by the president and secretary, the members signing later. Copies were struck off July 5, and it was publicly read in Philadelphia, with due fireworks and jubilation, July 8. A new nation was born.

During the next five years Sherman worked day and night on army and financial affairs. A dependable wheel horse, he rose at five every morning and toiled till ten at night.

He fought to support the war by taxation rather than by issuing paper money. "I know no better way to preserve credit than to pay debts and not run into debt more than is absolutely necessary."

He bought army supplies and was on a committee to investigate army frauds—the dismal concomitant of all wars—and presently on another to reorganize the whole army. He looked after every detail with such jealous concern that he was occasionally charged with creating petty difficulties, for army men are rarely able to lift their eyes beyond their own fancied needs and extravagances. Often he had to consult with General Washington, and he settled various jealous disputes between high officers that threatened the unity and effectiveness of the patriot army.

His blunt, honest speech was more tactful than the cleverness of others, and increasingly he gained the respect and admiration of his colleagues. "The decisive weight of his character, the inflexibility of his patriotism," said one fellow Congressman, "made him like a Roman Senator in the early and most exemplary days of the commonwealth." His early verbosity disappeared; he became terse, putting his points confidently in a pithy way, and at times he displayed considerable wit.

When it was moved that an inept representative in France, ordered home, "need not return until it suits his convenience," Sherman amended it to read, "He need not return, period." When an emotional delegate proposed that the patriots give up the language of the British oppressor, Sherman moved to retain English for the patriots and let the British hunt for a new tongue.

"He was formed for *Thinking and Acting,*" remarked Ezra Stiles, new Yale University president, who found his treasurer a firm support at a difficult time. *"Law and Politics* were peculiarly adapted to his genius. . . . Calm, sedate & ever discerning and Judicious . . . with that Dignity which arises from doing every Thing perfectly right," he became "oracular" in Congress for the "deep Sagacity, Wisdom & Weight of his Counsels. An Extraordinary man."

He had a grasp of broad principles without the slightest pedantry; he was firm in his moral beliefs yet not dogmatic or intolerant; he knew law well, without being legalistic; he stuck to his guns stanchly but avoided arguments and never shirked reasonable compromises. He won men to reason and moderation by his calmness, knowledge, and sense of justice, and time and again headed off acrimonious debate by opportune delays to give participants time to cool off.

Sherman labored on the Articles of Confederation. He favored vote by states rather than by population, otherwise the three most populous states could govern the rest, but suggested that the vote might be taken both ways—that a majority of both the states and the popular vote be required. His idea was not adopted, but here was the germ of the later "Connecticut Compromise" that created the House and Senate and made final adoption of the American Constitution possible.

The Articles, presented in 1777, had to be accepted by all Thirteen Colonies. Sherman was eager to get ahead with the matter. "If it not be done while the war lasts, I fear it will not be done at all." But three states held out until all western lands were ceded to the central government. Virginia did not accede to this until 1781, whereupon Maryland, the last to resist, promptly ratified.

The Thirteen Colonies at last had a united central government and a written constitution. The nation was growing up.

4

One day Sherman announced that he had bought a piece of land he didn't need at a price well above its value. Rebecca was upset, for they were having a hard time making ends meet. "The man needed a coat," he said simply. He found time and means, even in difficult moments, for such kindly acts.

During all these years, the Sherman finances were most precarious. Rarely did he receive his pay on time, and, to help out, Rebecca and the girls made gloves, muffs, and tippets, some of which he placed with a Philadelphia concern. The situation grew worse with galloping inflation. Before the war was over, he was paying $90 for a shave instead of 33½ cents.

In October, 1781, when Cornwallis surrendered, Sherman wrote Governor Trumbull, describing the church services, official formalities, and gay illumination in Philadelphia. He also asked urgently for money long due him. He was without funds.

The war was over now, and Sherman returned to Connecticut, hoping to be relieved of duties far from home. He

resumed his place on the Governor's Council and the
Superior Court. He and Jonathan Law were asked to codify
the state laws. They worked for seven months, eliminating,
combining, altering, putting everything in simplified order.
Their compilation was published January 8, 1784, as the *Acts
and Laws of Connecticut*. Sherman had to wait six months
before getting the £78 compensation for his long toil.

Once more he was asked to return to the Continental
Congress. He arrived in time to ratify the treaty of peace.
Independence had been fully won, and the "man who had
never done a foolish thing in his life" had played a great part
in the achievement.

He worked hard on the debt question, taxes, tariffs, and
plans for setting up the western territory. He wanted no
"foreign adventurers or speculators"; the land should be sold
cheaply to bona fide settlers.

In absentia he was elected first mayor of the newly chartered
city of New Haven, a position he held until his death in 1793
and in which he showed the same care for every detail.

Determined to revive New Haven's trade, he had the town
made a free port for seven years and freed all ships engaged
in foreign commerce from all local taxes. He also sought to
attract new residents with capital, even if suspected of Tory-
ism. Merchants could bring in up to $10,000 in new capital,
or up to $15,000 in goods duty-free, without being taxed on
profits. A welcoming committee was organized to help such
newcomers find business locations, lodging, and homes on an
equitable basis.

Abel Buell, the onetime counterfeiter, was given a state concession to make coins with a new machine he had invented;
he set up a "Mint" on Water Street. Sherman was on the
committee to inspect the coins.

Under his guidance, the city took new pride in its appearance. To wipe out Royalist memories, street names were
changed: Queen Street became State Street. New ones were
cut through. Trees were planted. Elms were set out, and the

green "restored from its primitive savagery." New schools were built.

Ezra Stiles described some of Sherman's formal duties—the ceremony of laying the foundation of a new bridge over the Quinnipiac in the "XV year of American Independence." A cavalcade of "fifteen Chaises, besides single Horses," participated, and the entire party took tea at the home of Henry Dagget, son of a former Yale president. A year after that, Sherman participated in the laying of the cornerstone of a new university building.

After he left the Congress he was described as taciturn and aloof, "excessively reserved and aristocratic." At teatime he took his cup alone into his study and talked to no one. In the street, a young law apprentice observed, Sherman saw nobody, but wore "his broad beaver hat pointing to the horizon and giving no idle nods."

But those who knew him well thought him amiable. "There was no arrogance in his manner," said one. Rather was he diffident, humble, shrinking from prominence. He always preferred an inconspicuous back pew in church. A man of deep sentiments all his life, he was devoted to poetry, particularly the sonorous cadences and moral depth of Milton. He also liked Joel Barlow's contemporary poem, "The Vision of Columbus."

5

Once more he was sent back to Philadelphia, to the Constitutional Convention of 1787 to revise the Articles of Confederation and give the central government more stability and financial support.

During the Revolution all but one of the states had adopted new constitutions that abolished the indentured-servant system, swept away property and literacy restrictions on office-holding and voting, and provided other far-reaching popular reforms.

For the first time, the city mechanics and workmen had

obtained the vote. Representation shifted from taxable property to population. Legislative control over the executive was strengthened. Virginia adopted a thoroughgoing Bill of Rights. Tory lands were split up and sold to small farmers.

But even before the end of the war, an entirely new crowd —the speculators—were pushing into power in many places. James Bowdoin of Boston wrote in the year of the peace-signing, "When you come you will scarcely see other than new faces." After peace, reaction—the trend that follows all wars— came rapidly. In nearly all the states more conservative elements, even pro-Tories, edged back into high office. Everywhere the pendulum was swinging away from the democratic idea, away from "human rights," to order, property, and power. Little was done to ameliorate the lot of veterans, suffering from inflation, unfair taxes, and mortgages with accumulated interest. Shays's Rebellion in Massachusetts, in true Sons of Liberty style, closed down the courts that were foreclosing on farms. It frightened the governing groups, the commercial and mercantile elements everywhere, although in eastern Massachusetts it was joined by business elements and small shopkeepers rather than farmers. It came within a hair of taking over the commonwealth because of mass desertions by the militia. The Federal Government had no resources and was afraid to put arms back into the hands of the veterans. The reaction to this violence was a call to reform the existing Federal Constitution.

Actually the secret plan afoot was to dump the Articles overboard and write an entirely new document. Jeremiah Wadsworth, the other Connecticut delegate, was worried that Sherman, not a man to go in for "schemes," might balk, for Sherman always put principles above expediency, and Wadsworth feared he merely wished to "patch up the old scheme" —the Articles. "That was not my opinion of him when we chose him," he remarked wryly. "He is cunning as the Devil ... if he suspects you are trying to take him in, you may as well catch an eel by the tail."

Fifty-five delegates gathered. Not many were schooled in the great ideas of French and German liberalism that had provided the minds of the Revolution with inspiration. Jefferson was absent in Europe as minister to France. Most influential delegates were worried by democracy and widened suffrage. Gouverneur Morris felt that if "the western people" got "power into their own hands," they would ruin the East. This was the old exclusivism of theocratic Boston in early days, unable to grasp the true meaning of western empire. Elbridge Gerry feared suffrage would put seaboard interests "at the mercy of foreign immigrants," another failure to grasp the country's future greatness. James Madison wanted to disregard "the unreflecting multitude" entirely. Alexander Hamilton, who had no faith in the people at all, was an outstanding exponent of Hobbes's theories: the Leviathan State and all.

But among more prominent leaders were a few stanch survivors of the Revolutionary period. George Mason, of Virginia, who, with Washington, as early as 1769 had put through the House of Burgesses a resolution practically setting aside British authority and penned the great Virginia Bill of Rights in June, 1776, was one of the most valiant speakers in behalf of human rights at the Constitutional Convention, along with enlightened James Wilson of Pennsylvania, who had been in the forefront of the fight for independence.

Sherman for the most part stood between the extreme positions. Though a conservative, he was a thoroughgoing believer in democracy as expressed through representative government and bitterly opposed to the Leviathan, or all-powerful State, superjealous of local rights. His influence was great, for no other man present had had longer or more varied experience of parliamentary affairs. No one knew the law better. Few were more versed in religious and political philosophy, particularly the great stream of German and French thinking that had nourished the ideas of the independence leaders. His notes contain numerous excerpts from Rousseau, particularly

Lettres Écrites de la Montagne, and he often cited Frederick the Great's enlightened laws and luminous concepts of education and culture. Among his favorite books were Cicero's works, Winthrop's *Journal,* and Vattel's *Law of Nature and Nations.* But unlike Vattel, Sherman did not wish a too-powerful executive and believed in popular representative government. He did not want the executive or the courts to be able to countermand popular or congressional will.

As, in his day, Roger Williams had had a clear concept of the proper spheres of each branch of government and, similarly, the respective spheres of federal and local government and of those individual rights on which no government should trespass, so Sherman, though he wanted a central government that would function efficiently, with adequate revenues and the dignity and strength to maintain respect abroad, was determined to safeguard state rights in the matters of militia and defense, taxation, trade, and the judiciary.

On the other hand, he did not believe that the people "immediately" should have much say—in fact as little as possible —in the actual operation of government. "They want [lack] information and are constantly liable to be misled." Often he was asked whether this or that measure corresponded with public opinion. He saw no way to gauge public opinion accurately; it was subject to extreme and mistaken short-range passions. Those who claimed to reflect it merely found there the mirror of their own improper ambitions. He was sure that if a representative followed his judgment and conscience honestly, the people would support him.

His steady hand brought order out of conflicting proposals He soothed hotheaded adversaries and steered the delegate toward reasonable compromises. There were ticklish question of slavery, of how the population should be counted: whethe it should include only voters, i.e., free men only as in Massa chusetts, or all adults; or whether it should include slaves. Th fear felt by smaller states of being dominated by the large continued. Here, when deadlock resulted, it was the Cor necticut compromise, devised by Sherman, that saved the day, producing the House and Senate elected according to the opposing principles and satisfying both the extreme democrats and the more conservative factions, the small states and the large states.

Sherman was tireless. He delivered 138 speeches. Delegate William G. Pierce from Virginia gazed amazed at this "oddest shaped character" he had ever seen, "unaccountable strange in his manner." His "vulgarisms . . . that strange New England cant . . . make everything connected with him grotesque and laughable . . . and yet he deserves infinite praise . . . no man has a better Heart or a clearer Head."

The "New Roof"—the American Constitution—was put on. The final document bears the impress of Sherman's ideas and his terse phraseology. Lord Bryce contended it was "above every other written constitution" in the excellence of its scheme, its simplicity, brevity, and precision, and for its "judicious mixture of principle with elasticity of details."

It was, of course, the product of the experience of all Thirteen Colonies, of the steady growth of free institutions, democracy, and governing experience for more than a century and a half. In New England those institutions were based on the bedrock of the *Mayflower Compact*, the Eleven Fundamental Orders, the broad tolerance of Rhode Island law and charters, the early experiment of the New England Confederation, hundreds of democratic church covenants. They rested on the growth, spreading out in widening circles from Plymouth, Providence, and Hartford, of the vital town meeting and of representative legislatures with ever broadening suffrage. All these institutions and procedures were deeply ingrained in the life of the Republic. They had provided the sinews for resisting autocratic encroachment by England; they had provided the organized force of resistance; they could not be set aside easily, and in the strengthened Federal Government, as mirrored in the Constitution, they came, in spite of Hamilton and a few others, to retain their virility and to be respectfully guaranteed.

That this was so was also due in good measure to Sherman. No man present was more steeped in the legal and social structure that had evolved from those first faltering essays in popular government—their history and essence—than Roger Sherman—the awkward, grotesque shoemaker-statesman, almost incredible for his honesty and devotion, his unfaltering faith, his knowledge and clarity, who appeared "to have known the science of government and the relations of society from childhood."

Yet if experience supplied this mighty platform, some of the bright luster and moral fervor of earlier democratic experiments failed to shine through the new document. It carefully preserved a balance of powers, it respected state and local rights, it was basically democratic. It was competent, efficient, but it contained no Bill of Rights. Only indirectly did it mirror the great ideas of the Declaration of Independence. The rights of the individual, the rights of man, so fundamental in the struggle against England, found no direct expression there, and many felt those basic rights were not being properly safeguarded. The new document left too many ways in which they could be abused or overthrown. As a mechanistic instrument, it was well-nigh perfect for its day, when agriculture and straightforward politics largely held the stage, but it lacked moral stature.

No one believed more ardently in civil liberties than did Sherman. He made his stand clear on that time and again. He recognized completely the realm of personal individual rights, sacred and inviolate. They should be beyond the reach of government, and to encroach upon them would mean the abridgment of basic liberties and the end of free government. In spite of this, he was opposed to writing such a bill of rights into the Constitution. A guarantee of that nature, he contended, would last only as long as a "honeymoon" and would be ignored by any ruler wishing to oppress the people. The only true safeguard was for the citizenry to elect those who had their welfare and that of the nation at heart. If they failed to do so, no bill of rights, however explicit, could save them.

He was only partly right. The survival of individual rights depended not merely on custom or on electing enlightened representatives but also on the day-to-day conduct of affairs at lower levels: tax collectors, police, judiciary, the bureaucracy. Without guides or legal signposts, more abuses would creep in. The bitter experience with overseas bureaucrats was too fresh to be forgotten.

It was on this issue that final adoption by the states of the Constitution almost foundered. In few states was there an overwhelming majority favoring the new document. Even where it passed, the vote was very close. In many states only after promises of revision were made could a slim majority be secured. It was voted down decisively in Rhode Island, and when ratification was submitted to popular vote, only 237 people in the entire state favored adoption. South Carolina gave a majority of a single vote. Madison won out over Patrick Henry in Virginia, but only by attaching a rider proposing a bill of rights. North Carolina had to hold two conventions; not until proposed amendments were included did it give grudging assent.

In view of the overwhelming strength of public opinion revealed by such contests and by the many popular demonstrations against the Constitution, the Congress at once took under consideration twelve amendments. The states quickly ratified ten of these, and thus the Bill of Rights became an integral part of the Constitution, December 15, 1791.

Thus was the oversight in the original document rectified by popular will. Thus was it provided with the universality and humanitarianism it lacked. The weak corner of the great edifice was shored up, and thereby freedom was joined with strength.

Sherman was a member of the Hartford convention that ratified the new Constitution on January 3, 1788—"the grandest Assemblage," said Ezra Stiles, "of sensible and worthy characters that ever met together in this State."

Sherman considered his great task done. He wanted to retire from public life, take up the threads of his life in Connecticut, and be with his family.

6

Once again he was not permitted to indulge his Cincinnatus-like desires, for he was sent back as congressman (later as senator) under Washington's administration to help shape the laws and undertakings of the new government. He drew up House rules, helped establish the census, legal copyright, a naturalization law, and examined the accounts of outgoing treasurer Robert Morris, who turned $21,986.72 over to the new government to start it on its way. But there were colossal debts. These, Sherman insisted, had to be shouldered and honorably paid.

One of Sherman's first efforts was to have President Washington declare a national Thanksgiving Day. The early celebration of William Bradford's flock at Plymouth more than a century later became part of the pleasure of the whole land.

The temporary Capitol was in New York City. The old City Hall on Wall Street had been remodeled by Pierre Charles L'Enfant with "an elegance hitherto unknown in America." Upon the open portico of that building, George Washington delivered his Inaugural Address to the people. The reply from Congress was drafted by Roger Sherman—the one man in America who had helped shape and who had signed every great document of war and independence, of peace and government, from the first days of the First Continental Congress.

XI. Exploring New Horizons

WHEN EZRA STILES, pastor in Dighton, Rhode Island, read the Declaration of Independence at noon, July 13, 1776, he recorded in his *Literary Diary* that "CONGRESS" had "tied a Gordian knot" the British could never "cut, nor untie. The thirteen united *Colonies* now rise into an *Independent Republic* among the Kingdoms, States and Empires on Earth!"

He was at that time forty-nine, a refugee from Newport, which was occupied by British troops and Hessians. "The violent, oppressive & haughty measures" of "the Ruling Powers of Great Britain" had "alienated the affections of three millions of People.... Cursed be that arbitrary policy," he exclaimed. "Let it never poison the United States of America!"

For twenty years, Ezra Stiles had been quietly carrying on his pastoral duties at the Newport Second Congregational Church. He had emerged as a noted scholar—one of the most universal, enlightened, and tolerant minds of the Thirteen Colonies. Only Jefferson approximated his vast range of scholarly interests.

Their backgrounds were worlds apart, they were engaged in different tasks, but both worked in the vineyard of human freedom, knowledge, and reason. Both belonged to the great new enlightenment that created independence and now flourished more brightly because of independence. When, after the Revolution, the two met—thanks to a letter of introduction from Roger Sherman—it was epochal in the life of each.

Jefferson, nourished far less on religious and ethical literature, drew his inspiration from the great German, English, and French liberals. The New England leader was molded and glazed in the precious clay of dogma as it had been formulated for more than a century by narrow-minded divines, and he seemed, in manner, far more the aloof aristocrat than the scion of the Virginia plantation world. Son of a preacher, Stiles remained in the clerical profession most of his life. Dragging the chains of his dour Calvinism, he searched indefatigably for his own truths and imperishable beliefs, which was more than New England "thinkers," apart from the political leaders of the Revolution, had done for a long time, and in the end he stood forth free of most of the chains, a free man in his own right, his sinuous scientific mind able to reach out for knowledge in all directions without prejudices, from the religions of the East to the philosophers of the enlightenment.

For expediency, but not untruthfully, according to his own definition, he continued to call himself "a moderate Calvinist." Even this concession to current shibboleths did not save him from bitter criticism and attack. For though New England had progressed toward political freedom and had come to permit all denominations, his church—whose adherents outnumbered all others—was still bound by the dark creed of innate sin and predestination, the same gloomy doctrine that had led John Cotton to such grave violations of the human spirit. Man, it was contended, was a vile creature, inherently sinful, predestined to salvation or damnation regardless of how he conducted himself, yet he had the duty to fear and constantly placate his capricious Master. It was a perfect mirror of feudal serfdom. God was shaped in the image of the lord of the manor. Except here and there, the New England churches had never let in the light. Their leaders still gnawed the bones of a dead creed that had stifled intellectual and creative cultural growth during most of the colonial period.

Stiles, unable to entomb himself in any such cold and cruel dogmatism, came to believe in the possibility of personal perfection and personal will—a position he reached long before Unitarianism became popular, and fifty years before "Perfectionism" was to unfurl its loud banner. As a contemporary noted, his heart and mind belonged to "no sect." Above all, said one Newport follower from his congregation, "he carried into his religion the spirit of liberty which then stirred the whole country. . . . He worked to break every yoke, civil and ecclesiastical."

He hailed the *good*, not the *sin*, in all men—how remote this is from Calvinism and Puritanism! He searched for the inner moving power, much as Emerson later did, and, in a more scientific way, derived just as much inspiration from Nature as did the Concord sage. Stiles found God, not merely in poetic wonder at Nature's beauty and innate manifestations of divinity—thus anticipating Wordsworth—but perceived in the scientific processes an expression of God's will, a part of His orderly plan, a point of view even more modern than Emerson's.

For all Stiles's dedication to theology and philosophy, he tried earnestly to see the world as it really was. Primarily he was a scholar with scientific rather than didactic inclinations, eternally thrilled by the advance of the natural sciences, every technological discovery. Scarcely anything in Nature, man, or the eternal mystery escaped his restless curiosity: the tribes of Siberia, wasps' nests, new flour grinders, the population of a Chilean city, mammals' bones, the invention of a new telescopic lens, Fitch's first steamboat, the similarity of Egyptian *sacerdotes* and Scotch presbyters, public finance, the writings of Mary Wollstonecraft. No man was ever more avid to see the world as it is, more enthusiastic in heralding new inventions.

His mind was open to every new idea and phenomenon, and he was never afraid of change or growth, knowing—though never passionate about it in the precise, poetic Emerson way —that blind tradition and fixity were man's will to death not life. Unless Man kept moving valiantly up toward the "great purpose," the eternal Godhead, he must perish. Man's mission was to fill in the divine purpose with deeds, to create and build. Not to do so was merely the security of the coffin. When the sap ceased to flow, the tree died.

Above all, he was excited by the new technical possibilities of the young Republic. Unlike Jefferson and Emerson, he saw no grim portents in industrialism; rather, a great opportunity, a liberating force providing self-reliance and freedom for the new nation.

He was also concerned—always—with statecraft (though not much with politics). Economics and currency questions interested him more: the ratio of gold and silver, price levels, taxation, the federal debt, theories of wealth. He tried, when president of Yale, to broaden the curriculum in these directions. "This day," he noted, "I introduced for the first time Montesquieu's Spirit of the Laws as a classical book in Yale college . . . never was used before."

In all social fields he had the modern approach, using rational and scientific methods, and this led him increasingly toward the new practical techniques rather than abstract problems of government or society. The new technology tugged at him strongly. Perhaps—though science had been a vital interest since boyhood—this was in part an unconscious evasion in an era when men were crucified more than usual for new opinions; perhaps also an escape, after stirring over so much stale hay of metaphysical niceties, into free air where his imagination could roam without restraint, penalty, or undue controversy. Avenues of fresh knowledge were opening up on all sides. With almost childish pleasure, Stiles took note of every new wonder that swam into his vision—faster and faster. His enthusiasm was genuine.

2

His passion for facts, facts, facts, often unrelated and unsystematized, his intense preoccupation with minutiae, likely would have aroused the scorn of Emerson as the toil of a mechanistic, not a creative, mind, of thought, not "Man Thinking." It would have been an unfair criticism. Stiles reversed Emerson's metaphysical process. For Stiles, first of all was the fact, outside and inside the mind. Once the over-all universal scheme with its relation to God had been selected, conceived, believed in, the edifice could be constructed only with mortal bricks, with facts. There was no use trying to suspend a sublime roof in the air without any walls.

Thus Stiles's choice of detailed materials was a mosaic in his sublime concept of man's creative earthly and spiritual mission in the universe. As did Blake, as also did Emerson, he knew the universe was in a grain of sand—quite as much as in philosophic generalization. A lizard's footprint ages ago in soft lava, just as his own more perishable footprints, had a meaning in the interrelation of all things and the divine purpose. The shifting of a single grain of sand altered the ongoing process, became a creative act.

Thus precise measurements always excited him. They were helpful guideposts on the road. They were pivots in his concept of an orderly universe.

He made the first scientific survey of New Haven and of New Haven Harbor.

"February 7, 1780. This day being pleasant, Therm° 33, I surveyed the Harbor of New Haven upon the ice." Thereafter follow notations of points, angles, degrees, and distances. "We used a Six Rod line instead of a chain . . . allowing for stretching . . . 4 rods per half mile." He carefully checked the amount of stretching under different conditions of temperature and wetness.

He made sketches of both the town and the harbor, for mapmaking always interested him. His diary is sprinkled with sketches of towns, rivers, battlefields, and diagrams. He particularly mentions the fine copper-engraved map of Vermont by Amos Doolittle, the brilliant early engraver and musician of New Haven. Doolittle also provided the engraved maps for Stiles's *History of Three Judges of King Charles I*— the "regicides" who fled to the New World, one of whom was a brother of Roger Williams's first love.

Mapmaking tied in with Stiles's ever verdant interest in geography and the peoples of the world. He never missed an opportunity to talk with persons who had traveled to far places, and ask them about customs and institutions. Sea captains were his special delight. He talked at length with one who had been a prisoner of the Barbary pirates. In his diary he mentions with pleasure that his wife (the second Mrs. Stiles) and his two daughters had completed their lessons of geography on the globe. He makes frequent mention of the various editions of *Geography Made Easy* by Jedidiah Morse, "the father of American geography," whom he knew well. Stiles had it adopted as a sophomore text at Yale.

Paleontology—the study of fossils and ancient bones—lighted a fire in him. Something of an anthropologist, he delved into races and origins, and he organized perhaps the first anti-slavery society in America. An amateur naturalist, attentive to all plant and animal life, not so much in the poetic, adoring way of Emerson, but with the eye of a scientist, he records his observations of the antics of insects. He tells wonderingly of picking "a spongey vegetable substance" that shot up in his yard with an eleven-inch stem and bell-shaped top. By noon it began to dissolve and drop black liquid. Emerson would merely have looked at its shape, color, and divine essence. Stiles describes the aloe tree, its remarkable thirteen-inch round spire that grew thirteen feet in thirteen days. Let the Scots have their thistles and the South Britons their Glaston-bury thorn—"much finer things may be said of the aloe Tree of America."

An agronomist, he experimented with insecticides and tree grafting. He treated Roger Sherman's apple trees for canker. Stiles's farm in Cornwall—160 acres—had a 60-tree orchard and produced 20 tons of hay a year.

"Viewing the College Farms in Norfolk and Canaan," he wrote, "the Tenants had this winter past Eleven sugar works and maple sugar orchards, 150 to 250 & 300 Trees each." On one seven-acre tract, he counted "about 300 Maple Trees of phps 100 & 150 years old; yielding up to 4 lb sugar each."

With his first wife, he raised silkworms—3,000 "cocooing" this winter, he wrote in 1771—and he sent the silk to Benjamin Franklin, colonial agent in London, to have it made into a "striped and sprigged" green silk gown. His academic robe was made from his own silk. Later, in New Haven, he grew mulberry seed and distributed it to every corner of Connecticut—enough to get a million trees growing. He founded an extensive silk industry in New Haven and Northford; by 1789, there were 300,000 silkworms. Because of his pioneering, the great Connecticut silk mills, some of which still operate, were started.

Industrial processes always aroused his keenest interest. He visited cotton mills, foundries, powder mills, and other plants. He carefully jotted down the amount of powder manufactured during the Revolution in Isaac Doolittle's powder mill in North Haven. He was excited when Doolittle built the first commercial printing press in America.

Statistics about any- and everything always ministered to his love of preciseness, his idea of a well-ordered universe. At Mount Carmel, he inspected his cousin Munson's new type of gig mill—a Connecticut invention—able to grind "a bushel of wheat in 11 minutes and a half by the Watch.... There are but four of these mills in the world, all in Connecticut." He was thrilled by every sign of the technical revolution and its progress.

He went to Berwick to see copperas refined from Lebanon ores. In 1791 he looked over Lamberton's "Lead Mine," took samples, also got "stone-cotton or genuine asbestos from a neighboring Mountain." He records the process of making cobalt, or "China Blue," with flint and potash, undertaken by Grosuinus Erkelins, who had bought the "Winthrop Ring," northwest of East Haddam—about 8,000 acres "abundant" with ore. Erkelins was taking "Twenty Tons," worth $90,000, to China; trade with the Orient was just getting under way.

During the Revolution, Stiles wrote: "It is wonderfully ordered in divine Providence that so many Things should conspire toward establishing the Independence of America. Heaven opens Resources and Supplies within ourselves. The Discovery of our being able to make *Saltpetre* and *Copperas* lately, as well as *Potash* formerly, and these in great abundance, is of this kind." Now that West Indies trade had been cut off, he noted, "Heaven has led us to the Successful Experiment on Corn Stalks, from which it is probable may be made an Abundant Supply of *Molasses & Rum* for the whole continent." He was excited by receiving a Vermont newspaper printed on homemade paper from the inner bark of the "Bass Wood Tree . . . the first ever so made," at one third the cost of rag paper, and he was interested in the efforts of the local newspaper publisher, Thomas Green, to make paper out of seaweed. From New Hampshire, during the war, he secured a fine specimen of isinglass from a newly found deposit at Dartmouth College—"almost as clear and much stronger than common glass." Many houses were using it. "A wonderful Discovery at this time!"

Well before the Revolution, he helped Abel Buell get a type foundry started in New Haven, and when the boycott of British goods made metals scarce, he sent out pleas for antimony to help keep the enterprise going. He encouraged Eli Whitney during college days and in his later efforts to manufacture his cotton gin. Though never of the market place and always avoiding unnecessary controversy, Stiles always put his shoulder to practical and humanitarian undertakings.

3

When Stiles was thirty, a year after becoming a Newport pastor, he married Elizabeth Hubbard, the sister of a leading New Haven physician famous for his great brick mansion and his fine blooded black horses. During courtship, his lengthy letters were rarely personal, merely scientific or philosophical ideas he was pondering. One in 1755 dealt entirely with eclipses and the moon's influence on tides—matters that absorbed him his entire life—a textbook discourse that he signed, "I am, my dear, Your Affectionate Philosopher." For all its lack of moonlight and roses, his letter—and apparently Elizabeth knew it—was a passionate love call and most complimentary, showing he considered her his intellectual peer.

It was a happy, helpful, and fruitful union. They had eight children, and she participated in many of his experiments, particularly with silkworms. For years after her death, he affectionately recorded her birthday and his sorrow in his diary.

He was born December 10, 1727, in North Haven, son of Reverend Isaac Stiles and Ruth Willis, of Hartford. When Ezra was inducted into the ministry, Isaac, one of the more broad-minded leaders of New England Congregationalism, preached the ordination sermon: "Hold Bigotry in abhorrence." Ezra owed much to his early family life.

When he was a student at Yale, his interests went beyond the curriculum. At sixteen—a sophomore—he compiled a "chronological compendium of the Old and New Testaments" and calculated the movements of stars, carefully recording "the numbers, periods, distances, velocity and other properties" of a comet of that year. At eighteen he used Newton's theory to calculate the true position of the sun and moon— a landmark in the progress of American science.

Graduated in 1746, he delivered in Latin the Cliosophic Lecture and the valedictory. In 1749 he was appointed "tutor."

The high light that year was the gift from Benjamin Franklin of "an electrical apparatus." Stiles performed many experiments with it—"the first in New England," although John Winthrop IV at Harvard had begun lecturing on electricity three years before this. Stiles's later diary has frequent technical references to electricity; it was always his favorite lecture subject. In 1781, he read Carvallo's historical treatise on science, noting that "Muenchenbroek discovered the Leyden Phial in 1747," but that—unmentioned in the text—in Philadelphia Benjamin Franklin and Ebenezer Kinnerly (still a neglected genius) had done "more" in the field than anybody in Europe.

When Jefferson passed through New Haven, electrical discoveries were among the chief topics in his talks with Stiles. In 1765, when Franklin came to New Haven to get the city's first printing plant and newspaper started, Stiles was asked to deliver the Latin address in his honor. The encounter was thrilling, with much conversation about electricity. They remained friends for life, corresponding, doing mutual favors. Franklin got Stiles awarded a doctorate of laws by the University of Edinburgh long before he was so recognized in America. Stiles remarked humbly that being "registered in those archives" was nothing compared to having his name written in the "Lamb's Book of Life."

His beliefs were not wholly in harmony with those of Yale University, which disapproved of his published position on ecclesiastical government, and he participated in an unorthodox ordination ceremony. The trouble became serious when he protested against Yale's refusal to accept a private library donation containing works on deism, this nearly fifty years before Thomas Paine's *Age of Reason*.

"Deism," Stiles wrote President Clap, "has gained such Head ... that it would be in vain to stop it by hiding Deistical writings; and the only Way left to conquer and demolish it, is to come forth into the open Field, and Dispute the matter on open Footing.... Truth, and this only, being our aim ... open, frank and generous, we shall avoid the very appearance of Evil."

He soon found it convenient to leave the university to preach in West Haven, then did missionary work with the Stockbridge Indians. He had been studying law and was admitted to the bar in 1753. For two years he practiced in New Haven.

4

Unable to accept ideas or religion blindly, not happy in the practical duties of law, he was filled with doubts as to his true calling. His closest confidant, "an amiable and virtuous character" who was a complete skeptic, raised painful "scruples," and Stiles sought feverishly for the true meaning of the universe and man.

He delved into theology, all the eerie, shadowy dialectic stemming from medieval sophistries and evasions, which still, after more than a hundred years, held most New World divines bemused. He pondered questions of "divine grace," the Half Way Covenant on baptism (what stale rehashing!); and all the heresies that John Cotton thought he had buried—Arminianism, Arianism, Antinomianism, Pelagianism, Socinianism. Though these doctrines sought to modify or set aside bleak Calvinism, their balderdash concealed rather than clarified spirituality and screened off knowledge and reality.

Stiles, however, faced up to the basic question of whether there was a God and the truth and falsity of the divinity of Jesus and of scriptural revelation. But he learned, after his Yale experience, to keep many of the answers to himself.

He moved on to study all denominations and religions, and he always went to first sources. His historical and exegetical survey of the Scriptures and other religions led him on a lifelong search. He was obliged to study Hebrew to get at the wellsprings of biblical lore. He learned it by himself, with some help from Rabbi Isaac Touro, one of his intellectual friends in Newport.

His interest in Judaism and its contribution to Christianity was profound. He attended the Newport Synagogue whenever he had an opportunity and was personally acquainted with every rabbi in America and with the Jewish philosophers of Europe. He spent much time translating the Syriac Bible, which he considered more authentic than the Greek version on which English translations were based.

These efforts made him one of the New World's most renowned linguists—"a living polyglot." Not only did he read and write Hebrew, he delivered Hebrew sermons, and also had a command of Syriac, Samaritan, Chaldean, and Arabic, plus some knowledge of Persian and Coptic. The morphology of several American Indian languages was known to him. He wrote and spoke Latin fluently and was well versed in Greek. After becoming president of Yale, he studied Italian and French. On November 22, 1784, he started reading the French translation of Robertson's *History of America* and in three days had translated 210 pages back into English.

At the time Stiles was trying to make up his mind, the Congregational Church, along with other denominations, was being shaken by the Great Awakening. This dark, emotional revivalism, in his church, took on the habiliments of reactionary Calvinism of the worst sort—what became known as the struggle between the "Old Lights" and the "New Lights." President Clap fell out of favor with both factions and had Yale University build its own independent chapel. In this conflict, many people veered off to the Episcopalians; the more democratic elements wandered off to the Baptist church.

Stiles's approach to religion was that of the great philosophers, so remote from current folly that he scarcely noted the controversy. Though he does not mention them, his ideas were closer to those of the new rationalist school of 1750, led by Jonathan Mayhew and Charles Chauncey, which stressed "reason" apart from "revelation," and thereby laid the basis for Unitarianism three-quarters of a century later.

Stiles came finally to a concept of a universe of perfect order that was the expression of God's design and will. From that concept, he postulated faith, peace of soul, and individual striving for spiritual enlightenment. It was the opposite of conventional Calvinism; it was essentially Emerson's formula —though his point of departure, methodology, and emphasis were different—which had to wait for another fifty years of scratching the dead hay of doctrine where few kernels were left. Emerson walked those dry, exhausted gullies with his poetic divining rod, and it was perfectionism, as envisaged by Stiles, refined to transcendentalism, the immanency of God in all things and all life, that gushed forth from underground beds as a pure crystalline stream in the Concord master's glistening, concise prose to nourish the long-starved minds and souls of men. Thus, religion, for Stiles, became the effort to understand and obey that universal holy will and to harmonize himself with its superior perfection. Emerson said, find it in your own mind and in Nature. Stiles said, find it everywhere. To the extent he was able to discover this higher harmony and be part of it, he could teach others to share his ideas and faith.

No church, no denomination, no single mind could possibly discover all truth about God. "I set out in Life," he declared, "with an extensive Charity to all Protestants, supposing their Differences founded in conscientious Judgment and wishing All to live in Forebearance, mutual Love and Harmony, and All to joyn in their several ways in promoting Righteousness and Virtue."

At a later date, he discussed religious tolerance at length with John Adams. The Continental Congress, in drawing up the Articles of Confederation, had been cautious about religious matters. But by that time, beginning with the Virginia Declaration of Rights in 1776, all the southern states had "established universal religious liberty," and it was "easy to foresee," said Stiles happily, that it would come for "all religious sects in America."

This open-mindedness, so unusual in his day, especially in the mouth of a leading divine, did not preclude his making caustic comments on the failings of this or that denomination. He never achieved personal tolerance for "Popery"; and the Church of England, at least in America, where it received the human "cast-offs," was particularly "unanimated with a love of Jesus" and was concerned chiefly with the "love of Dignitaries and Preeminence," making the Church an asylum for "polite Vice and Irreligion." Nor could he sympathize with the way newer sects distorted the deeper meaning of Christianity by pettifogging, fanatical adherence to this or that detail of doctrine or ritual. Physical baptism, exaggerated out of due proportions, was like a false loyalty oath, unnecessary to the enlightened spirit. Though aware of shortcomings in his own denomination, he felt it had a broader tent, for, whatever the Calvinistic thunderings, it accepted all who loved God without asking members embarrassing questions about dogma. Above all Stiles was indignant at the lack of charity between denominations more interested in self-aggrandizement and power than in advancing the faith—zealous to "build up sects rather than make Xtians."

More than any man he knew he felt "ALONE—unconnected with the world," for he had "an inward consciousness and Cordial Union with all the *good*, with those who love & those who hate me, with the numerous Millions who know me not, with the whole Collection of Characters in all Nations ... of every kind & degree of Excellence ...; above all, my soul unites ... with the whole body of the Mystical Church, with all that in every Nation fear God and love our Ld Jesus Christ. ... These stript of all the peculiarities which eternally separate them from one another & from me, I embrace with a true spirit of universal Love."

He was unable to love *everything* in every person, nor could he love "a whole Church, or any whole Fraternity, whether literary, religious, or political," for none could achieve complete truth and goodness. There were always too many "inconninities [inconsistencies] & am disgusted too much for Acquiessence in any here below. I never shall cordially & externally unite with Mankind in any of their Affairs, Enterprises and Revolutions. There is a preference of Systems, but no perfect one on earth."

This is Emerson long before Emerson, except that Emerson demanded that those he loved also be intelligent and creative. Stiles, closer to primitive Christianity, made such demands only of himself.

He sought identification with the ultimate harmony and, when he reached fifty, wished to retire to become "more & more a Recluse—waiting for the Rest of Paradise, where I foresee my soul will unite with perfection & acquiesce in eternal universal Harmony."

5

In 1767 Stiles expressed antipathy to diaries. They contained "not what we really are and have been," but "what we would wish to be esteemed ... for." But two years later, on January 1, he started keeping one as a personal record, not for posterity, for it was written without literary affectation, not to indulge his personal opinions or feelings, but to record everything that aroused his interest and influenced him, plus the usual details of work and family life.

He had already been at Newport fifteen years when he started it, and he continued it at home and when traveling, with few days omitted, until a week before his death. However troubled or ill or busy, he found time and energy to record, if nothing more, the temperature and weather. The first entries were a bare-bones record of the Bible texts of his sermons, routine pastoral duties, baptisms, marriages, deaths, ordinations, occasional church squabbles—and the weather, always the weather. The words glow when some unusual phenomenon occurred, as though the clear skies, the eclipses, the comets and falling stars, the precise periodicity of Algol, the cold, rain, snow, and winds were all personal messages from God.

As the trend toward independence set in, more and more he recorded contemporary events and spelled out his wholehearted devotion to freedom. Increasingly alarmed by British coercions, he wrote a London acquaintance that there were still "many means of redress"; should they fail, the American colonies would call a congress and issue their own joint Magna Charta and Bill of Rights that England could not withstand and which would endure. There would be "a Runnymede in America," and the outcome would be liberation from British rule.

When hostilities began, his diary became a faithful record

of military action for the duration of the long struggle. He was indefatigable in interviewing eyewitnesses, civilians, soldiers, generals, and would write to participants to gain exact details of a battle. He often described tactics in detail and made sketches of the deployment of opposing forces. He visited the front during the Boston siege and was pleasurably surprised at the strength of colonial defenses. He talked with Washington, who invited him to dinner. In 1776 he looked over troops at Fairfield, nervous because of British seizure of Westchester and threats of Tory treachery in their rear.

His diary is full of intimate items about the struggle. On July 18, 1776, he noted that 600 carpenters were being enlisted to go to Crown Point and build floating batteries and "Gallies" upon Lake Champlain: "The wages high, 33 dollars per month.... The whole continent is alive...100,000 men in the American army."

During the first British occupation of Newport in 1775, Stiles remained in town to succor the few of his flock who could not flee. To add to his sorrow, that year his wife Elizabeth died, leaving him with eight children. Soon, instead of receiving his stipend, he was obliged to solicit money to help his distressed exiled parishioners, most of whom went to an encampment in Middletown. He visited it whenever he could, preaching, solacing, bringing food and money. Nor did he forget them after he became president of Yale.

March 14, 1776, he moved to Dighton on the Taunton River, near the Massachusetts line—"landed safely"—to take over a tiny, struggling second church in a place already supplied with two ministers. He rented a house for "sixteen dollars a year."

About midnight two days later, Saturday, they heard "afiring at Boston," thirty-six miles north—"very heavy about Sunrise" and lasting all during Sabbath services. The next day, news came that the King's troops, "struck with Terror," had evacuated the port. On Bunker Hill they left straw images "dressed as Sentries standing, with a label on the Breast...."

'Welcome, Brother Jonathan.' " Five hundred "of ours having had the small-pox [hence immune from the epidemic raging in Boston] entered and took possession."

On the last day of April—the British having withdrawn from Newport also—he preached in his old pulpit amid alarms of a second invasion. Through the dense fog after a snowstorm, twenty British ships were sighted. By Monday 15,000 men were on the march to Rhode Island to repel them.

A week later, cannon were dragged to the shore, and all except two vessels, one a hospital ship, were driven off. "I could scarcely discern the ships," Stiles records, "though I could hear the Shrieks & Distress and Confusion or Noise of Tumult on Board." With cannon sounding, he preached on Hebrews, 3:14: "For we are made partakers of Christ, if we hold the beginning of our confidence stedfast unto the end."

He noted down that the Governor of Maryland had treacherously sold out to the British for cash in hand, but had been allowed to depart in peace. Ninety Newport Tories were rounded up and given "The Test"—the chance to swear allegiance. The Baptist elder, because of his age and "pious and Inoffensive" character was allowed to stay on in town—his mind was "not strong eno' to digest this Revolution."

Though so devoted to independence, Stiles never displayed vindictiveness. When news came of Benedict Arnold's treason, he was upset—"a loss!" for he appreciated Arnold's dashing military ability—but he was philosophic. America was "so fertile in *many* patriots" it could afford to sell a renegade or two "every year without any essential injury to the Glorious Cause of Liberty and Independence."

Not all was devastation and death. "It has been computed, that this war, by Prizes, building of ships of War & the Navy has already within a year & half brought into Providence One million and a quarter of Dollars or near Three Hundred thousand sterling which is double the property of the whole Town two years ago in Houses, Shipping, Goods &&&."

He was not worried about financing the war. The two

hundred million acres within "the Inhabited Parts of the United States" were worth from one to three dollars an acre; total American property was worth at least half a billion, one-fourth that of Great Britain, but while England was "at a stop," in America expanding population and settlement were constantly "creating Property." Within twenty years the country could easily stand a $4,000,000 debt, so if the war created a $1,000,000 debt, "the Prize of Liberty will be well purchased." When later the debt went far beyond his maximum figure, he calculated that Connecticut's share could be paid off in four years by a mere tenpence a pound on the Grand Tax List.

Early in December, 1776, the British came back to Newport with eleven men of war and seventy transports. "The Town is in great Consternation and Distress. . . . Cannon were heard," he reported from Dighton. The twelve hundred American soldiers withdrew without opposing the British landing, and three-fourths of the inhabitants fled. Four hundred patriots marched through Dighton, with many evacuees and their tumbled belongings.

The British paraded before the courthouse and set up "the Kings Government & Laws," and the Episcopalians, again free to pray for the King, reopened their church, but Stiles's house and church were seized, "to make an Assembly Hall for Balls after taking down the pews." He was honest enough to report later that the Hessians had not made a stable out of it, as was rumored, but were holding services.

Even with such stirring events, he found time to make his usual observations of the weather and celestial phenomena. On January 9 there was "a solar eclipse. I observed it at Dighton."

On March 14, 1777, the anniversary of his arrival in the village with his motherless family of eight, he observed that though he received only sixty pounds a year, "a Gracious Providence" had so supplied them that he was "not in debt for sustenance the year past—& blessed be God there is some Meal in the Barrel and a little Oyl in the Cruse."

He jotted down one of those curious facts that always entranced him. "The City of Prague is situated on the Muldaw, a large and rapid River, divided in 2 parts, joyned by a *Stone Bridge 1700 feet long* . . . & 35 feet broad, supported by 24 arches." Why not a bridge to replace Howland's ferry near Newport? Distance only 1,350 feet. He drew a sketch map, on which he also indicated an American raid to the island.

6

On April 23, 1777, Stiles accepted a call to the Portsmouth church, where he would receive "£110, a House, Firewood and the Expense of removal. Generous! Kind! . . . Certainly God hath put it into their heads thus to provide for an Exile! *Deo opt max grates!*"

He took the opportunity to visit Boston in the company of fourteen newly arrived French officers; for the first time in years he could afford the five-dollar seat on the stagecoach.

The first night he put up at the pastor's house in Hampton, next day dined at Newberry, where the coach was delayed for repairs. They got only to Ipswich, so he stayed over the Lord's day and preached. In New Cambridge he visited President Samuel Langdon of Harvard.

Toward the end of the month, going again to Boston to deliver a sermon, he took along all eight children and his Negro servant "Newport." This lad had been a gift from a sea captain. One day Stiles found little Newport weeping—he wanted his mother. From that moment, Stiles, who had taken black servitude for granted—became an opponent of slavery.

The year 1777 saw terrible reverses for the patriots. The sad tidings of Washington's Long Island defeat caused "Discouragement" to sit "upon the minds of the pple at large." The Connecticut militia had shown cowardice at the beginning of the battle, but the next day fought well. We may be 'satisfied—at least not so mortified," observed Stiles, "as if we had been driven off thro' Cowardice and without good Fighting."

But the army was badly broken up, men coming home daily, and he noted with distaste that "600 officers are loitering & dancing in Boston only." In spite of such improper displays and general "Dismay," there had been a rush of new enlistments; there was no doubting "the spirit of the country."

A few lines farther on, he notes that he has "weighed a large tooth ... from the Ohio ... *fifty ounzes ... seven inches long ... three inches & an half across* the Top ... a grinder Tooth of some great Animal, but whether an Eliphant or a Gyant is a question."

In September he was notified he had been elected president of Yale. This was not the "Quiet solitude" he craved, and "150 or 180 young gentlemen students is a bundle of Wilde Fire not easily controlled or governed ... and at best the Diadem of President is a Crown of Thorns." His task would not be easier with war going on, students off fighting, restless, no money available. He wanted assurances that the lamentable state into which the college had fallen, though it now had a larger student body than Harvard, could be remedied.

Also, recalling his earlier difficulties, he did not want to plunge into controversies that would undermine his efforts. Most members of the Yale Corporation were opposed to his liberal ideas and had voted for him merely because he was preferred by the State Assembly, which had long withheld funds from the institution.

The day he set off to go there, in October, 1777, to discuss the matter, was auspicious. News came of General Burgoyne's surrender, "rejoycing universal." He found Cambridge lit with bonfires. He was greatly cheered and went on to New Haven.

To the Yale Corporation he argued that he was in poor health and lacked "Talents for Government." Without reservations, he set forth his "sentiments in Religion with respect to the *System of Theology* and *Ecclesiastical Polity.*" He doubted he would be acceptable to "the Pastors, the Assembly and the Public," and he could not accept the position without "unanimous acquiescence" and assurance of "Continuing Cordiality." They reassured him on every point and promised faithful support.

Would the bankrupt college secure adequate funds? He consulted with the Assembly and wrote Governor Trumbull. "Is there a *real* prospect of a Restoration of Harmony between the Assembly and the College, of new-building another College Edifice, augmenting the Library, completing the Philosophical Apparatus & endowing professorships?"

Most of the library, containing three thousand volumes, had been sent north "to be out of the way of the enemy." The Anatomy apparatus consisted of "Paintings of the body skin'd" and a human skeleton. Practically no new equipment had been added in forty years.

He held off until committees from the university and the Assembly had drawn up plans for closer union, with promises of proper aid. Nor did he feel morally free to take the post until he had obtained the assent of his scattered Newport congregation and that of Portsmouth, which had offered a substantial salary boost to try to keep him.

His letter of acceptance was written April 18 (dated March 20), 1778, the same day he went to the Portsmouth-island smallpox hospital, with three of his children, to be inoculated with weakened bacilli, plus doses of mercury and calomel. He broke out twelve days later and left, "having experienced the Divine protection," on May 13.

He freed his slave Newport (who later came to New Haven with his wife and child on contract) and paid all his Portsmouth bills. He had "some money left," plus $500 sent by the University to pay his traveling expenses. On June 9, he set out in a "caravan," or carriage, and a covered wagon, with his seven surviving children and household goods.

The "neat gentle caravan [provided by Yale] ... was suspended upon steel springs as a coach." They went via Boston, and lodging and supper usually came to twenty or thirty dollars, but sometimes they put up at the minister's house. At Leicester, a Jewish merchant gave him half a dozen bottles of wine. On June 16 they reached Brookfield, sixty-three miles beyond Boston. "Lodged at Mr. Hills. . . . Liquor £1 7 sh, being two double Bowls Milk Punch at 2 dollars each. 8 Suppers @ 3 sh. Lodging 8 sh." Expenses for the trip totaled $230.

They arrived in New Haven June 20 about noon *"Deo opt max grates* . . . I am now entering upon a new scene of life . . . done with the stated Labors of the ecclesiastical ministry, which for so many years past has been my great delight."

He moved into the President's house. On June 24 "fell a great eclipse of the sun . . . nearly 11 Digits," and that day he was inducted into office.

On July 2 he lectured on "the three great principles of Gravity." A "Thunder gust took place," so he interjected an account of "the electrical philosophy of Thunder and Lightning." The following day he lectured on Oriental learning.

His formal "instalment" was celebrated July 8 with eight receiving Fellows or "Messengers." In the procession were 116 undergraduates; the Beadle and Butler, bearing the College Charter Records, Key, and Seal; the members of the Corporation; all the professors, tutors, ministers, and "Respectable Gentlemen." A State Assemblyman presided, and addresses in Latin were exchanged.

"I sat down in the President's Chair at the Desk, put on My Hat, and called for the Orator"—another Latin address by a senior. Stiles responded with a "Latin Oration" on literature. "The Senior Class then sang . . . the 122d Psalm." The students wanted to illuminate the campus and fire cannon, but were "dissuaded."

Most of his worst forebodings were realized. Students were coming and going to and from war, though Joel Barlow, the poet, fought only during vacations. At various times the whole student body had to be dispersed inland because of lack of food. No money could be obtained while war continued. But as the years flowed by, Stiles brought order out of chaos, wheedled the Assembly successfully, got new buildings and new equipment, and built up the institution's reputation.

Besides such worries, he had to work on the curriculum, often facing opposition to the introduction of new studies and books corresponding to the progress of the times. How difficult this was is revealed by the fact that ten years later, when the famous surgeon John Jeffries tried to lecture on anatomy in enlightened Boston, he was driven off the platform by a mob. But resolutely Stiles laid the basis for a true liberal arts and scientific education with new dignity and vision—and, above all, with respect for free inquiry—which, despite the Calvinist, Tory-like period under his brilliant successor, Timothy Dwight, has tended to shape the university from that day to this.

He was also giving lectures in Hebrew, and on divinity, philosophy, and astronomy. At the same time, he kept on with his independent research, read vast amounts of literature, and studied new languages. His correspondence, always heavy, was now voluminous. He wrote to other college heads in Europe and America, suggesting co-operation, exchange of views and methods. To the head of William and Mary, he suggested building up a repository of the world's best literature to promote the development of American writers who would outshine those of Europe. One letter to a Hamburg professor, detailing the history of Connecticut, ran to sixty pages.

He had to spend much time entertaining celebrities, over the years—such men as Talleyrand, the Duc de Lauzun, Rochambeau, the Marquis de Castellnux, Baron von Steuben, Jefferson, Nathaniel Greene, George Washington, Francisco Miranda, who was trying to liberate all Spanish America.

In 1779 everything was interrupted by British invasion of New Haven under General William Tyron. On Sunday night, July 4, Independence Day, forty British sail appeared off West Haven, and warning signals and cannon fire flashed from the hills. At five in the morning, Stiles mounted the college steeple with a spyglass and watched the small boats putting troops ashore—about three thousand men. All over town, people were burying their valuables and fleeing inland.

But two-thirds of New Haven's male population was already getting ready to put up resistance. Yale students, including Stiles's oldest son, prepared to defend West Bridge. Former President Naphtali Dagget rode across the bridge past the Yale students on an old nag, coattails flying. With his rusty old flintlock, the aged gentleman took up his stand behind a venerable West Haven oak and refused to retreat when the others did. Taken prisoner, he was clubbed and bayoneted for five miles into the city. He was in bed for a month and died the following year.

Stiles hastened to send the more valuable university records and his diary and manuscripts out of town in care of his youngest son. The girls went on foot. He sent off "a horse load of Bags and Cloaths" another way. In Mount Carmel he hired a cart to go into the city and bring out four beds and a trunk.

A Yale graduate among the British officers halted the looting of the university and Stiles's house; only a looking glass was shattered by a pistol shot, but Stiles himself broke the precious thermometer which Franklin had secured for him in London.

Seeing that his family, belongings, and university effects were safe, Stiles rode among the militia at Neck Rock and Ditch Corner in the thickest of the fighting.

"Next morning, soon after the Evacuation, I returned to Town and visited the Desolation, dead Corpses and Conflagrations. It was a scene of mixt Joy and Sorrow . . . Plunder, Rapes, Murdering, Bayoneting, Indelicacies toward the sex, Insolence & Abuse and Insult toward the Inhab. in general. Dwellings & Stores just setting on fire at E. Haven in full view & & & . . . Joy and Rejoicing that the Buildings had escaped the Flames in the Compact part of the Town."

What angered New Haveners most was that the Hessians

had made off with nine hundred feather beds. But what grieved Stiles was the loss of the university records of former President Clap. He wrote General Tyron requesting their return. Tyron answered that war should not injure "the Rights of the Republic of Learning," but that he could learn nothing about the papers.

A few were found floating in the Sound off Fairfield when the British were burning that town. Stiles wrote with acid irony that Tyron need not bother to look any further.

7

On May 29, 1782, Stiles noted in his diary: "This day my wife has been dead seven years," and he added in Latin, "Seven Years Alone."

August 15, he spent "five hours incessantly communicating Instruction to . . . the Senior Class in Astronomy, the Calculus and Delineation of a solar Eclipse . . . the Trajectory & places of Comets both heliocentric & geocentric."

At great moments of his life, the comets and fiery heavens always seemed to whirl in his mind. The following day he put down in Latin and Hebrew that he had become engaged to Mary Cranston Checkley, a thirty-seven-year-old widow from Newport who was visiting in New Haven—*jejunis praecibusque contulli.* He was then fifty-five.

September 1, he held up his grandchild to be baptized, and three days later sent off "a Letter of great Importance" to Mary concerning his "last Decision after earnestly looking up to the Throne of Grace for Direction of Unerring Wisdom."

They were married in Providence on October 13, with five ministers and forty guests present—"Splendid Entertainment." By then a new building was going up on the Yale campus.

Mary proved a competent hostess, took a leading part in church affairs, and delighted him with her progress in Hebrew. Three weeks after she started to study the alphabet and grammar, she was able to translate the first Psalm, and Stiles glowed: "She has accurately parsed & resolved every word, looking out each Radix & declining it."

When she broke her ankle, he took her to Mrs. Mary Porter's in Wethersfield, where three bones were set. After six weeks, he rode to get her. Once while he was in Boston and heard that she was ill, he secured special permission to ride on the Lord's day and hastened home across country. In 1792, she was again apparently not well, and he took her once more to Mrs. Porter's.

During 1794 and 1795, terrible epidemics of yellow fever, smallpox, pneumonia, and typhoid hit New Haven, sweeping off a large part of the population. He was called on for extra duties, to give solace and to preach funeral sermons. In his diary for May 6, he made a long statistical record of United States commerce for 1794, but two days later he was taken ill with bilious fever, and his diary contains only a faint pencil scrawl. "Sick—omitted—fair." The following day he scrawled a faint entry at 2:00 P.M. "67. Fair." It was the last. Three days later, at the age of sixty-eight, he died.

8

Stiles had some blind spots. He had scant interest in music or painting, though he mentions John Trumbull, the historical painter, and he had his own portrait "taken" twice by Samuel King in Newport and "in wax" by Reuben Moulthrop of East Haven. But there were few American artists until after the Revolution.

An official Yale biographer has berated him for his failure to promote literary efforts among his students and for his lack of sympathy for the brilliant Yale men who became known as the Hartford Wits—Joel Barlow, Jonathan Trumbull, and others. But the Hartford Wits, if clever and caustic, were short on ideas and full of spleen against the slightest show of democratic expression. Timothy Dwight soon attacked Stiles in anonymous letters and schemed to supplant him. Their brash manners and Tory prejudices must have gone against

Stiles's grain when they were in college. Actually he lectured constantly on literary topics, often expressing hopes for a bona-fide American literature. Undoubtedly he did have a stronger bent toward scientific progress, and with students like Eli Whitney he encountered the type of free experimental mind that most appealed to him.

Stiles had the great, indefatigable universality of Aristotle and Bacon. Up to this time only a small body of scientific knowledge had been accumulated, so wherever he turned, he pioneered, treading original ground. At the time he studied plant and animal life, though the works of the great John Bartram of Philadelphia and half a dozen others in the South and West were in existence, not a single treatise had been published in New England except Cotton Mather's general and rather dubious observations, and Paul Dudley's exact and brilliant studies of swamp sumac, bees, and rattlesnakes.

No chemistry course existed until that given by John MacLean at Princeton in 1795, after Stiles's death. The New Englander's studies in paleontology predated all others, and he had been dead three years when Jefferson produced the first paper, in 1797, on the fossils of Big Bone Lick in Kentucky. Stiles predated most physics publications by a quarter of a century, though James Logan and Cotton Mather had accomplished considerable. Geology, in which he was exceedingly interested and active, did not begin to develop until a quarter-century after his death.

His method was scientific, and if he did nothing overly remarkable in many of these fields, the details he chose fitted in with his concept of human progress and ultimate perfection. They were part of his vision of a harmonious universe, and all helped round out the grandiose portrait of Nature and man that he had drawn and framed.

As a leader, he may be criticized for avoiding public debate on many current issues, though he did not shrink from standing up quietly for what he believed, but as a student and a teacher, he inspired all with whom he came in contact. This quality and his faculty for being far ahead of his times in so many directions were his true genius. His tireless observations and investigations were an embodiment of the awakening world long stifled by Calvinism and superstition, at a time when men were thirsty for fresh philosophical and religious approaches that would carry them toward the wider horizons being opened up. The colonial darkness was lifting, with the completion of some of the exhausting physical tasks of taming the frontier that had prevented proper cultural development and intellectual speculation.

Stirred by the new vistas of science, new inventions and machinery, in a world so long stagnant with stale doctrine, people on every side were demanding true knowledge of nature and man. It was a fine new ferment. With more economic security, independence won, faced with new problems of government never before known in history, America was beginning to discover both itself and the outside world in new ways. Stiles was the symbol of that enthusiastic search. The feeling of freedom now sent New England men forging west and around the seven seas. It sent others on a still more distant search in the wide corridors of learning and knowledge.

What particularly distinguished Stiles, what made him such a vital part of the new effervescence in contrast to his more conservative academic contemporaries, was that he did all things, as one of his church members described it, "con amore—in a spirit of kindling and generous enthusiasm." He helped sweep away the habit of parroting dogma and the prejudices that had passed for thought and dominated New England for more than a century. He marks the emergence of modern man and the modern mind, with its emphasis upon reason and humanitarianism, equality of human rights, science, and invention, freed now from the narrow Puritan discipline. He helped prepare the way for the perfectionists and transcendentalists and the mid-century flowering of New England. He helped the American mind to become an adult free mind.

XII. The Great Innovator

DURING THE hard times just before the passage of the Stamp Act, Abel Buell of Killingworth finished his seven years of apprenticeship to Ebenezer Chittenden, a leading New England silversmith, and set up in business for himself on the Post Road, the main King's Highway between New York and Boston. He was a craftsman of unusual ingenuity. No one equaled him in tracing a coat of arms or a fine monogram.

His great-grandfather had founded Killingworth, and, on finishing his apprenticeship at twenty-one, Abel traded the hill-country homestead for this tall house on the Post Road overlooking Long Island Sound. He and his wife, Mary Parker, niece of a Saybrook shipmaster, were well liked, and his neighbors commented favorably on their devout church attendance and Abel's persevering industry. When most of the village was asleep, his light could be seen high in the attic, like a lone star, attesting to his devotion to his tasks.

For nearly a year that light burned late. One winter night in 1763, when the bare trees were snapping with ice, a heavy knocking fell on his door. He was arrested by the Killingworth constable on a charge of "counterfeiting the King's money."

Few people had much respect any more for the King's money; it had depreciated badly and was a symbol of alien rule. Counterfeiting had become almost a respectable profession. But of late the severest efforts were being made to suppress this scarcely helpful pastime, and the Crown authorities had even threatened to intervene in local police and court jurisdiction if proper punishments were not inflicted.

The grand jury bound Buell over to appear in Norwich Superior Court. Ebenezer Chittenden, who looked upon Abel almost as a son, and another fellow silversmith guaranteed his bail bond.

His trial came up in March, 1764. The court found him

guilty of the "heinous" crime of raising the King's notes from two shillings sixpence to thirty shillings. He was condemned to life imprisonment, to have his property confiscated, to be branded on the forehead with a "C," and have one ear cropped.

He was taken to New London jail, where the sentence was executed, though seizure of his property was staved off, as a result of title tangles maneuvered by his friends.

Mary and Ebenezer managed to get up to see him. Ebenezer advised Buell to "pen a petition to the General Court in Hartford." He was going there on business and would present it through friends. Relatives of Buell by marriage—the Griswolds—held important positions in the colonial government: one was Killingworth's delegate to the General Court; another was State's Attorney.

With no great hope of favorable results, Abel wrote a lengthy appeal in fine, even lettering that looked "almost like engraving," saying that he and his wife were penniless, he had no money for food, he was grievously ill, shortly he would perish in these "gray damp walls."

When Chittenden agreed to put up the customary £200 bond, pay Buell's bill for jail keep, be responsible for his good conduct, and see he did not set foot outside of Killingworth, the court ordered the prisoner released.

Abel worked hard, paid off those who had received his bad notes, and saved all his property. Patiently he collected affidavits of good conduct from local notables and sent a second petition asking to be freed from bond. He was again reminded of his "heinous" crime.

He invented a machine to cut and polish precious "Amethysts and other native stones." He informed the General Court of this and, as proof of his invention and good workmanship, he sent the State's Attorney a beautifully mounted amethyst ring. As a reward for his contribution to local enterprise, once more he asked to have his full rights restored. The local minister backed his plea eloquently. "Our good Abell Buell" is an "inspired mechanical genius."

A legislative committee was sent down to look over Abel's invention. Its report was favorable, and all his citizenship rights were restored.

2

A few years later, the secretary of the General Assembly laid another remarkable petition before the august members. It was printed in red ink with flowing, thin-faced Long Primer characters. The initial flowery block "T" was a beautiful bit of engraving.

It was the first printing ever made from type manufactured in America. Abel Buell had designed that type; he had perfected a special amalgam and had cut it by a method all his own. He asked that the Assembly, in accordance with its law offering aid to new inventions and industries, authorize him to celebrate a lottery—a frequent method of raising capital— or assist him in any way it "deemed proper" to set up a shop to manufacture the type.

As before, his petition was accompanied by affidavits. The worth of his type was attested to by "the most notable divine" of Connecticut, Ezra Stiles, then in Rhode Island, and by the "most famous preacher" of Boston. Abel had also secured the endorsement of the Philosophical Society of Philadelphia, "the most learned body in the colonies," an opinion backed up by guarded praise from "the most outstanding printer of the colonies," who suggested minor changes in several letters.

At no time was printed matter more important than at this hour of intellectual ferment on the eve of the break with England. Newspapers were being started everywhere. Pamphlets and books were being circulated in increasing quantities. Everybody was hungry for reading material. It was a great awakening. But with the trade embargo, it was difficult to get printing presses, type, and materials; the cost was well-nigh prohibitive.

Abel Buell's petition pointed out that even in Europe there were only a few type-cutters, the supply could not begin to meet demand, and he claimed he would be able to sell his product at the same price as in London, thus eliminating heavy shipping costs and duties.

Once more an Assembly committee hastened to Killingworth. Abel was granted a £100 loan and promised an equal amount after twelve months' successful operation.

He rented a house on Chapel Street on the south side of New Haven Green, near the famous inn started in the first years of the colony by Stephen Goodyear and only a step from Roger Sherman's store. For his shop, Abel rented the Sandemanian Meeting House behind his home. The Sandemanians, or Glassites, were an unpopular Scottish sect, afraid to meet publicly any longer because of the animosity to their intense Tory feelings. Ebenezer Chittenden moved down and opened a gold and silver smithy next door to Abel's home.

Buell faced formidable difficulties. Because of the embargo it soon became almost impossible to get metals. Lead, tin, copper were in short supply, and bismuth especially, an essential part of the formula he had devised. Ezra Stiles was busy for several years appealing for the small amounts needed.

Small silver, jewelry, and engraving jobs helped Buell survive, and after Stiles became president of Yale, the inventor was given the task of engraving Yale diplomas. They were beautifully designed, with a fine Chippendale border, and were signed "A Buel Sculp." Abel's diplomas hung on the walls of many a New England personage.

He also designed and engraved a map of Saybrook, at the mouth of the Connecticut River, which was to be improved by means of a state-authorized lottery. It was the first copper-engraved map ever made in America, a fine piece of craftsmanship, clear-cut and elegantly designed.

But the most substantial help for Buell's new enterprise came from James Rivington, the big New York publisher, who advanced him money for metal and commissioned him to make copper-engraved illustrations for books, among the first ever made in America.

This profitable connection came to an abrupt end when a wagon driver lost one of Abel's plates, a rush order for a geographical treatise on Florida. Angered at having to bring the book out with a blank space stating that the engraving would be inserted in future editions, Rivington attached Buell's property and brought suit for £500. With Abel's record of past conviction, the matter was serious. To avoid debt imprisonment and utter ruin, he vanished from New Haven. Echoes came from New York, from along the Atlantic seaboard, from Florida, where, legend has it, he was jailed on an island off Pensacola by the British governor and later escaped.

Before he left Killingworth, his wife Mary Parker had died, leaving him with several children. He then married Aletta Devoe. Letty, a courageous, fiery girl, manned the barricades. In an advertisement in the *Connecticut Journal* she denounced Rivington as an "ingrate" and "inhuman varlet," pressing an unjustifiable, exaggerated claim. She received considerable sympathy, for Rivington had become marked as the most furibund Tory in the colonies.

Letty promised to carry on the business and meet every legitimate obligation. Hiring apprentices, she continued to work the type factory and kept on with his silver shop. By hard work, she managed to pay back the £100 to the General Assembly.

Rivington's attacks on those favoring independence grew more virulent, and a band of Connecticut Sons of Liberty galloped out of New Haven and rode into New York in broad daylight, bayonets fixed and glittering, defying the King's soldiers and officials. They headed straight for Rivington's plant. It was smashed to bits, and the type and metal carted off. Rivington fled to London. His suit against Buell was thrown out of court, and Abel was awarded damages.

Right after the Declaration of Independence, July 4, 1776, Abel was one of a Sons of Liberty band that pulled down

George III's lead statue on Bowling Green. Abel tried to get the lead for his type foundry, but it was sent to Connecticut to be made into bullets.

Back in New Haven, unable to keep the foundry operating, he resumed his silversmith trade and held weekly auctions—"vendues"—at which he sold everything from books to ships. Among the books were some that had come out of Rivington's New York plant.

Shortly "Abell Buell and Company" secured a commission from fighting Governor Jonathan Trumbull to outfit the privateer *Porcupine* with a crew of eighteen. Later, Abel was bonded for $20,000, to run the sloop *Tiger*, with a thirty-six-man crew and two cannon. Several prizes were brought in.

As things quieted down, Abel brought his foundry into full production, hiring as many as twenty apprentices. Presently he had enough type to set the entire front page of the *Connecticut Journal*, "a refreshing contrast" to the heavy black type fuzzy from long use. Soon the whole paper appeared in Abel's type. The New London paper also bought his type, and a Hartford publisher put out several books in the "fresh, clean-cut" characters he produced.

Letty never lived to see this success. Their two children died in infancy, and she passed on soon after his return to New Haven. He married a third time—Rebecca Parkman Townsend, of a well-to-do, aristocratic family, widow of a member of the great shipping family. She bore him four children, three boys and a girl.

Abel's fortunes were on the rise now. He started a regular packet-boat line between New Haven and New London and operated a stone quarry. But best of all he loved his silverwork and made silver services for churches. Those for the North Haven Congregational Church still exist and are among the finest specimens of the period, sturdy yet delicate and with exquisite engraving. He still held his "vendues" on the Green, and "no man was cleverer at boosting the bidding."

3

Peace brought new opportunities. In his handsome house on the Green, the property Benjamin Franklin had originally purchased to set up a printing plant, in 1783 Abel engraved the coat of arms for the first edition of the laws of the free State of Connecticut, which Sherman had compiled. He was also engraving a wall map of the new United States. The idea had first come to him when George Washington complained bitterly to the Continental Congress that lack of maps was seriously hampering his military operations.

Abel issued his map in March, 1784, advertising with pride that it was "the effect of . . . long, unwearied application, diligence and industry." It was the "first" map ever "compiled and engraved and finished by one man, and an American. . . . Every patriotic gentleman and lover of geographic knowledge" would "encourage the improvement of his country" by buying a copy.

It was indeed a remarkable one-man accomplishment. Singlehanded, Abel had assembled the data. Legend has it that he explored the entire Atlantic coast. More likely he assembled it mostly from the charts of sea captains who put in at New Haven Long Wharf and from venturesome explorers of the interior. He recorded various names that had never before appeared on any map, among them "Muscle Shoals."

It was "a milestone in cartography," the first single-sheet map of the whole United States ever made in America, the first in history to bear the American flag, thirteen stars and stripes flowing through a flamboyant cartouche beside two trumpeting cherubim and a lean Goddess of Liberty seated under a spreading oak. This map, based on the Treaty of Ghent, was reprinted by the Library of Congress and was used in later treaty negotiations to fix boundaries between Florida and Louisiana.

Five months after issuing the map, Buell invented a

machine that could turn out 120 coins a minute, doing away with laborious molding, punching, or stamping by hand. The days when Connecticut relied on Indian wampum for small change were long past, and since the Revolution, British, Dutch, and other metal coins had disappeared, making retail transactions except by barter almost impossible. Small coins were urgently needed.

His invention pointed the way toward power-made interchangeable parts soon to be pioneered by Gideon Roberts and Eli Terry in making clocks—the principle that Abel's neighbor, Eli Whitney, was to incorporate into the manufacture of cotton gins and guns, thereby laying the basis for future mass production.

Abel went to see New Haven's eager promoter, wealthy James Hillhouse, "the Great Sachem," a "tall big-nosed Yankee," said to be part Indian, who had set out the elms around the green with his own hands. He was the first of a new type of financial genius, with the vision and daring needed to put the new skills of America to work to tame the continent. Hillhouse was enthusiastic about Abel's machine. He put up money, got others to participate, and secured a state contract to manufacture copper coins.

Abel set up his "mint" on Water Street, facing Long Island Sound. He held only an eighth interest but retained control of his invention and was paid to manage the plant, design and engrave, make dies, and strike off coins.

His AUCTOR CONNECT pennies, bearing the motto INDE ET LIB, encircling a figure of Liberty holding an olive branch, were the second or third issue of metal coins in Connecticut, and the first ever made by machinery. During the next few years Abel and his helpers made three hundred engravings and dies for copper, silver, and gold coins.

The small-change famine was not confined to Connecticut. Congress contracted with James Jarvis of New York to make coppers. Buell's shop had the only "modern" equipment, and Jarvis put in capital to enlarge it. Buell retained a twelfth interest, ownership of invention, and his previous employment. Thus the man who had faced life imprisonment in the days of the colony for counterfeiting became the first maker of coins for the new United States Government.

The "Fugio ... 1787" Federal pennies he designed and minted bear a sundial and meridian sun and the good American motto MIND YOUR BUSINESS.

His restless brain soon drove him on to new adventures. He borrowed $500 on his share of the business, left his son Benjamin in charge, and departed secretly, for he was bent on a mission that might be blocked were he to divulge it. Not a single power-driven textile mill existed in the former colonies, and the British forbade the export of machinery and the emigration of textile workers and experts. Abel was determined to overcome these obstacles.

In England, he worked in British mills to get the know-how for the plant he intended to erect. He had already picked the ideal spot—on West River in New Haven.

While in England he also designed and built iron bridges, among the first ever constructed.

In London he met Tom Paine, acting as American representative, and they became good friends. Abel's admiration for the great American patriot was boundless. Many of their ideas were similar. Buell asked Paine to help him figure out a way to get around the severe British textile restrictions. Buell saw Andy McIntosh, the Scotch textile expert, who was enthusiastic about going to America. They schemed how to avoid arousing the suspicions of the authorities.

In 1793 Buell sailed triumphantly into New Haven Harbor to Long Wharf with a boatload of British machinery, his Scotch expert, and two New York capitalists.

He helped erect a four-story $50,000 mill, the first or second successful power-loom cotton mill in America. But Abel wanted his own establishment. He secured a $3,000 subsidy from the State Assembly and soon had a smaller mill working on the spot he had planned on long before. President Ezra

Stiles of Yale visited both establishments and predicted that
Abel's smaller mill would prove the more successful. He was
right. It kept on many years after the other had failed.

Abel Buell had another important visitor, his neighbor Eli
Whitney, whom he had met some years before. Eli had been
greatly interested in Abel Buell's minting machine. He had
also been interested in an automatic machine invented by
Ebenezer Chittenden, with Buell's help, to manufacture bent
pins for carding machines. Chittenden's machine could turn
out 86,000 pins an hour.

Whitney was now making the cotton gins he had invented
in a plant on the street back of "The Mint." His invention had
spread millions of acres of yellow cotton blossoms over the
South, making mills like Abel's possible. Clumsy imitators,
pirating Eli's machine, were charging that the fine wire
brushes on Whitney's models injured the long cotton fibers.
Eli wanted affidavits from successful millowners like Buell
that such charges were not true.

4

Most men would have been content to push one notable
enterprise to success, then rest on their laurels and their
money. But Abel was too full of new ideas. He disposed of his
share in the mill and set to work on new projects. In his free
time he liked to tinker with the two fire engines Chittenden
was building for New Haven.

Often Abel looked in at Amos Doolittle's engraving plant,
doing book illustrations and maps and engraving bank notes.
Doolittle had made famous illustrations of the Battles of
Concord and Lexington, popular all over America, and he had
engraved the first paper currency in New Haven, put out by
the new Chamber of Commerce to help relieve the short-
change crisis. He was also engraving sheet music—he was a
passionate musician—and started the first music magazine in
America. Among other books, he illustrated Jedidiah Morse's
Geography Made Easy and designed the maps.

Abel's projects took a different direction, quite down to earth. He invented a corn-crusher, and then, foreseeing the increased demand for corn in the expanding nation, invented a mechanical corn-planter, the first ever made. He paved the way for Iowa, "the great corn-growing, hog-raising upsurge of the Midwest." He also built a mechanical onion-planter.

Buell also kept on with his craft work, making more silver services for churches. He loved this patient artisanship better than his more ambitious undertakings. One of his advertisements read:

"Mariners and surveyors instruments cleaned and rectified; engraving, seal and die sinking, seal presses; enameled hair-worked mounting, rings and lockets; fashionable gold earrings and beads, silver and silver plated; gilt and polished buttons, buttons, button and other casting models, plating mills, printing blocks; coach and sign painting, gilding and varnishing; patterns and models of any sort of cast work; mills and working models for grinding points as used in Europe; working models of canal locks; drawing on parchment, paper, silk, etc. . . ."

This varied list is a compendium of technical advances in American skills during the two decades following independence, many unknown previously. His "coach painting" told of the new industry rapidly making New Haven the carriage capital of the world. It was given a big impetus when Jonathan Mix invented and patented the elliptical spring, the first satisfactory steel spring used on horse-drawn vehicles. Up to this time the bodies had hung precariously from leather straps that were always breaking. Later, adapted by Joseph Ives, Gideon Roberts's apprentice, the leaf spring that resulted from Mix's invention provided a revolutionary new principle for timepieces.

Buell's canal-lock models were part of a new urge in America soon to bear fruit. Buell and Hillhouse visualized a canal across central Connecticut, a grandiose project that eventually "might reach into Massachusetts and cross Vermont to the St. Lawrence and the Great Lakes," and in time "be hooked up with the Mississippi." It would help open up the back country and the whole West; it was attuned to "the growth of farms and cities on far plains." Such were the early dreams of American men, seemingly fantastic and impossible, yet which soon were to take on actual form.

But when Abel's famous friend and backer, James Hillhouse, started such a canal in 1825, Buell was no longer alive. The sixty locks that lifted boats more than three hundred feet above the Connecticut hills, were modified versions of the original model Buell had brought to Hillhouse's home.

5

Abel moved on to Hartford and set up a shop on the Commons, opposite the Meeting House, where he made military equipment and turned out silverwork and jewelry, printing blocks and ornaments.

His wife died there in 1800, and at the age of sixty-one he remarried. His young wife died three years later, and growing lonely now, he moved on to Stockbridge, Massachusetts. His family was scattered. Most of his old friends had died.

Parson Swift induced him to read the Bible. One day Abel burst out of his shop, waving a pair of red-hot tongs and shouting, "They have altered the Bible! This is not the same book which Tom Paine and I used to ridicule. This is beautiful! All beautiful, beautiful, beautiful!"

In 1813 his nostalgic memories drew him back to New Haven, where he opened another shop. There he kept on until his death in 1822 at the age of eighty-one.

By then a still larger tide of people was moving west; a mighty empire was arising. The industrial upsurge of America had started. It was the patient, eager work of artisans and craftsmen, inventors and promoters, such as Abel Buell, that had made it possible for the new nation to march ahead to greatness. Abel Buell's life was the very essence of Yankee enterprise, ingenuity, and freedom.

XIII. New England Discovers the World

LATE IN September, 1787, the *Columbia*, a 213-ton ship fresh off the ways in Plymouth, lay alongside Boston wharf, being outfitted for a trip around the world. When all stores were stowed aboard, Captain John Kendrick anchored off Castle Island, where they were joined by a consort vessel, the nine-ton sloop *Lady Washington*, under Captain Robert Gray.

The two vessels were headed for an adventure into the unknown. American vessels had already circled the Horn and visited Chinese ports, but the Pacific Northwest, which was to be the main theater of the two vessels' operations, had scarcely been explored by anybody. James Cook had sailed into those waters a few years before, touching here and there, but his map of the Pacific coast line was very vague from Cape Mendocino to Nootka Sound (located on what presently was discovered to be a large island, in due course named Vancouver Island). From there north to Sitka, Alaska, his map had been left blank. The two Boston vessels would be sailing into dangerous, uncharted waters.

The various accounts of Cook's voyages had inspired Joseph Barrel, a wealthy Boston merchant, to get together a trading expedition to the area. It would barter with the Indians for furs, then sail on to Canton to exchange them for tea, nankeen cloth, and silk, and return to Boston via the Cape of Good Hope and the Atlantic. He and five other merchants and shipowners put up £50,000 to buy and outfit the two vessels.

The enterprisers were looking for fresh opportunities. Since the Revolution, West Indies trade had been largely cut off; frequent seizures of ships by the British and French spelled ruin for many owners. Even European trade was dangerous. Barbary pirates ranged all along the French coast to the

English Channel. The present undertaking was fortunate in having as first officer under Kendrick, Simeon Woodruff, who had been a gunner's mate on Cook's last voyage. Though no longer spry, he could be most helpful.

Kendrick himself was a seasoned officer of forty-seven, known to be a courageous and competent navigator. He was born in 1740 at Harwich on the south side of Cape Cod, near fabled Nantucket Sound. At twenty-one he joined a whaling expedition to the Gulf of St. Lawrence, and, except for a short enlistment in the French and Indian Wars, never left the sea. During the Revolution, he had commanded three large privateers that had brought in valuable prizes. Afterward he had captained coast vessels between Boston and southern states. He had never lost a ship, his word was gold, his reliability unquestioned.

Though he was a man who never hurried, and this at times irked his employers, they had appreciated his caution and care for their ships and cargoes. Indeed, he was such a perfectionist that he trusted no man's judgment but his own and often performed even menial tasks to be sure they were done right, which often occasioned serious delays. He was an iron disciplinarian, quick-tempered, brooking no opposition, and rarely accepting advice from others; he could be explosive, drastic, even brutal, though he was the first to acknowledge his own mistakes even to underlings, and he bore no grudges.

Only his intimate friends knew that secretly he nursed lofty, unfulfilled ambitions. He thought in cosmic terms, of colossal geographic projects and new empires. Dreaming of such "Gargantuan Grandeur," he was apt to neglect minor obligations, and this also made him slothful at times. This venture into the Northwest was the first that seemed to match his vast dreams.

His subordinate on the daring enterprise, Robert Gray, captain of the *Washington*, was only thirty-four, but he had been in the naval service of the Continental Congress and had already captained a trading vessel owned by two backers of the Pacific undertaking. No one had ever proved more satisfactory.

He was born in the seafaring town of Tiverton, Rhode Island, May 10, 1753, grandson of Edward Gray of Plymouth, who had married the niece of Governor Edward Winslow. Some years before going to the Pacific, Captain Gray had married a girl named Martha of Martha's Vineyard, where he made his home; they had four daughters.

Gray's clear, terse, exact logbook reveals a practical, direct mind, an energetic spirit, decisive, efficient, self-confident. He was self-contained, and though straightforward and truthful, was a man of tact. Having great and justified confidence in his own resourcefulness, he was always willing to take risks and in moments of danger was calm to a point others thought reckless. Having the true feel of the sea, a canny awareness of weather and currents, always quick to act, he was able to ride out perilous moments coolly and find his way among uncharted reefs in a forthright way that caused more timid, less experienced officers to grow terrified and question his judgment. He liked getting things done quickly, and he never faltered. He was a born leader of men.

2

After the "mirth and glee" of a Sunday-night farewell shipboard party, with "a great number of Merchants, Gentlemen and others of Boston" singing "Jovial Songs," before dawn Monday morning, October 1, the two vessels "weighed and came to sail and by sunrise were out of the harbour."

The ships headed through "boistrous" seas for the Cape Verde Islands. The weather improved, both vessels sailed "exceedingly well," and had proper sail been set to take advantage of the favorable winds, a quick crossing could have been made, but Captain Kendrick never hurried, so it was November 8, before they anchored off Maio Island to take on animals. Seven days drifted by before Kendrick moved on to the port of São Thiago, where everything was unloaded to give the *Columbia* a thorough overhauling. Kendrick insisted on doing nearly everything himself, so this job also dragged.

"Discord" had "subsisted" between him and his officers ever since departure from Boston. Angrily Kendrick now kicked off his Chief Officer Woodruff, the only man who had ever visited the Northwest, and the ship's surgeon asked to be discharged on account of illness and ill treatment. Kendrick refused to give him his effects, and this brought on a quarrel with the governor, which obliged the *Columbia* to leave port in such a hurry that the crew had to cut the anchor cable.

Otherwise there is no telling how long Kendrick would have loitered there. Captain Gray complained to Barrel, "We lay there forty-one days, thirty-six more than I thought necessary." He had repeatedly warned Kendrick they would have to face Cape Horn gales at the worst season—"all to no purpose, he being absolute," unwilling to "hear to reason."

As they plowed the five thousand miles to the Falkland Islands, Kendrick still refused to speed up their trip. The officers fretted, and though Gray kept things running smoothly on the *Washington*, there was near mutiny on the *Columbia*.

It was February 16 before they skirted Jason Island in the Falklands. They missed magnificent Port Egbert and had to put into Brett's Harbor, where the anchors scarcely held in the kelp on the stone bottom.

Kendrick decided to winter here rather than round the Horn in such dangerous weather. Every officer "expressed . . . disgust at the Very Idea." Gray pointed out that there might be even greater danger in Brett's Harbor, where there was no anchorage and not a stick of wood with which to face what promised to be a severe winter. For once Kendrick gave in.

3

The two vessels "stood out of the Harbour" March 3, 1788. They hit unfavorable "flawey tides," then mountainous cross-currents, finally one "continuous tempest" climaxed by the worst gales any had ever experienced. "Almost continuously under water," their bunks and clothes were soaked with no chance to dry them out and often became frozen to their skin. They plowed on through fog, rain, hail, sleet, and snow, and —to add to the danger—icebergs.

They gave Cape Horn a wide berth, sailing south almost to the Antarctic Circle and swinging back far west of South America. On April 1 they hit their worst gale. The vessels floundered in hundred-foot waves and had the smallest struck them it would have "infaillibly ... put an end" to their existence.

The storm separated the two vessels, which pleased Captain Gray, for he could now set his own course and pace. More terrible storms hit them, but north of the west end of the Straits of Magellan they soon enjoyed moderate weather— "that beautiful serenity this Ocean is selebrated for."

They headed for the outermost Juan Fernández Island off Chile, avoiding the main Spanish penal colony, but their small boat could not get through the pounding surf for water and wood, nor were they able to find water in the desolate red hills of San Ambrosia Island, hundreds of miles north.

Water rations had to be cut to two quarts a day per man, and they had to piece out with rain water. Off Central America they made only twenty miles in twenty-one days against headwinds and a strong south current.

For two months more they moved north, never once in sight of land, but on August 2 at 10:00 A.M., to their "inexpressable joy," they sighted the northern California coast above Cape Mendocino.

Off the Oregon shore, ten Indians paddled out in a big, hollowed-out tree trunk, making "very expressive seigns of friendship." They smoked tobacco in small tubes "about the size of a Child's whistle."

The *Washington* moved north in a gale, laid up in a safe cove, pushed past Cape Blanco, and at the Alsea River, warlike natives waved white moose skins—their armor against arrows—and shook their spears at the boat "with hideous shouting."

There were other contacts with more friendly Indians, and on the fifteenth they anchored in Tillamook Bay. Indians came out in a canoe, bringing berries and boiled crabs. These probably saved the lives of three or four crew members far gone with scurvy. Good sea-otter skins were purchased with "knives, axes, adzes, etca." The Indians wanted copper, which the ship did not have, but with buttons the crew bought more boiled and roasted crabs, also "dryed" salmon and berries.

The Indian braves wore skins; the women were naked except for white cedar-bark tasseled skirts, which covered them "only when standing, as in other positions the tassels separate." Trouble soon developed over a stolen cutlass. Two crew members were killed with arrows and spears; others nearly lost their lives. All that dismal night they heard the "hoops and houling of the natives," dancing around beach fires. "It chilled the bludd in my vains," said one of the mates. They named the place "Murderers' Harbor."

They moved up the coast through drizzle, stopping here and there to buy otter skins. They saw Juan de Fuca Strait and hove to in Barkley Sound to mend sails.

Forty-six people came out in three canoes. "They paddled with exceeding great haste, singing an agreeable air and keeping stroke in time to the tune with their Paddles and at the end of every cadence, all together they would point their paddles first aft then forward, first hooping shrill then horce. They went three times around the vessel performing this manual exercise, and then came alongside without further seremony."

The *Washington* beat on north through fog and bad weather, unable to take locations, until they found themselves under strange "Craggey Barren Cliffs." Pinned down by large beds of kelp, they were almost wrecked on dangerous shoals, but finally reached Nootka Sound, agreed upon as the rendezvous with the missing *Columbia*, and anchored at Resolution

Harbor on a small island well inside, where they hauled the boat on shore and "payed her bottom."

That was on September 16. Not a single Indian showed up to trade, and they were soon in a bad way for supplies.

In port were two "snows," or brigantines, belonging to Captain John Meares, an Englishman who operated them out of Macao under the Portuguese flag in order to evade the South Sea and East India Company monopolies. In two months their crews had traded in 750 otter skins. They had also erected a small fort and had almost completed a new thirty-ton schooner. Meares generously loaned his blacksmith to the *Washington* to help repair the rudder chains, badly damaged crossing Murderers' Harbor bar.

On September 23 Captain Gray looked through his spyglass at a "sail in the offin." It was the *Columbia*. Kendrick's boat was in a bad way. Her topsails were reefed, and her topgallant masts were down on the deck in disorder.

Gray went out in the longboat to help them, and about five in the afternoon, the *Columbia* anchored alongside the *Washington*.

4

Two of Kendrick's crew had died of scurvy, the rest were "in an advanced state of that malignant Distemper." John Nutting, "the ship's astronomer," no longer able to endure the hardships or, it was hinted, Kendrick's abuse, had gone insane and had jumped overboard.

Any trading had to be done before winter set in, but Kendrick showed little inclination to get things shipshape to go out. October 1 rolled around—the weather getting colder and stormier. They celebrated the anniversary of their departure from Boston with a thirteen-gun "federal" salute, which the British answered from their new "Fort Defense."

Some provisions were obtained by going inland to Indian villages, and presently a few came to the shore with fish oil, venison, and skins. They were powerful men, though with crooked, ill-shaped legs, for they rarely walked but went every-where by boat and always sat cross-legged. They wore goat's-hair and pounded cedar-bark garments and kept their skin constantly covered with red paint and oil, on which they threw sparkling sand.

Soon the season was too advanced to trade, and Kendrick put all hands to work converting the rigging of the *Washington* into that of a brigantine, but soon dropped the project and had them start a winter house on shore. He soon abandoned this also, ordering them to tilt up the longboat as a shed to keep their water casks and a few cannon, with the result that presently the Indians made off with five small cannon and fifteen water casks. He spent several weeks "up to his elbows in mortar, building a brick chimney" or "cabuse" where the mizzenmast had stood and a shelter big enough to house every-body. He had a good brass stove, but "its consequences we all dreaded and endevered to diswade" him from using it, "but for no purpose." In due course, fire broke out that almost reached the magazine bulkhead before it could be extin-guished.

5

Early in the spring, on March 16, Gray took the *Washing-ton* out, heading south, putting in wherever it was possible to trade, and getting many skins. They found the villages in Clayoquot Harbor well built and cleaner, the people at-tractively clad in furs or cedar-bark capes edged with fur, sometimes in a hand-woven "Cleptanick" blanket, with a hole in the top for the head.

Opitstat, the main summer village, had two hundred large houses with elaborate totem poles. "Their Clums or carved pillars are . . . so large that the Mouth serves as a doarway into their houses. Some of their ridgpoals . . . are of incredible length and bulk . . . neatly Fluted. Others are painted in resemblance of . . . beasts and birds . . . [or] the Sun both painted and carved the rays shout out from every side of the orb which like our Country Sign painters they picture with eyes nose and mouth and plump round face."

They made friends with the chiefs, attended musical fiestas, where the Indians sang and struck hollow chests and shook pebble-filled instruments shaped like men or birds, and were invited on a whale hunt.

The *Washington* beat on down the coast, entering Juan de Fuca Strait several times, once sailing fifty miles inside, but usually only to Poverty Cove, on the north shore near the entrance, where they were offered curious blankets woven from dogs' or childrens' hair.

Tatoosh Island, outside the entrance, was a profitable trading point; and at Nittenat village, on the shore just south, they could have secured 200 otter skins for five chisels each, but had only chisels enough left to buy fifty.

They returned to Nootka Sound on April 22, expecting to leave at once for China, only to find that the *Columbia*, which was supposed to have gone out trading, was still "mearly a Hulk," not graved or calked, and that all the guns were on shore.

The *Washington* set out on another trading cruise, north this time. At the harbor entrance they were hailed by the *Princesa*, which fired a warning shot and hoisted the red-and-yellow Spanish colors. It was commanded by Stefano José Martínez, who had orders to explore as far north as the Bering Straits, take possession of Nootka Sound in the name of His Catholic Majesty, and seize all British ships.

He was hugely pleased to learn that a British ship lay in port, and he sent Gray presents, "brandy, wine, hams, sugar, in short everything he thought would be acceptable."

Salutes were exchanged, and the *Washington* continued north, rounded Cape Scott, on the upper tip of Vancouver Island, and entered Queen Charlotte Sound—the first American vessel ever to do so. The mainland natives were friendly, and thirty otter skins were purchased for "a trifling number of chizels."

Gray sailed along the Alexander Archipelago of Alaska and sought shelter in a small cove, but a terrific gust off the snowy mountains tossed them back. They tried to tack, but their jib boom and bowsprit were smashed on the rocks, and the surf lifted the boat into a "nook in ... craggey cliffs nearly as high as our mast head," surmounted by pines that darkened the water to fearsome blackness.

Every swell dashed the vessel higher against the rocks "with the utmost fuery." The wind "Increased violently," and they were left "on the pinnacles of this murciless Iron Bound coast" among "a most horrid race of savage canables [not true] in whose hands we could not hope for life ... and so destitute of everything ... requisite to sustain life that a European could not exist." A situation "more critical could not be imagined."

There was no help this side of Nootka Sound, five hundred miles away, and they worked desperately. A hawser was carried out in the "kedge" and held tight every time the sea rose and the ship "fleeted." Inch by inch they got her so she "seldom struck the rocks" and put out an anchor. But while clearing away the wreckage of the bowsprit and boom, their "kedge" became wedged and they had to abandon it, so were unable to examine the damage done before pushing out to sea again. "This disastrous place we called Distress Cove."

They headed for Nootka Sound, but, finding the vessel was not too badly damaged, they continued trading. At one point in the Queen Charlotte Islands they bought two hundred skins in "a fue minutes" for only one chisel apiece.

They found a fine cove in Barrel Strait, named after the owner, and did some lively trading. The Indians here were stark naked, and the women wore only "a Lethern apron" and pearl-shell and wooden labrets rimmed with copper, "the most prepostrous ... orniment ..." imaginable, held by an incision in the lower lip, with a groove cut for the lip and the other part "formed to Lay against the gums." This "huge trencher" was the size of "a barber's Lather box." When the women spoke, it flew up and down, hiding half the nose; hanging down, it covered "all the chin." In spite of these "lip pieces ... enough to disgust any Civilized being ... some of the Crew was quite partial," for the women, who came aboard freely, were "willing to gratify the amorous inclinations of any who wish it."

On June 17, they caught a breeze that "wafted" them into Nootka Sound. Martínez, in full possession there, had seized the British *Iphigenia* and was holding the crew prisoners. Later, he seized Meares's other vessel and three more, sending them to San Blas for "tryal." The Spaniards paid Kendrick ninety-six otter skins to carry Meares's crew to China.

The damage to the *Washington* was repaired, and Kendrick ordered both vessels south to Clayoquot Bay. There he turned the *Columbia* over to Gray, with orders to take the cargo of skins to China, while he kept the *Washington* to do more trading.

Gray lay up in Hawaii three weeks, salting pork and taking on board 150 live hogs. He and his crew were captivated by the beauty and flowers and the colorful cheerful people. The women were "beautiful" and "in a state of Nature except a small covering around the middle." Not many of the *Columbia*'s crew "proved to be Josephs," Gray's mate recorded.

Gray sailed on to Canton, arriving nine weeks later, on November 17, 1789. Meanwhile Kendrick got a fine cargo of furs in the Queen Charlotte Islands and also crossed the Pacific, reaching Dirty Butter Bay in Macao near the end of January, 1790, where he sold most of his skins for $18,000, saving out 200 to take to Japan, where he hoped to get a better price. This was the first time the American flag had been flown in a Japanese port.

Kendrick traded hither and yon for five years with incredibly bad luck. One typhoon off Macao tore away his masts and rigging, sweeping the deck clean. He took part in an inter-island war in Hawaii, with the King as "Admiral" of his ship.

He was promised a full load of sandalwood, but the King never kept his promise.

On his trips to the Northwest, Kendrick purchased five tracts on Vancouver Island from the Indians, boasting that while other nations *stole* the land, he had *bought* "his Territories." He planned to carve out an empire. Northeast America was Lilliputian; he intended to build the Northwest on a Brobdingnagian scale. To improve the climate, he proposed diverting the Gulf Stream into the Pacific by digging a ditch across Mexico. No wonder "the paltry two-penny objects of his expedition were swallowed up in the magnitude of his Gulliverian views!" wrote his mate, John Howel. "But with all his fooleries he was a wonderful man, and worthy to be remembered beyond the gliding hours of the present generation."

He was killed accidentally in Hawaii, when a neighboring vessel, giving a salute to the King, neglected to remove the grapeshot from the cannon and the charge tore through Kendrick's cabin. Perhaps the King was saving himself some sandalwood!

6

Robert Gray, after leaving Hawaii and anchoring at Canton, wrote the company that the ship was "much out of repair, and the expense, I fear, will exceed your expectations." He was having grievous difficulties selling his 1,209 pelts. The smuggling price was fifty to seventy dollars, but the risk was too great. The local merchants and officials were cunning wolves. Starving river folk in the junks threw poison to the hogs so they could eat the carcasses thrown overboard. The lower-class Chinese were "the worst thieves in all Christendom."

Not until January 4 was Gray able to take the cargo ashore in a "chop boat" guarded by eight men with muskets. One crew member smuggled a skin under his jacket for First Mate Coolidge.

But it was nearly a month more before the Hoppo, or customs official, would put his "chop" (seal) on the shipment, and final sale and delivery were not made until January 30. The skins brought $21,400 after customs, but half went for warehousing, expenses, and the 7½ per cent commission. The sum of $11,241.50 was invested in a cargo of Bohea tea for the return trip.

Gray circled the Cape of Good Hope, reached St. Helena "in good order," and entered Boston Harbor August 9, 1790, almost three years after setting out. The *Columbia* had covered 48,889 miles; and Gray, trading in the *Washington*, many thousands more.

He was the first American to carry the Stars and Stripes around the world.

7

The *Columbia* received a royal welcome. As it slid past Castle Island, thirteen-gun salutes were exchanged, and cheering crowds lined the wharves. The *Columbia Sentinel* lavishly praised the merchants for backing an "experiment . . . before unessayed by Americans." The "intrepid Navigators," by their "urbanity and civility," had "secured the friendship of the aboriginals," and their "honour and intrepidity" had "commanded . . . respect . . . to the American flag."

But more than half the tea was damaged by salt water and at auction brought only £76/15. The total wages of officers and crew came to £1498, of which Gray, paid £3/12 a month, received £132.

Financially the venture was a fiasco, and one ship had vanished over the horizon forever. Two partners dropped out.

But Gray and two new investors put up money, and six weeks later, he took the *Columbia* out again, with £1519/10 of supplies and trading goods for a four-year voyage. Gray carried a personal letter from the President of the United States, putting the vessel under the protection of the government and asking the officials and citizens of all friendly nations for courtesy and assistance.

In his instructions to Gray, merchant Barrel expressed harsh feelings over the conduct of the first expedition. This time, to keep an eye on everything, he was sending John Box Hoskins, a twenty-two-year-old lad he had adopted and brought up in his own home and countinghouse. Gray considered Hoskins a spy, and the fastidious young gentleman, uncomfortable among "rough" and "ignorant" men, repeatedly accused Gray of "intended" shady doings. During his life-time, Gray won the loyalty and respect of everybody except Hoskins.

Thanks to the experience gained in the first trip, the *Columbia* set out better equipped at far less cost, with tools and equipment for every contingency and a large supply of objects craved by the Indians.

Port Collector General Benjamin Lincoln (who had put down Shays's Rebellion) made a cursory examination of the cargo and certified that it carried, among other things, 2,000 bricks, 30 barrels of tar, 1,500 pounds of gunpowder, 6 tons of bar iron, 27,000 pounds of bread. But according to the detailed purser's list, it carried 5,470 bricks. Nor did Lincoln mention four tons of iron already made into "chissels," nor copper sheets for trading, nor the oak and spruce framework carried to construct an additional vessel on arrival in the Northwest. The "thirty packages of merchandise" he mentioned contained clothing, rope, canvas, 800 large sail needles, 1,000 ordinary needles, brass, rivets, nails, spikes, kettles, coffee pots, twine, tallow, glass, and putty. The vessel carried carpenter, blacksmith, and ship tools; bear traps, whale irons, and mackerel, cod, and shark hooks.

Adventures were similar to those on the first expedition except that Gray kept up a faster pace. Cape Horn weather was ideal, and the passage was made in half the time.

They traded busily along the Northwest coast all season, wintered in Clayoquot Bay, where they built the new boat which they named the *Adventure*. Early in the spring, First

Mate Robert Haswell took it north to the Queen Charlotte Islands and on to Sitka, Alaska. The *Columbia* turned south.

All day, Saturday, April 28, it traded at Kenekomit village near Juan de Fuca Strait for "a fine lot of skins" bought with copper. Near Destruction Island at 4:00 A.M. Sunday, they were hailed by Captain George Vancouver, commanding the *Discovery* and the *Chatham*. He sent a small boat to inquire how to get to the Juan de Fuca Strait.

Out of helpfulness, curiosity, or perhaps rivalry, Gray followed the British vessels, all sails set. He stopped to "drain" Kenekomit of its last skins, then pressed north full tilt and followed the British ships through the dangerous, foaming passage between Tatoosh Island and Duncan Rock.

In the morning, Vancouver moved on into the Strait, and the *Columbia* put out to sea again. For a week Gray traded at Tatoosh Island and shore villages.

Sailing south from La Push, at the mouth of the Quilayute River, on May 7, he sighted what appeared to be a large harbor and sent the cutter to investigate. The breakers at the bar were too heavy to enter, but Gray refused to give up and ordered the small boat to make soundings and signal the best channel. Tacking about, he boldly headed through the wild spray against a strong current. He found himself in an enormous bay at the mouth of the Chehalis River. It was duly christened "Gray's Harbor." He was probably the first white man ever to visit the place. The Indians were open-mouthed.

"The men were entirely naked," said Boit, "and the women, except a small apron before, made of Rushes, were also in a state of Nature . . . and very ugly."

During the second night, a fleet of war canoes attacked them but was dispersed by musket firing. The attackers returned at midnight, ignoring volleys, and the *Columbia* let go with "a Nine pounder, loaded with langerege," and "about 10 Musketts, loaded with Buckshot." A large canoe was blasted to bits, probably killing the twenty men aboard.

In spite of this, the next day many canoes came alongside

to trade. The Indians pointed excitedly at the cannon, trying
to explain to friends the noise it made. "Those natives
brought us some fine Salmon and plenty of Beaver skins and
...had we staid longer among them, we should have done
well."

On the tenth, at one o'clock, Gray's logbook declares, the
crew "began to unmoor, took up the best bower-anchor and
hove short on the small bower-anchor. At half past four (being
high water) hove up the anchor, and came to sail and a beating down the harbor."

From the natives they had learned about a great bay not far
south. They sighted it at 4:00 A.M. on the eleventh. Gray lay
inshore till after sunup, then sent the pinnace in to feel out
the channel. At eight o'clock, the *Columbia* bore away,
wheeled about, and ran in under short sail through the heavy
breakers, brunting a powerful current that brought fresh water
to the very mouth of the harbor. He kept on upstream for ten
miles and anchored half a mile out, off a north-shore village
called Cenoak. The river at this point was three miles wide.

Gray had rediscovered the long-lost mouth of the Columbia
River, which thereafter bore the name of his vessel. The upper
reaches had been explored by the French seventy-five years
earlier, and a Spanish navigator, Bruno Hecate, had entered
here seventeen years before Gray, but Captain Meares, following Hecate's astronomical observations in 1788, had
declared no such river or harbor existed and dubbed the nearby point, Cape Disappointment. Vancouver, recognizing Cape
Disappointment, only three weeks before this, had confirmed
Meares's opinion. Gray sailed in.

The *Columbia* moved upstream, but went aground on a
sandbank. Gray and a mate went ashore "to view the country"
and—as a later writer inserted in the record to back United
States territorial claims—"take possession."

Many canoes "from all parts of the river" came alongside.
The men were "straight limb'd, fine looking fellows," wrote
the mate, and the women "very pretty...all in a state of

Nature, except the females who wear a leaf apron (perhaps *'twas* a fig leafe). But some of our gentlemen that examin'd them pretty cloase and *near*, both *within* and *without*, reported that it was not a leaf but a nice wove mat! !"

During the stay, the *Columbia* collected 150 otter skins, 300 beaver skins, and nearly 500 "land furs." The river abounded with "excellent Salmon" and most other river fish, and the woods with "Moose and Deer, the skins of which were brought to us in great plenty." It was a beautiful spot, and if a "factory" were set up here and another . . . in the Queen Charlotte Islands, with the help of a few small coasting vessels, they "wou'd engross the whole trade of the NW Coast."

More than a quarter-century later, Timothy Flint of Massachusetts, noted missionary chronicler of the new West, published an imaginary Fourth of July editorial in the imaginary *Gazette* of 1900, a newspaper in an imaginary city of 100,000 at the mouth of the Columbia River. "Church and school" were words that "flourished" in its ads to sell lots to the rush of people moving west. A rich old lady traveled to the Columbia all the way by new roads or river boats without having to abandon her carriage. There, Emily Evergreen, aged seventy-five, was rejuvenated "by a transfusion of youthful blood into her veins."

Not Kendrick alone dreamed of a great northwestern empire. Whether Gray also foresaw great cities on the Columbia and Puget Sound is not recorded.

Next, Gray sailed back north to look for the *Adventure*. Haswell had been doing a brisk business in the Queen Charlotte Islands and off Alaska. The two vessels arrived at the agreed rendezvous off northern Vancouver Island at the same moment and sailed into harbor together.

More trading was done, but in the Queen Charlotte Islands the *Columbia* hit a rock. The bad hole was patched up, but the ship had to put in at Nootka Sound for repairs.

The Spaniards had built a fort—"no great thing" though it had forty-two mounted cannon. Of the many houses built, only that of the governor was "rather grand." Governor Juan Francisco de la Bodega y Quadra was cordial, gave them every assistance, and insisted that Gray stay at his house until repairs were made. Two Spanish botanists already lived there as his guests. He gave a "grand entertainment" for all officers in port. "Fifty-four persons sat down to Dinner, and the plates, which was *solid* silver, was shifted five times, which made 270 plates," for none of the soiled ones were reused. "The Dishes, Knifes and forks and indeed everything else, was of Silver ... and always replaced with spare ones."

The Governor was astonished at the rapidity with which Gray made repairs, and praised his ingenuity.

After more trading to the north, Gray re-entered Nootka Sound and sold the *Adventure* to Governor de la Bodega for seventy-five otter skins valued at $4,960.

The *Columbia* secured last-minute wood and water at Poverty Cove in Juan de Fuca Strait; a "full allowance of Grog" made "our worthy Tars join in the *generall* Mirth," and on October 3, they "weighed for the last time on the N. W. Coast," bound for Hawaii and Canton.

By early December a pilot was taking them up Macao roads; on December 12, they anchored at Whampoa, at the mouth of the Canton River, a rough free port where a better price could be obtained, since many buyers evaded the customs. The pirates in junks there were less terrifying than the merchant pirates and officials of Canton. Repairs cost the *Columbia* $7,000, but the furs, selling at $45 each, brought in $90,000. They loaded up with tea, nankeen, sugar, and china ware.

By May, 1793, they were at St. Helena, and they sailed triumphantly past Castle Island into Boston Harbor, July 25.

8

By the time Gray returned from his second voyage, American vessels were swarming around the Horn to China. It was part of the freedom of independence, the burst of energy from new opportunities. The former manufacturing and trading restrictions were now gone, and men invented and built and manufactured new goods. They hurried west. They took to the sea. They circled the globe and ranged deep into the frozen south and frozen north. New horizons were open on every side. New England suddenly awoke from its century and a half of isolation and ingrowing creeds and discovered the world.

Before the Revolution, American shipping had been limited largely to coastal trade. Though in some ports every vessel was lost during the war, within a few years tonnage was greater than ever. Shipyards were busy from Connecticut to Maine. New and bigger boats slid down the ways constantly.

New Haven was typical. Cattle were carried to Boston as early as 1639. During its first twenty years, a group of ship-owners and traders—Lamberton, Mabron, Goodyear, Allerton —put it on the map as a shipping center. All that first century, numerous ships were built there and in Derby on the Housatonic. A Derby fishing company built up considerable West Indies and Mediterranean trade.

By 1763 New Haven had the longest wharf in the world and a thriving trade with Europe and all the way from the French and British islands in the West Indies to Newfoundland. During the Revolution its shipping, though privateers were outfitted, was wiped out, but it came back fast and soon exceeded prewar tonnage. From 1783 to 1793 seventy ships a year came into port.

In spite of British and French trade barriers after the war, American ships edged back into West Indies ports. Then war between the two European countries brought worse trouble. In April, 1794, 52 American vessels were seized and held in British West Indies ports, awaiting decision by Admiralty Courts; 102 were held by the French at Guadeloupe and Martinique.

One French war vessel took off the cargo of the New Haven brig *Anne*, not even leaving provisions. "Eat pine shavings," the French captain told the master; "that is proper food for Yankees."

The Americans fought back and quickly learned to build faster boats. Many heroic sagas were lived and written. Captain Gad Peck of New Haven, captured by the French, broke from below decks with his crew and retook his ship. One New Haven captain fought off Barbary Coast pirates against incredible odds. Others were not so lucky. A ransomed ship's captain told Ezra Stiles that he and six hundred other American sailors were lashed to work as slaves. Some would never see home again.

Such difficulties caused New Haven boats to turn increasingly to the China trade. A few went northwest, following the track of Gray and the *Columbia*. But most found their own three-cornered trade in which they had ten fine, well-armed ships. They sailed south to the Falklands and there, on islands south as far as Antarctica, and on Juan Fernández, they clubbed seals on the beaches, extracted the oil, salted or pickled the meat, and "breached" the skins, removing the fat and drying them. One favorite drying spot in Patagonia was called the "New Haven Green." The skins were sold in China for around $3.50 each, and the vessels were loaded up with tea, silks, and other goods for the return.

Hartford, Wethersfield, Middletown, East Haddam, Farmington, Derby, Litchfield, Milford, Branford, and Stratford—all had sealers in the China trade, not to mention other New England states, and particularly such centers as Boston, Salem, and New Bedford.

One of the first New Haveners to send a ship to the South Seas was Ebenezer Townsend. His trusted captain, Daniel Green of Boston, who had commanded a ship before he was twenty-one, was one of the most successful and daring navigators on the high seas. One trip he brought back a load of pepper that netted $100,000 profit.

Townsend had the 350-ton *Neptune* built at the Olive Street boatyard in New Haven. It carried twenty guns and a forty-man crew, besides surgeon, supercargo, carpenter, black-smith, and cooper. Townsend sent his son along as supercargo to hire the crew and keep accounts. His logbook is an incredible story of trials, tribulations, adventures, new sights, and commercial sagacity.

The *Neptune* carried a general cargo and $500 in gold for emergencies. In the West Indies, Green bartered for rum and sugar; at Rio de Janeiro, for indigo, fustic, sandalwood, and other Brazilian products. He sailed on to the Falklands, visited the seal island, and at Juan Fernández dried 80,000 skins. In the South Seas, he traded cotton goods, brass wire, and old iron for pearls and pearl shell and divi-divi pods for New Haven tanneries.

From China he brought back 3,000 chests of tea, 54,000 pieces of nankeen, $24,000 worth of silk, 547 boxes of china-ware, also lacquer and ivory. He was gone thirty months, reaching New Haven July 14, 1799, with his gold untouched.

Duties totaled $75,000, 30 per cent more than Connecticut revenues. Townsend and his son made a net profit of $150,000; the other partners came in for $100,000.

Such trips were a bonanza for those who first ventured, but many met disaster, and later expeditions grew less profitable as seals were exterminated and the price of skins dropped.

New Haven, along with most of New England, turned to whaling, which also returned astonishing profits—plus such by-products as sperm oil for the lamps that were replacing candles in better homes, and that classic novel, *Moby Dick*.

Trade with the Orient settled down to a more orderly exchange of normal products, less spectacular but more certain. By 1800 New Haven alone was bringing in annually several hundred thousand pounds of tea, more than a million pounds of sugar, and nearly 400,000 gallons of rum, as well as goodly quantities of wine, gin, and brandy.

The last ship to follow the old seal route to Antarctica and China was the *Zephyr*, out of Middletown, shortly after the war of 1812. It found no seals and went north to Nootka

Sound. It picked up a few furs, then put in at Hawaii for sandalwood, an increasingly important trade item.

The era of the Yankee clipper ship was fast approaching.

9

Thus did Gray's pioneering open up the whole Pacific to American enterprise and eventual settlement. He was the trail blazer who sailed uncharted seas on rough coasts through storm and ice. Besides being the first American to take the flag around the world, he was the first to explore the coasts of Oregon, Washington, Canada, and part of Alaska, the first American master to enter Queen Charlotte Sound and Juan de Fuca Strait. He discovered two great harbors in Washington State. His exploration of the mouth of the Columbia was a landmark in American history. He opened the way for the great upsurge of Pacific trade for the rising young Republic, and his explorations and landings helped establish claims to the Pacific Northwest against those of other nations.

The tide of exploration set in motion a new overland wave of enterprising people to the Northwest, many of them New Englanders, to trap, trade for furs, and settle. Soon after the Louisiana Purchase, President Jefferson sent out the Lewis and Clark expedition, which reached the mouth of the Columbia on November 14, 1805. For a time John Jacob Astor, extending his ramified fur enterprises to the Pacific, maintained a trading post, Astoria, near the mouth of the Columbia.

Before long the "Oregon Trail," starting from Independence, Missouri, was jammed with streams of caravans, often with two hundred wagons or more, settlers braving the rough country, the blizzards, the Indians with "paint and war plumes, fluttering trophies and savage embroidery, bows, arrows, lances and shields," as Francis Parkman described them in the Black Hill country. The "Oregon fever" continued for decades.

In 1818 England and the United States agreed to hold the northwest empire jointly, then in 1846 it was arranged to divide the region at the forty-ninth parallel, except for a southern dip to follow Vancouver Harbor and the Juan de Fuca Strait. Idaho, Oregon, and Washington thereby became permanently part of the United States.

Thus the name of Yankee captain Robert Gray from Tiverton, Rhode Island, later of Martha's Vineyard, looms large in the story of America's rise to greatness. He symbolized the century and a half of Indian trading, shipbuilding, and seafaring in New England, knowledge that had held the colonial territory inviolate against the French, which had sent privateers forth to rip great holes in British control of the seas, which had brought prosperity and world products to provincial, isolated shores, and which made it possible for the nation to march on to the Pacific.

XIV. The Father of Mass Production

ELI WHITNEY, inventor of the cotton gin, was in New York sick with fever when his New Haven plant on Wooster Street, back of Abel Buell's mint, caught fire early one morning. Chittenden's two fire engines galloped up, and men worked the long pump handles, but the feeble streams failed to check the blaze. Half a hundred men and boys started a leather-bucket brigade, passing buckets of water from hand to hand.

A new, unoccupied building was saved, but the cotton-gin plant was burned to the ground. The machines, a lathe, treadmill, and several other "engines" Whitney had invented, were destroyed.

He did not learn about this disaster until the packet boat from New York docked at Long Wharf. His eyes were sunken and still glazed with fever; he was emaciated, and his big nose stuck out from his hollow face bigger than ever. But though harassed by debts, lawsuits, and other troubles, he took the loss with a shrug and a smile. Things, he said confidently, would be far simpler with the previous clutter cleared away. The new, empty building was all he needed.

While ill, he had worked out in his head an entirely new method of production. He intended to toss hand production out. This would require new machines he must invent and make. He would be able to manufacture dozens of cotton gins while his competitors made one, and his would be better and more reliable.

Even so, the fire was a staggering loss that would have floored most men, a blow on top of many blows. Imitations of his gin were flooding the market, an avalanche he could not stop no matter how hard he fought the numerous patent infringements. He had put every cent into such court cases, taking long trips to press futile suits in distant parts of the South. Southern judges laughed at his claims. All the South wanted was gins and more gins. Whitney scarcely had a free moment, he was always hard pressed for money and fighting off creditors; for a long time he was unable to afford even decent clothes and proper food.

Though his invention had been on the market only a few years, already it had transformed the South. The slow labor of cleaning seeds out of the fibers had long blocked large-scale production. Right after the war, the British had confiscated eight bales of cotton from America, declaring that so large a quantity could not have been produced in a single place, as the manifest stated, hence must be contraband. But now tens of thousands of new acres were going into cotton. Any amount of cotton could now be handled, and everybody who could get hold of a quarter-section planted the bonanza crop. The tide of yellow blossoms moved across Georgia and the Carolinas and on into the wilderness. Never in history had a single crop shown such rapid expansion; never had so much wealth been added to a nation so quickly.

The year Eli invented the gin, fewer than two hundred and fifty thousand pounds were exported, and shipments abroad were to keep on growing till more than two thousand times that amount would go into the world market from American shores. Soon new cotton mills were being erected in England and all over New England. Tens of thousands of people were finding new jobs, north and south. Country girls, "fresh-scented with cedar and checkerberry leaves," came in from backwoods villages and farms to work at the shuttles and looms.

On his visit to Abel Buell's mill, Eli saw the end operation of his great accomplishment: "The buzzing, hissing, whizzing pulleys, rollers, spindles, and fliers," the carding, dressing, weaving, and dyeing rooms. In their bright calico and gingham dresses and aprons, the "wilderness-shy" girls moved among the looms, gracefully lifting their arms to change the bobbins on spindle frames or to replace full spools with empty ones.

Thanks to Whitney, a whole empire of new production was opened up, the first truly national hookup, aside from some trade, of American enterprise: a team in which southern farmers, gin mills, and plantation owners were yoked with New England millowners and workers.

2

Eli Whitney was the son of a Massachusetts farmer in Leicester, who believed that "book learning" was nonsense. But when Eli, always whittling and making new things, became dead set on studying law, his father shook his head sadly and mortgaged his farm to help out. At Yale, Eli paid a good share of his expenses by making nails, ladies' hairpins, and walking sticks.

In 1749 Yale University received an exciting astronomical instrument from London, an orrery, a clockworks with very delicate balances, to teach the movements of the planets. The fine mechanism had been damaged. President Stiles closeted himself with the new apparatus over the Christmas holidays but could not repair it.

Dr. Elizur Goodrich, a former tutor or instructor, brought Eli Whitney to see the new instrument. Whitney soon had the pieces spread over the table. His ability to fix it saved the university a good deal of money and time. Stiles doubted if anybody else in America could have done it except David Rittenhouse, the talented instrument maker of Philadelphia, who a few years before had himself made an orrery.

Whitney was broadened and inspired by coming under the influence of such an extraordinary man as Stiles, through whom he met such personalities as James Hillhouse, "the Great Sachem," New Haven's early wealthy promoter, David Austin, Pierpont Edwards, and other notables interested in backing new enterprises.

On Eli's graduation in 1792, Stiles suggested that before he

settled down he should see the country; he secured a teaching
post for him in South Carolina. He asked Eli to escort his
close friend, the widow of Major General Greene, and her
family, to their plantation, twelve miles from Savannah.

Before leaving New Haven, Whitney visited the new industries that had sprung up: forges, carriage shops, button
factories, Abel Buell's mint. As he was packing to leave, he
tore up some plans and drawings of inventions he had made.
A friend was horrified, but Eli laughed, saying he had already
remade them better in his head.

When he reached the South, he listened to planters be-
moaning the toilsome process of cleaning seeds from cotton.
It set him to "thinking on the subject," and he "struck out a
plan of a Machine." He showed it to Mr. Miller, executor of
the Greene estate.

"He was pleased with the plan and said if I would pursue it
and try an experiment to see if it would answer . . . he would
be at the whole expense . . . we could share profits."

Eli forgot about teaching and, telling no one of his project,
shut himself up in a small workroom. In about "ten Days," he
had a small, one-man model that could clean "ten times as
much cotton as . . . in any other way before known and also
. . . much better." The machine could also be turned "by
water or with a horse with the greatest ease."

Miller thought it would fill the bill, and Whitney went to
work on a larger one that would do the work of fifty men. It
seemed promising, and he perfected it.

A year and a half after going south, he was back in New
Haven with a model to be sent to the patent office. He rushed
to show it to Ezra Stiles.

Bent steel hooks, similar to those made by Chittenden's
carding-pin machine, were set in a rotary drum that pulled
the cotton through a screen that kept the seeds back. Brushes
on a second drum, revolving in the opposite direction, cleaned
the cotton off the hooks. Later he made it work better, with

a simpler mechanism, by having both drums run in the same direction at different speeds.

3

New Haven was a long way from the Georgia cotton fields, and Eli found it hard to interest anyone in putting up capital. Nobody had the imagination to foresee that his invention would remake the map of the United States, particularly New England, and change the clothing habits of the world. A classmate finally put up a little money, and Whitney rented the Wooster Street shop, hired helpers, and set about designing and making necessary tools and "engines." Even before the patent, with its big gold seal, arrived from Philadelphia in March, 1794, he had already shipped a few gins south.

He kept improving his models till he had a machine with six-foot drums that would clean, not fifty pounds, but a thousand pounds a day.

In making "engines" to manufacture the gin, he perfected a metal lathe, an invention he considered far more important. The cotton gin served only one purpose; the lathe could turn out parts for the gin or for ten thousand other machines. The lathe gave him no world-wide renown, but in improved form it created not ten thousand but millions of new products. His first lathe was destroyed in the fire, but by then he had perfected a better one in his head.

Since the courts could not protect his patent, his only hope was to make a better gin faster and in larger quantities than any competitor could. The new method toward which he had been groping, and which he worked out during his New York illness, was to make every gin exactly alike, with identical interchangeable parts. Any part could be used in any gin. When it wore out, the machine would not have to be junked or require a costly handmade replacement. The secret of doing this was a perfect pattern with power behind it—almost the same story as Abel Buell's coin machine. Buell's coins fitted into any pocket. Whitney's identical parts would fit precisely into any gin.

Here was the process hit upon by clockmakers Terry and Roberts, but Whitney, coming upon the same idea independently, applied it to a factory-sized process and product. Here, in the discoveries of the clockmakers and Whitney, was the birth of mass production, the beginning of America's industrial might.

This meant an end of handwork, and, though his men had stood by him loyally after the fire, working for weeks without pay, now his skilled workmen began quitting in disgust on finding they would no longer make a complete gin but only a single part, and not by hand but by machines. His ablest mechanic threw up his job angrily, loaded his household goods onto a covered wagon, and started west.

Though handicapped by such desertions while getting his production line ready, Whitney was not greatly upset. The old-style handicraft mechanic had little place in the new setup. Men with stubborn habits, unable to visualize his new method, could not take hold properly and became misfits. It was preferable to train younger men without preconceived ideas who were willing to work in new ways.

All New Haven was impressed by the spunk Whitney showed after the fire. His "crank" ideas and shabby dress had aroused doubts in conservative minds. He had knocked in vain on important doors for help, meeting shrugs and tolerant smiles. But local people were now awake to the tremendous revolution his invention was making in America. As he rolled into bigger, faster production, prominent businessmen began saying, "Here is a man to watch. Here is a man who can be profitably helped." It is ever the way of the world: men with brilliant new ideas rarely get help when they most need it.

Invited to dinner at the home of wealthy Pierpont Edwards, New Haven's most prominent lawyer, he was asked if he had ever thought of making guns. The country needed guns badly. It needed them to open up the West, to kill game and

Indians. It needed them for national defense. Here was the
royal road to profit—big profit.

The art of handicraft gunmaking was well known. As a boy,
Whitney had often watched the Leicester gunmakers at work
in their small forges: how they hammered a white-hot piece of
crude skelp or flat iron into a welded gun barrel; all the pains-
taking boring, filing, fitting of parts. The gun was a more
complicated mechanism than a cotton gin, he remarked. It
had to be made with closer tolerances and much greater care.

His eyes strayed to Pierpont's pretty daughter, and he
became conscious of his frayed cuffs. Clearly she was attracted
by him, but he was too engrossed, too poor, with too many
bitter problems for courtship, his future too clouded to aspire
for her hand. When he failed to respond to her interest, she
became engaged to someone else. In the end he married a
friend of hers, but it was she, people whispered, whom he
really loved.

As he kept on with his heartbreaking struggle to make gins,
the gun idea kept revolving in his mind. Could he apply the
same principle of interchangeable parts? Little by little he
solved problem after problem in his head, figuring out
methods and costs.

4

In spite of his efforts, competition made the cotton-gin
business daily more difficult. After years of struggle, he was
no better off than when he had started. All his profits had gone
down the drain of those endless, fruitless lawsuits. Worse
disaster threatened.

In perverted form, the French Revolution was stalking
across Europe behind the plumes of Napoleon. All Europe
was at war. Cotton shipments declined, and sales of gins fell
off. He might have to close down entirely.

One winter day he drew out a sheet of paper and wrote to
the Secretary of the Treasury, Oliver Wolcott. He offered to
manufacture ten or fifteen thousand stand of arms at $13.40

a stand—far below any previous price. Even had he asked more, this would have been a startling offer. The biggest producer, the Springfield Arsenal, had nowhere near that capacity.

Wolcott, a man of ability and understanding, who had played an effective role alongside Roger Sherman in the Continental Congress, was from Litchfield, Connecticut, and inclined to favor anything from his native state, for he had tremendous faith in homespun Yankee ingenuity and integrity. He was duly impressed by the letter from the famous cotton-gin inventor. Though Whitney had never made guns, the offer could not be tossed aside lightly when the needs of American defense, badly neglected, were so great at this moment of world danger.

The United States might be drawn into the European struggle. Its rights were being flagrantly violated. American shippers were furious at the way the British seized American cargoes and forced American crewmen into service on British gunboats or threw them into dungeons. The United States needed to be in a position to enforce respect for its rights on the high seas. It had to arm—and arm fast.

But the cupboard was bare, and with trade cut off, economic conditions were deplorable. Whitney's offer came at the psychological moment, at an hour of dire peril for the young Republic.

He was called to Philadelphia. Wolcott and other government people wanted to know about his qualifications to make guns. How could he produce so many so quickly at such low cost?

His technical explanation of his new system of manufacturing was beyond the grasp of his hearers. Army people were especially skeptical. Only Vice-President Thomas Jefferson, himself an inventor, who long ago had carefully examined Whitney's cotton gin, seemed to understand the inventor's talk and believe he could carry through. Wolcott at least had faith—besides, time pressed. The contract was made and signed. This was in 1798.

The government advanced $20,000. Senator James Hillhouse, Edwards, Goodrich, Austin, and other New Haveners put up $10,000 more.

Whitney had already picked out the ideal location—"a wild romantic spot," with adequate water power, at a natural traprock dike on Mill River where a gristmill, set up soon after New Haven's founding, was still running. The site lay under the noble red face of towering East Rock, near the little hamlet of Hamden. Beyond, Mount Carmel stuck out boldly from the end of high-timbered Blue Hill Ridge. Whitney bought ample land so that workmen's houses could be built nearby and they would be able to farm when work at the plant was slack. He held the deep conviction—a century and a half before such ideas became current—that workmen were entitled to all-year security and that considerable advantage would be gained by holding together a trained group of workers.

Winter rolled in upon him before he could start construction, an unusually bitter winter that delayed everything. Cement froze, and a wall fell down. A terrible epidemic swept away a fourth of the town's population. Some of his best workmen died, and for long periods he could get nothing done.

Tooling-up took longer than he had anticipated. But, step by step, he worked out the necessary patterns, lathes, jigs, and "engines"—machines for rolling, boring, grinding, and polishing. His jig—to guide moving tools—was in itself one of the most notable and valuable of inventions. As in the case of the cotton gin, he got little help from experienced gunmakers. Bench workers, they did not understand what some of the machines were for, this assemblage of flyers and belts driven by the big water wheel. Again, he lost good workmen by this affront to their handicraft skills.

At the outset, Whitney bought everything he needed for the entire contract—stacks of iron and steel, copper, brass, lumber, masonry materials—thereby getting better terms. Government inspectors criticized his "poor judgment," though once in operation he would need everything double-quick.

But the days slipped by. Only a few months were left, and he had not yet produced a single gun. Friends urged him to get in a few good gunsmiths and slap enough guns together to make a showing.

The shop was not laid out for bench work, and he considered the idea dishonest. His gun was designed in a new way, with new parts. It had to be made in a new way.

By the old method, after the crude barrel had been welded and bored, the gunsmith had to grind it carefully, a little here, a little there. This required skill, a trained eye, patience without end. Whitney was preparing to forge a thousand barrels at once and bore them by machine—each barrel perfectly gauged, identical, superaccurate.

Handicraft gunmen had to chisel out each individual wooden stock, carve it, smooth it by hand, gradually fit it to the barrel. Whitney was using machinery and power lathes to turn out identical stocks to fit any barrel without special adjustment.

Making and fitting the complicated lockplate and pan was an even more ticklish task. Whitney simplified the mechanism by making pan and plate separately. The old-style gunsmith had to fit the lockplate, with much careful hand filing, to the other parts, then screw it fast. After being assembled, the gun had to be taken apart to temper and harden all metal parts. With Whitney's method, since there was no problem of fitting, all parts could be pretempered, and the gun, once assembled, would be complete, ready. All parts would be identical, precise, reliable.

5

The national government was in a topsy-turvy state when Whitney wrote to request an extension of his contract. Most departments were still in Philadelphia, the others in Washing-

ton, where the new capital was being built. A fire had wiped
out all War Department records, the agency was provisionally
housed in a moldy cellar, and Whitney's contract could not be
located. He was called to Washington, where President Adams
had just arrived, to explain.

He made the trip with his good friend and sponsor, Elizur
Goodrich, now a Congressman, whose eloquence could be
depended upon. Goodrich was an impressive dandy, the best-
dressed man in or out of Washington, impressive for his
elaborate lace sleeves, starched neck stock, and embroidered
waistcoat.

As they rode south through the Maryland forests, they saw
the government in motion: endless trains of oxcarts bearing
furniture, archives, supplies, even bird cages.

The new capital was a crazy-quilt of boiling energy and
confusion. Few buildings had been put up yet. The White
House gleamed shiny-new at the end of a long, staked-out
slough in which oxcarts and carriages floundered and almost
vanished. Real-estate agents were frenziedly hawking lots at
fantastic prices. There were few places to sleep. Tuncliffe's
Tavern, the only decent gathering place, buzzed with noisy
crowds night and day, making sleep there, even for those lucky
enough to get accommodations, well-nigh impossible. Even
Congressmen were obliged to sleep on straw pallets, three or
four to a room, in all sorts of shacks.

The gun contract was discussed before Whitney's arrival in
President Adams's office, where even the furniture had not yet
been properly arranged; desks, chairs, mahogany tables, a bedroom wardrobe, washbasin, and other undignified objects were
heaped in disorder.

Most officials present, it was said, wished to cancel the
contract and try to recover the money. Senator James Hillhouse, who had put in capital, told them in his slow, stern
way, looking down his massive eagle nose, that Whitney could
be depended upon, the guns would be made. Wolcott,
responsible for the contract, argued that if anything could be

salvaged, if the guns could be delivered, even with delay, it would be a loss to everybody to hold strictly to the agreement. What was paramount was guns, more urgently needed than ever.

Inspector's reports were examined. One enthusiastically praised Whitney's new techniques as a tremendous contribution, not only to gunmaking, but to industry in general, but the technical language was not easily understood, and the inspector himself admitted he had no idea what some of Whitney's "engines" were supposed to do. A southern Senator, when it was suggested that Whitney's great contribution to the country's wealth by the cotton gin entitled him to confidence and all possible help, testily snorted that the New Englander had not even invented the gin, and he pounced on an inspector's phrase that the East Rock gunshop was still in a confused state. In general, the atmosphere was hostile to Whitney.

Into this heavy unfriendliness, Whitney and Goodrich stepped. The lawyer did the talking while Whitney quietly began removing gun parts from a chestnut case. He had managed to make a small test run on the eve of the trip. The guns had come up to all his expectations, and he had brought the unassembled parts of ten of them to Washington. He proceeded to arrange them in neat piles on a side table. When he was asked for his own explanation, the inventor merely waved his hand toward the table, saying he preferred to let his work speak for itself.

The group gathered around. They were confused at seeing no finished guns, only parts. An ordnance general examined them closely. He was perplexed at finding the lockplate with no pan. The parts were different from any he had ever seen, and he thought them defective, though they were finely made, more like precise clock parts. He jumped to the conclusion that they must be too costly and would require too much time for quick production.

Whitney suggested he assemble a gun. The general laughed

out loud, saying he could not keep the President and important personages waiting that long. There was no bench. He needed a vise and file, proper tools.

"All you need are the brass and steel screws and the screwdrivers," Whitney answered.

The General, to his own astonishment, had the gun assembled in a few minutes. It went together without a hitch. Excited now, he tried it again. The gun he balanced in his hand was finely designed; it had a smooth, streamlined perfection; it was the best gun ever made by man up to that moment. But it merely made the General more doubtful that Whitney could ever produce such guns as cheaply or as quickly as he claimed.

The atmosphere cooled again when Whitney admitted he had been able to make only a small trial run. But, he assured them, the rest could be turned out very quickly, the cost would not exceed that contracted for $13.40 a gun. But he urgently needed an additional sum to pay his workmen, and for fuel and other costs. He explained his difficulties thus far, the bad weather, epidemics, mechanics moving west. These difficulties no longer existed. There would be no reason for further delay.

The questioning turned directly to his new methods. Those present seemed unable to grasp what he was doing. Whitney was curt, overtechnical, seemingly indifferent to what they might think. He had been unable to make highly skilled workers understand; these political people would be even less likely to. He was not a schoolteacher, he intimated.

Goodrich stepped into the breach. The story goes that he seized a rule, drew a straight line, and said, "The principle is as simple as this, gentlemen. Once a ruler was invented, anybody could make a straight line easily and quickly. Whitney had invented rulers to make guns quickly and accurately, without guesswork, at great saving of labor and cost. With his rulers, anybody can make guns—many of them—rapidly."

President Adams made the final decision. Whitney would get more time; he would get more money.

He completed his contract; he completed many more contracts, from the Federal Government, from state militias, from frontiersmen and private hunters. His factory grew; it became the world's largest gunmaking plant.

David L. Dodge, a pious merchant, visited the establishment in 1809. People often traveled "fifty miles out of their way to see it," he commented. A hundred men were then employed. It had "a cheerful, tasteful appearance—like a tidy village.... Every part ... was made by machinery ... any lock or stock would fit any barrel ... remarkable ...no similar establishment in the country." And he added, "What a bound did my ideas make in mechanics from the operations of the penknife to this miracle of machinery."

Thus, Eli Whitney opened the door of mass production through which all American industry could move ahead to greatness. A line down a ruler. A pattern moved by power. Precise, interchangeable parts. These were to become the key, the implements to all production in quantity by which goods could be made cheaply, swiftly, of superior quality—above all, reliable quality. Thus the discovery by Whitney made possible the great factories of Pittsburgh and Chicago, the auto works of Detroit, the airplane factories of California. It made possible the high standard of living for all Americans, equality of opportunity and luxuries, not merely for the favored but for everybody. It multiplied individual human energy thousands of times over, made fine goods available on a mass scale. Thereby it made possible—it assured—not a class system, but a working democracy. It assured greater well-being for all the people of the nation.

XV. The Giants Meet

EARLY EVENING, April 3, 1850, a group of influential citizens drove up in their fine carriages to dine at Foster's Tavern on Farmington Avenue, in Bristol, Connecticut. It was an old edifice with impressive columns, put up soon after the start of the century to serve as the stagecoach stop. It was famous for its excellent oyster dinners and pretty waitresses.

To its doors, the stagecoach driver was wont to roll up in grand style, with a last flick of his long, silk-tipped lash over his horses' ears and long blasts from his six-foot tin horn. Here at Foster's horses were changed and passengers descended to have brandy flips, dine, and rest before proceeding on their rough way. In 1850, large herds of cattle were still being driven past the tavern, headed for the Hartford slaughterhouses—perhaps the most important meat-distributing center in New England—and Foster's was still the stagecoach stop, although that year the railroad finally pushed into the city on the Pequabuck.

By then quilted silk "pumpkin" hoods had given way to jaunty, elaborate leghorn bonnets, lavishly trimmed with ribbons, purple lilies, French bouquets, and ostrich plumes. Black Flemish or Spanish mantillas were popular; the newest mode was the basque, a bodice with short tails below the pinched-in waistline. Indian muslins were coming into favor, but the pleated skirt, so snug and fluid with the motions of thigh and leg, had given way to elaborate flounces from waist to ankle. Men were wearing cutaways, cream-colored satin waistcoats, and tight trousers.

The gentlemen who handed over their tall gray hats this particular evening included all the successful clockmakers of Bristol, Plymouth, and Forestville; also a foundry man, a brass maker, and a Waterbury banker. The object was to set up a big modern brass foundry in Bristol, by this time the clock factory of the world and the biggest user of brass of any city in the country.

Prime mover was Elisha Welsh, local foundry owner, cited in the confidential report of that year (which still reposes in the vault of the Bristol Public Library) as a businessman certain to make a success of whatever he undertook. But the key individual, knowing the brass industry inside out, its founder, its greatest producer, was Israel Holmes. He was inventive, daring, a man of great technical knowledge and of proven business success. In off moments he wrote political verse.

2

Israel Holmes was born in Waterbury in the Naugatuck Valley, December 19, 1800. His father died when he was two, and he was brought up in the home and tavern of his grandfather, Captain Samuel Judd, on west Main Street. At sixteen, Israel was teaching school but soon went to work in a hat factory, and before long was sent to Augusta, Georgia, to run a retail hat store for the firm.

Two years later he returned to Waterbury to work for the Scovills (related by marriage to the Barneses of Bristol), manufacturers of metal buttons. Their product was expensive because brass had to be imported from England. Holmes persuaded them to send him overseas to try to get machinery and skilled workmen to make brass in Waterbury.

He encountered the same difficulties that Abel Buell had faced in securing textile machinery and experts. After lengthy negotiations, Holmes obtained an export license for machinery, but no permission to take out workmen. Discreetly, he persuaded twenty workers to emigrate, among them a die sinker, a gilder, and a burnisher. The British manufacturers tried, too late, to get his machinery export license revoked. Emigrating workers, who might arouse suspicion, he had concealed in empty wine casks till the vessel left Liverpool. Fearing arrest if he embarked there, he traveled incognito across Wales and took ship at Holyhead.

He organized the firm of Holmes and Hotchkiss and, in 1831, began rolling brass. Desiring to add wire drawing to his operations, he made a second trip to England, dodged the police, and successfully returned to America with a wire drawer, a tube maker, and other artisans.

Hardly had he returned than he learned that a pending tariff law would remove all duties on brass and brass wire. This would mean ruin, and with Isaac Coe, another brass maker, he rushed to Washington. They were too late to block passage, but Holmes persuaded the Secretary of the Treasury to draft a special law protecting brass products. It was squeezed through on the last day of the session.

The disaster Holmes averted was nothing compared to the one that did strike. In his absence, the old Judd tavern burned down on a night of wild, swirling snow, and two of his children were burned to death, two saved. When he reached home early morning, he found his wife Ardelia kneeling barefoot in the snow, weeping beside the blackened ruins.

Unable to endure Waterbury any longer, he sold out and moved to Wolcotville (now Torrington) in northwest Connecticut, where he began making brass kettles in a mill acquired by Isaac Coe and two associates. Holmes soon found American brass unserviceable for kettles and for the third time returned to England to get more workers who could roll the right kind of brass.

The British manufacturers, fully aware of him now, kept close tabs on him. A detective, posing as a brass maker, tried to get himself hired to go to America. His soft white hands told Holmes instantly he had never been near hot brass in his life. Aware that he was being followed, Holmes persuaded his landlady in Birmingham to warn him the instant anybody came looking for him.

He got thirty-eight persons aboard a vessel for Philadelphia, but just managed to slip out the back door of the boardinghouse as the police came in the front door. He hid out in the slums of Liverpool and, for a high price, got a small boat to put him aboard ship on the high seas.

Even with this skilled help, the brass did not turn out right, and, in 1842, Coe went to England and succeeded in getting the correct formula. Hiram Hayden, a relative of Holmes's wife, hit upon a new processing method. The road to good American brass in quantity was now open.

Holmes returned to Waterbury and organized the Waterbury Brass Company, with himself as president and manager. He put up the East Mill, the biggest yet, and later, the larger West Mill. In all, he was the guiding spirit of five Waterbury brass companies and built five mills. He set all the Naugatuck River towns on the way to great industrial prosperity. Waterbury became the world's major brass center, the supplier for clocks, bullets, shells, and other armaments. "He found Rome brick and made it marble," said an admiring associate.

His political verse was printed in local publications. At great length, he narrated sarcastically the political race of 1840, one candidate on a "dun colored nag," the other steed "black as your hat." Another poem mourned the death of President Harrison:

> He's gone to his home life a well ripen'd sheaf,
> The ear in fulness, and sere in the leafe,
> The angels have borne him with joy to the skies,
> The portals of heaven have closed on their prize.

But he was a good brass maker and a good businessman. In Bristol, he was teaming up with another shrewd metal producer and a much better businessman.

3

When Elisha Niles Welch was twenty-one, on February 7, 1830, his father George made him a full-fledged partner of the small family foundry on West Street in Bristol—"the old Porridge Pot"—where Elisha worked at furnace, forge, and bellows, hot, heavy work that singed off his eyebrows and kept his skin red and peeling.

The Welches, fervent Baptists, had come to Bristol from Chatham, Connecticut, four years before this to start the foundry. Elisha's mother, schoolteacher Zelinda Niles, had died two years previously, and his father had married Thalia Wildman, daughter of Bristol's first Baptist minister. Elisha married Jane Buckley, and a child was now on the way.

The Welches had done well, making bells and weights for clocks. Some were sheathed in brass, so they had learned to work other metals as well. Mostly they traded their products for finished clocks. From clockmakers Samuel and Ralph Terry, who had a large Pequabuck plant near the old Barnes tavern (now run by another family), they took twenty long mirror clocks in exchange for 4,400 bells. Elisha decided to go to Pennsylvania and try selling clocks himself.

He was an unusually successful salesman and traveled repeatedly after that. Often he traded clocks for scrap metal, which he brought back to the Bristol foundry by team. Sometimes he was accompanied by his brother Harmanius, who later put up a trading post at "Bristol Basin" in Plainville, when the Farmington canal reached there in 1838, and became the owner of packet boats. Later Harmanius founded the First National Bank of New Haven and became that city's Civil War mayor. Another brother, Henry Welch, built up big textile mills in Waterbury and Plainville—one of the biggest figures in the industry. All the Welches had great talent for promotion, business, and industry.

Several of the Ives brothers, apprentices of Gideon Roberts, began making brass clocks on a big mass-production scale, and the traditional wooden clock was doomed. After 1837 all the clockmakers able to survive the technological revolution and depression turned to making brass clocks. Elisha saw a fine opportunity. Bristol, besides being the largest user of brass, had a rich, undeveloped copper mine that had been worked briefly after the Revolution. It was on Yale property near the north Bristol line. Local copper, plus brass, plus the biggest market, seemed an unbeatable setup.

Land was leased from the Yales and neighbors, and a copper concern started that same year of 1837. Test diggings showed 70 per cent copper that needed merely to be hammer-trimmed to go into the smelter. A branch of the Pequabuck was damned for water and power, and a deep shaft with laterals was sunk. The ore proved spotty, but for twenty years the deposit was worked profitably.

Several small brass foundries were started, but Welch desired a large up-to-date plant that could supply all clock needs. Every day wagons toiled over the steep ridge from the Naugatuck Valley, bringing bright rolls of the copper alloy to the Ingraham, Manross, and Brown factories. Many teams passed Welch's home on West Street when he was tending his garden, and he talked to the teamsters in their leather pants and broad hats. They were working for Israel Holmes.

Welch had a long consultation with the Waterbury brass maker. Brass and clocks belonged together; Bristol offered a better opportunity than Waterbury; they should pool their energies in getting a big mill started. Holmes agreed to try to make a go of it. He could get the backing of the leading Waterbury bankers. Welch could round up the clockmakers.

4

Sixteen men were gathered around the table at Foster's Tavern to discuss the brass mill. Present, besides the Waterbury men, were Eli Terry, Jr., from Plymouth, a big name in the industry; Jonathan Clark Brown, "The Plunger," from Forestville, a bold industrialist making forty thousand clocks a year, always on his toes, seeking new inventions, coming out with new designs; Ebenezer Hendrick (of Hendrick and Hubbell, the world's greatest marine clock manufactury); Nathan L. Birge (who made "Puffin Betsy" clocks); Smith, Goodrich, Brewster, Manross, Boardman, all the great names of the clock world except Chauncey Jerome, the world's biggest mass producer, who had moved to New Haven.

Another interesting personality at the table, Colonel Edward L. Dunbar—nephew of Moses Dunbar, who had swung for treason—was making clock parts and clock wire and experimenting with spring making. Shortly after, with Wallace Barnes, descendant of Ebenezer, as partner, he struck a bonanza by making hoopskirts from clock wire when that extraordinary feminine fashion hit the country and crowded insignificant males into corners.

Elisha Welch took charge of the proceedings at Foster's Tavern. He was a big man, and beneath his broadcloth coat could be seen the bulge and ripple of muscles developed in the days when he had toiled at the old Porridge Pot. His massive forehead was bald well back; he had intense deep-set blue eyes, and a patch of beard emphasized his powerful jaw. It was his business tonight to introduce "the biggest brass man in the world" and set forth the mill project.

Holmes told what he had done, what he needed to start a mill in Bristol, what he could accomplish. He would not lift a finger unless he had $100,000 cash to start—a lot of money those days when the clock concerns needed every dollar to expand operations as the tide of people rolled west and the American market widened. But Holmes agreed to bring in his best workmen. In Waterbury, he had branched out, making German-silver tableware. He promised to set up a similar plant in Bristol at once, and he would roll the needed metal at the brass mill, thus providing another reliable local market. All was dependent on going ahead with the project at once.

Several present wanted time to consider. Holmes and his banker agreed to wait over one day, no longer. In the morning all signed up for stock. Papers were drawn up, and the Bristol Brass and Clock Company was born.

In less than three weeks after the tavern meeting, Holmes bought the necessary land on the Pequabuck. It included the Ebenezer Barnes property, and Holmes turned the tavern into a boardinghouse for his Waterbury workers. Several were key men smuggled in from England. The company archives reveal that wages ranged from 67 cents to about $2.50 a day for skilled men.

The brick factory and equipment were ready to start operations one year after the Foster's Tavern agreement. The first order was for 784 pounds of brass from a Plainville factory. Soon orders were placed by nearly all the local clockmakers. Two Bristol foundries asked for over a thousand pounds each.

Holmes soon had his German-silverware plant—Holmes and Tuttle—in operation. Later known as the "Spoon Factory," it carried on with great success until it was wiped out by the depression of the thirties in this century.

Brass at the Bristol Brass Company was made in large crucibles, copper melting at 1,800 degrees, zinc at 700. The amalgam was poured into iron molds to make three-quarter-inch slabs two feet long, four to eight inches wide. These were heated cherry-red in a muffle furnace, put through heavy cast-iron rollers from twenty to twenty-five times to thin them, and then were coiled into rolls for shipping.

Power was provided by an overshot water wheel, but a few years later a bad drought forced the installation of a 200-horsepower steam engine fired by wood from the surviving Pequabuck forests.

The first year was successful but difficult, for the clock men were slow in taking up their stock options, and Holmes had to use money from his Waterbury company to meet payrolls and keep afloat. He called the directors together. Stock had to be taken up in sixty days or canceled.

The more opulent clockmakers, headed by Welch, bought up all outstanding stock. As a result, Holmes was pushed out of control. By then Welch had the know-how and took over as president and manager. It was a crude squeeze play, the old story of two powerful men not being able to ride the same horse. Elisha Welch, though not a brass maker, was the shrewder operator.

5

The concern was destined to succeed. Industry was expanding fast in Bristol, everywhere. In the first two years the company earned 60 per cent on the investment. But Welch plowed every cent back into expanding operations. Even by 1855, the stockholders received their first dividend in stock bonus, not in cash.

Welch's canny business instincts led him to reef before the impending 1857 depression. He gave no credit. If payment could not be made promptly, he took merchandise, which he disposed of through his New York store, thus keeping a fluid cash backlog.

He expanded the Welch factory to make machine tools, gained control during a slump of Bristol's largest textile mill, "the Satinet," which originally he had helped organize, and bought up the fine Manross clock factory in Forestville, with a 30,000-a-year output of high-grade clocks.

Soon he took over several small clock-parts suppliers and the enormous but bankrupt Jonathan Brown clock factory. He acquired not merely plants but the best technical knowledge, the finest skilled workers, and broader sales outlets. His control of brass gave him a big advantage over his competitors. He merged the various clock plants to create the second largest clock concern in the world. It survives today as the Sessions Clock Company, makers of electrical clocks and timers.

When depression really hit, closing down most Bristol industry, he was able to gain complete control of the brass works and the Spoon Shop. Other enterprises and factories supplying clock parts toppled and fell into his net.

During the Civil War, Welch became a "Copperhead" in an almost literal sense. He was bitterly opposed to the war because the South was his most lucrative market for clocks, and the antislavery agitation—Bristol had more than its share of firebrands—was hurting business. War would be ruinous.

He watched the Bristol volunteers (most of whom were to

be slaughtered in their first engagement) march past the windows of Bristol Brass with dour eyes. He was hard hit, with a huge inventory of clocks for which there was no market.

He rushed them to England, made successful deals, and got payment in gold. By converting this into depreciated wartime currency he turned a neat additional profit. Also he was able to buy supplies more cheaply than his competitors and could pay all wages in the cheap domestic money.

Soon the war called for brass for cartridges—more and more brass. It called for spoons, knives, and forks, for the boys in blue had to eat if they were to fight. Welch, the former foundry worker, emerged from the war the wealthiest man in Bristol, one of the wealthiest in the country.

Presently he bought up a brass-lamp plant and got in on the ground floor when the discovery of oil brought the general use of kerosene for lighting. The demand for brass lamps swept around the world, providing an endless call for more brass. The "Bristol Burner" salesmen added to the demand by sharp practices. As told in the official history of the company, they broke so many glass lamps on trains that the railroad companies had to go in for brass lamps. There is no doubt that they were better and safer.

Welch was a frugal, tight-fisted man. He kept an eagle eye on his workmen. Woe betide the employee who put a rug in his parlor or went in for newfangled luxuries—it meant he was living too high and had no place in the Welch empire.

But he was generous to the Baptist Church, put down for large amounts on every subscription list, and erected a new church, one of the finest in the city. At times he served on the church committee that surveyed the morals of its members. Those older records provide racy details of fancy and plain sinning, even incest, but perhaps no spicier than some of Elisha's difficulties with sundry ladies, accounts of which make the old archives of the company sizzle.

But no breath of scandal ever touched him. He stood before his fellow citizens as an exemplary paterfamilias—he raised five children—as a fine church and civic leader, and one of New England's most successful manufacturers.

His daughter started to erect Brightwood Hall—a great castle on the commanding hills of Bristol, to be her residence and a memento to her father's wealth, power, and achievement in that ostentatious gilded era. It was a place that was to surpass the palaces of the Vanderbilts and Astors and Goulds, the finest mansions of Newport and Nob Hill. She was never able to finish it.

Welch symbolized the epic of American industrial growth. He had come to Bristol when it was a village of small handicrafts on numerous little streams, and had worked at a crude bellows. Clock companies came and went, a fluid pattern as new inventions came along. He watched the industry become stabilized, and a number of stronger mass-production enterprises take over. He, too, became a shaper of big business. Boldly he seized upon the opportunities provided by the 1857 depression that destroyed less canny men, to weld concerns into larger units.

Some people called him "a black spider," others praised him for keeping industry going, making it more efficient, and providing jobs when others were unable to do so.

His efforts heralded a new division of labor in American industry. The early men, like Roberts, had been craftsmen and inventors rather than businessmen. Gradually early craftsmen had to learn also to be businessmen and form companies. Elias Roberts, Gideon's son, founded the first Bristol clock company. Not until industrial techniques had greatly improved, not until the West was opened up to create a vast market, did the larger mass-production units become profitable.

Holmes represented this early ideal combination of technical knowledge with business acumen. To a high degree he combined the talents of both. Welch, although close to pristine skills, represented more the era of enormous mass-production plants requiring new executive ability of a high order, in which the promoter, the financier, the so-called industrialist assumed full control and relegated the skilled worker, the inventor, the researcher, and the engineer to secondary roles. As bedrock, Welch had his muscle-and-sweat experience at the old Porridge Pot, but his real genius lay in financial manipulations and large-scale management.

But though the scientist and engineer thereafter became a lesser cog in the forward march of industry, in the last analysis success depended upon trained skills and inventions even more than before, and this was increasingly true as industry became more complex. The newer type of businessmen, once large-scale consolidation took place, who could combine his wealth and power with real technical progress, was the man who survived. Upon this type of sound leadership—which Welch had to a greater degree than many so-called "Robber Barons" of his day—depended then, and depend still, the stimulation, preservation, and progress of the inventive and creative genius of America.

He contributed in his particular community, and in the country at large, to the creation of orderliness and efficiency in industry. He brought the organizing genius without which the discoveries of Whitney and others could not have come to true fruition. He helped shape the final industrial revolution in New England and move it on into the modern era and to make Connecticut even today the most highly skilled and industrialized state in the union.

In the year 1953, the brass company he and Holmes founded in 1850 had spanned the continent with its sales organization. A sales company was set up in Los Angeles, California, which was not even a state of the union in 1850. The New England way had literally jumped across the continent.

And Bristol, the town of Ebenezer Barnes, of Gideon Roberts, of Wallace Barnes and Elisha Welch—inventors, workers, builders—by that year had become, among other things, the maker of the finest-quality steel in America, the spring-making and the ball-bearing capital of the country.

XVI. Black Magic

IF YOU see a man with an India-rubber coat on, India-rubber shoes, an India-rubber cap, and in his pocket an India-rubber purse with not a cent in it, that is he." Such was the description given a visitor to New York in 1837 of Charles Goodyear, the inventor who discovered how to vulcanize rubber to eliminate its natural stickiness and make it one of man's most useful products.

This was before Goodyear had discovered the true secret. Whenever he hit upon a new formula, he made up wearing apparel and tested it on his and his family's persons. Once his wife and little girls wore rubber aprons and bonnets to church and thereby created a new fad.

The story of rubber began in the dim past when loin-clothed Amazon jungle Indians discovered the remarkable qualities of the sap of the noble *Hevia brasilensis* tree and used it to make river boats, sandals, and water bottles; idols, birds, animals, and figurines.

Christopher Columbus saw Indians playing ball in the West Indies with a round lump that *bounced*, and made a gift of rubber to Queen Isabella. Later Hernán Cortés watched Aztecs, playing *tlatchli*, toss a rubber ball through carved stone rings.

Early Spanish and Portuguese chroniclers mentioned the rubber tree, but two centuries flowed by before rubber came to Europe's attention again. In March, 1736, Charles-Marie de la Condamine, a French naturalist, one of the first outsiders ever admitted to the great Spanish colonial empire, sailed down Ecuador's coast on the *San Cristóbal* to the jungle port of Las Esmeraldas, where the natives brought him a strange "stretching cloth" called caoutchouc. They took him to see how they tapped the giant tree by slashing zigzags on the pale bark, from which the viscous, dark milk dripped into gourds. He fashioned a waterproof rubber pouch for his delicate quadrant. As he crossed the Andes and traveled down the Amazon tributaries, he came upon more lofty trees and marveled at how the Indians poured the sap into clay molds, which then could be broken and the finished objects removed. He collected samples of Indian "pumps," or syringes, and some raw chunks and reported his findings to the French Academy in 1745.

The first experiments sought solvents. Two French scientists hit upon turpentine. In 1768 another discovered ether. Frederick the Great had boots made by the ether process. A descendant of Magellan, the early Portuguese navigator, discovered that caoutchouc, *peau-de-nègre* the vulgar called it, erased marks better than bread crumbs. In England, Joseph Priestley, first to isolate oxygen, hit upon the same use, and artists were soon paying three shillings a square inch at "Mr. Marnes, Mathematical Instrument Maker, opposite the Royal Exchange." Thus it became "rubber." No other practical use was found except to amuse children until Dr. M. Grossart of France succeeded in using it to make surgical tubes.

Experiments were made in France and England to produce a rubber varnish for waterproofing silk, leather, cloth, and paper. The first patent was taken out by Samuel Peal in 1791. Professor James Symes, who discovered naphtha, found this to be a good rubber solvent, and in 1823, the Scottish manufacturer, Charles Macintosh, following in his footsteps, began manufacturing rubber coats by smearing benzine rubber between lengths of cloth, thereby immortalizing his name as part of the English language. Purchasers were warned to keep away from the fire, and doctors soon denounced such garments as causing colds. This antagonism all but wrecked his business, but nevertheless he made rollers, printers' blankets, machinery belts, billiard cushions, fire hose, and beer kegs.

Another early experimenter, Thomas Hancock, also manufactured waterproof cloth and invented the first "masticator," a machine for salvaging rubber waste. Later, he cheated Goodyear out of his British patent rights.

In America rubber bottles were brought in from Brazil as early as 1800. Twelve years later, a Boston sea captain brought back several pairs of rubber shoes made by Indians on clay lasts repeatedly dipped into liquid gum. A Boston merchant imported five hundred pairs and sold them, coated with gilt foil, for five dollars each. Clumsily made, with pointed toes, they became hard as boards in cold weather and melted on hot summer days, but imports soon totaled half a million pairs annually. American lasts were sent to Brazil for Indians to copy in clay, and an enterprising individual in Providence, Rhode Island, began making rubber shoes. Others soon competed.

Edwin Chaffee, foreman of a Boston patent-leather factory, made a mixture of rubber with turpentine and lampblack to smear on cloth, and invented two machines, still found in improved form in every rubber factory—the steam-heated, two-speed rolling mill and the calendar, or press-coating machine, nicknamed the "Monster." With others, in 1833, he formed the Roxbury India Rubber Company, which began manufacturing shoes, wagon curtains, coats, capes, and other articles, and opened a New York store. Within a year they expanded their capital from thirty thousand to nearly a quarter-million dollars. Other companies were soon organized. But the products would not stand cold or heat over 100 degrees. They suffered from the same drawbacks as the primitive Amazon wares that had been made for a thousand years.

On a rainy day in 1834, Charles Goodyear, then a young man of thirty-three, took refuge from the wind and wet in the entrance of the Roxbury store in lower Manhattan. It was a dreary moment. All day this thin scarecrow of a man had been trudging from bank to bank trying to get a loan to salvage the bankrupt hardware business he and his father, Amasa Goodyear, ran in Philadelphia. Unable to collect outstanding bills because of hard times, their business was thirty thousand dollars in the red. Young Goodyear had not been able to raise a penny.

His eyes roved over the coats, caps, shoes, and wagon curtains and came to rest on a round tube with a metal valve—a life preserver. His chance discovery of this article coincided with a terrible sea disaster in which many passengers had perished. Here was an object to prevent such tragic loss of life.

He pushed inside, and the manager, helping out because of the rush of customers, lifted the life preserver from the window —the only one in stock—and spread it out under the oil lamp. But when he tried to inflate it, the valve stuck, and he had to belabor it with a wire. That would not be much use for a drowning man, and it occurred to Goodyear that if he could make a foolproof valve, the Roxbury company might pay well for it. Both Charles and his father had the instinct of inventors and had developed useful new farm tools.

Charles fingered the change in his pocket, then resolutely put two one-dollar bills in the manager's hand and added a fifty-cent piece. Riding home on the jerky train back to Philadelphia, he pondered the problem of the valve and sketched out a design.

He came back to a home almost stripped of furniture, curtains, and rugs—all sold to get money for food—and all he had to extricate himself from his debts and feed his wife and small children was an idea in his head.

They managed to pull through the rest of the spring, and by midsummer he had perfected a valve that opened unfailingly and closed automatically.

It was a steaming-hot day when he rushed to New York with it. The Roxbury store was a shambles. It stank. All the rubber goods had been reduced to sticky goo. There were no customers and no clerks. The distraught manager told Charles that $20,000 worth of goods had been returned. Impatiently he brushed Goodyear's valve aside—also the inventor's hope of saving himself from a desperate situation—and in an excited outburst told him the company could guarantee a huge reward to anyone who could make rubber resistant to heat and cold.

When Goodyear got back to Philadelphia, the bailiff was waiting to take him to debtors' prison.

2

Years before this, Amasa Goodyear, fourth generation from Stephen Goodyear, the early New Haven settler and promoter, bought an interest in a Naugatuck button factory, but presently moved to his own plant in New Haven. Many soldiers of the War of 1812 wore Goodyear buttons on their uniforms. Amasa invented a machine for cutting pearl buttons, the first person in America to make them. He soon branched out into making hardware, spoons, a few clocks, whatever people wanted. His main interest became farm hardware, and he invented the spring-steel pitchfork that revolutionized farm work.

His son, Charles Goodyear, born in New Haven on December 29, 1800, was the eldest of six children. Very early Charles began helping his father at the plant. When Charles was seventeen, Amasa apprenticed him to Roger and Brothers of Philadelphia to learn hardware merchandising. As soon as he was of age, Charles came back to New Haven as a full-fledged partner of his father. Three years later, he married Clarissa Beecher.

In 1826 Amasa, and his sons Charles and Robert, opened their own retail outlet in Philadelphia, a center closer to southern and western markets, the first hardware store to sell only domestic manufactures. Money rolled in—"a handsome fortune was accumulated" within a few years.

Charles was too generous with credit to southern merchants. Money tightened, and worry gave him serious dyspepsia, an ailment that plagued him the rest of his life. When financial stringency developed from 1830 on, the concern became increasingly hard pressed. The end was debtors' prison.

Debtors were accorded some privileges, and Charles was allowed to make wooden objects to get enough money to feed his family. He worked on new farm gadgets so he could sell the rights and persuade his creditors to release him.

He kept on thinking of the rubber life preserver that would prevent loss of human lives—and of the gooey, stinking debacle at the Roxbury Company store. As a boy he had scaled off a sliver of rubber from an imported Brazilian bottle and had thought then that if it could be made less adhesive, it would "constitute a beautiful fabric for many purposes."

He persuaded his jailer to bring him some crude rubber and turpentine and there, behind bars, began his first experiments. He marveled, as he did all his life, at its "wonderful elasticity. . . . It can be extended eight times its ordinary length . . . when it will again assume its original form. There is probably no other inert substance, the properties of which excite in the human mind an equal amount of curiosity, surprise and admiration. . . . Who . . . can reflect upon the property of gumelastic without adoring the wisdom of the Creator?"

Being religious-minded, his chief reading the Bible, he believed that his attention had been redirected to the material at the opportune time "by his Maker." God's purpose included, along with "the highest elevation of mind and morals, the highest improvement of things material."

From then on, his one enduring passion became rubber. It was his Holy Grail, the pot of gold in the rainbow, the everlasting chimera of beauty and hope, the essence of God's mystery, the mistress of his dreams who never abandoned him day or night, rain or shine.

It took Goodyear three months to make enough money to obtain his release. He and Clarissa sold the last of their furniture and moved to New Haven. There, over Clarissa's cookstove, sometimes using her rolling pin, he continued his experiments. His most hopeful mixture was with magnesia, which resulted in thin sheets superior to any on the market. He bound a book with his "cured" or "tanned" rubber, but this, too, softened in hot weather. He tried different proportions and got better quality. A boyhood friend loaned him a hundred dollars. He bought shoes, and he and Clarissa embossed several hundred pairs with rubber in brilliant colors and novel designs. But hot weather ruined them.

By then he did not have a penny or any credit. If he could only reach New York with samples of his best magnesia rubber, he might get help. He sold the furniture, pawned Clarissa's jewelry, and persuaded the landlady of a small country boardinghouse to take her in for a roll of home-woven linen. Clarissa was pregnant.

In New York a friend gave him the use of an inside skylight room on Gold Street and introduced him to a druggist who let him have chemicals on credit. He tried boiling the magnesia rubber in quicklime. The product was firm and smooth, better than any yet seen, and he exhibited it at two New York Institute fairs—this was in 1835—and won medals.

He patented the process and began making rubberized cloth and other articles, earning enough to bring Clarissa, the two girls, and his newborn son, William, to join him. But one day juice from an apple he was eating fell on a rubber sheet and made it sticky. He discovered that any acid, even dilute vinegar, ruined the rubber. His customers soon demanded refunds.

He tried more lime, but to knead it burned his hands. He had to have machinery and power. After endless search, he found a small Greenwich Village shop where he was allowed to work free. Every morning, he trudged the three miles to the place with a jug of turpentine. But all he got was rubber that crumbled, and his despair was compounded by the death of his infant son.

To remove the bronze coating from a piece of rubber, he applied nitric acid. To his astonishment the rubber was tanned, no longer sticky. He did not realize he had made a basic discovery. Not the acid, but the sulphur in the compound, plus the heat of chemical change, had given results. He labeled this the "acid-gas process."

He sat feverishly to work making table covers and aprons

with fine designs and earned enough to support his family. Clarissa made rubber globes for school geography classes. This was around the time when she and the girls wore rubber bonnets to church.

Goodyear took his new product to Washington in the form of calling cards, maps, and surgical bandages in order to get a patent. Samples were presented to Henry Clay, John C. Calhoun, and President Andrew Jackson. All sent helpful personal letters. Jackson spoke highly of his "useful discoveries" and wished him success.

With such evidence, Goodyear was able to interest William Ballard, a wealthy New York investor, and the firm of Goodyear and Ballard started working on Bank Street, later in an abandoned rubber plant on Staten Island. A Broadway warehouse was rented.

Prosperity seemed within Goodyear's grasp. But he was badly gassed in the factory and for two weeks hovered on the brink of death; then the 1837 panic put them out of business. Goodyear made one last disconsolate trip through his ghost plant, musing on the irony of fate. To get back to Manhattan he had to post his umbrella with the ferry master, Cornelius Vanderbilt.

He struggled on alone, selling or pawning furniture, books, dishes, and making rubber products by hand. Utterly penniless again, he stood under the gilded globes of a pawnshop preparing to sell a cherished watch, when a friend happened along and loaned him $15. When that was gone, he reluctantly called on his brother-in-law, William de Forest, for help. William had tutored Charles, then had married Goodyear's sister; he came of the family which, a century later, produced the inventor who revolutionized communications and ushered in the electronic and atomic age with the vacuum tube. William was doing well in the wool business and loaned Charles a hundred dollars.

Charles and Clarissa made bandages, maps, toys, and other articles and had better luck. But to continue his experiments he needed proper facilities. He wrote to the Roxbury rubber people.

The factory was idle because of the business collapse and the public's lack of confidence in rubber goods, but the plant manager, John Haskins, sent Goodyear a cordial invitation to come up, plus money for his fare.

In Roxbury—the town across from Boston made famous by John Eliot, the "Apostle of the Indians"—the first person to greet Goodyear was Henry Willis, fellow-apprentice from Philadelphia, who proceeded to provide him with living quarters. Helped by Haskins, Goodyear at once began making rubber goods. The demand grew, and neighboring manufacturers asked for license to use his "acid-gas" magnesia process. By summer his profits totaled $4,000, and he sent for his family, then his aging parents and his two brothers, who helped him in his work. A seventh child was born, so he had a big household to support.

Haskins left to open a factory in Lynn, and Goodyear went to Woburn, a small community ten miles northwest of Boston, to work in the idle factory of the Eagle Rubber Company, where a foreman, Nathaniel Hayward, one of the most capable rubber men in the country, was still making a few rubber objects on his own. Goodyear secured a contract to make 100 U.S. mail sacks, and hired Hayward to help him. The finished product was sturdy and elegant. Elated, Goodyear took Clarissa on a vacation to New York, Philadelphia, and Washington. When they got back, it was hot summer, and the warehouse where the sacks were hung reeked of putrid rubber. Decomposed rubber was dripping off the handles.

His process had not tanned the rubber to the depth required for mailbags. Another ruinous setback! The story got around, orders fell off, licensees quit using his patent, all sources of income stopped. As penniless as the day he started, he had to close down.

3

Going to the plant in a despondent mood, he found Hayward still doggedly making a few rubber objects.

"What is that yellow stuff you smear on?" asked Goodyear.

It was sulphur. Rubber, smeared with it and exposed to the sun, seemed perfectly tanned. "The idea came to me in a dream," Hayward said.

Sulphur had been tried in Europe, and one Hollander had marketed a few "sulphur-cured" products, but the experimenters had never realized its importance or how to use it to harden rubber through and through.

Goodyear had Hayward patent the "solarization" process and assign the patent to him, promising to pay when he could. He set to work feverishly, trying out different proportions of sulphur, tanning many rubber strips in the sun. From the best, he made up more articles. But the rubber was not cured to any depth—the same drawback as with his acid-gas method.

While experimenting at the dwelling where he stopped whenever he visited the plant, a rubber article was "carelessly brought into contact with a hot stove." It charred the rubber "like leather," but did not melt it.

He paid no attention at the time, but later, thinking about it, remembered that the rubber, which always melted with heat, had merely charred. At the edges of the charring, he found that the rubber was perfectly cured. He nailed a piece in freezing weather to the outside of his kitchen door. Early in the morning, he rushed out in his nightshirt and greatcoat. The rubber was still flexible. He had discovered the true vulcanization process!

He soon found that "India rubber would not . . . melt . . . in boiling sulphur" at any heat. For some reason, perhaps both physical and chemical, hot sulphur altered the gum's structure so that it became immune to temperature changes and thus truly serviceable. Because rubber melted so easily, none of those previously experimenting with sulphur had thought of applying heat.

His discovery, he always maintained, was not the result of "chance" but the outcome of years of close "application and observation," otherwise he would never have been able to draw the proper "inference" from the charring that "divine Providence" had caused.

More extensive experiments were now imperative. By repeated trials, he learned that the flexible rim of cured rubber around the charred places could tolerate 278°, that no heat would melt it, that it would not stiffen between blocks of ice. But to work out the right proportions he needed to handle larger quantities under controlled heat—perhaps steam.

This seemed impossible. He had little money for materials. Food was scant, his children frequently ill. He became so gaunt that he, too, was taken sick.

He wrote to Haskins in Lynn. His friend said he was welcome to use the steam plant there. Goodyear managed to get to the flourishing seaport. Using steam to cure the rubber, he tried to find ways to make the hardened product adhere to fabrics. He needed the stickiness he had eliminated. Every attempt failed, though he made rubber cloth by mixing in cotton fibers before the rubber was treated with hot sulphur.

He returned to Woburn and struggled on. Everything was gone. He sold the children's schoolbooks for five dollars and persuaded an idle mason to accept some rubberized bricklayers' aprons in payment for building him an oven. With his brothers and sons, Goodyear scoured vacant lots and abandoned factories for the needed bricks.

With the oven he made more rubber but, unable to control the heat properly, spoiled many batches. Things got worse— no food, no credit. Scarcely anybody in the village would speak to him any more. It was doubly tragic because he knew that he had the whole problem about solved.

He wasted much time going to far places to get wood for the oven and to keep the family warm. When he was pulling home a heavy load through deep snow, the sledge runners ran off the path. Too weak to pull the load back, he collapsed.

A stranger came along and offered to help. He introduced himself as O. B. Coolidge and said he lived three miles out of town.

Goodyear fell ill again, and the family was hemmed in by a bad storm. There was no fuel, nor a bite to eat. Over Clarissa's protests, he struggled out of bed and walked through a raging blizzard to Coolidge's place. The last of the way, he had to crawl on his hands and knees. He collapsed inside the Coolidge door.

They revived him. Coolidge got out the team and loaded up with provisions. All winter, he gave the Goodyears small sums, enough to keep body and soul together.

Goodyear now had perfect rubber. Who would back him? The best hope was in New York. He walked to Boston, where Nathaniel Hayward now lived, to ask him for a loan of fifty dollars. Hayward was out of work and penniless. Goodyear tried other friends, but ended up owing a week's hotel bill and was thrown into jail.

His father scraped up enough to get him out. Goodyear walked out of Boston weary and hungry. In Cambridge, his friend Harry Willis fed him and put him up, but had no money. Goodyear walked on to Woburn.

His youngest boy was dying. Two days later, he and Clarissa walked alone behind the small casket to a lonely hillside grave. Shortly after, their fifth daughter, Clara, was born.

The tragic succession of poverty, death, and birth brought $7 from a Boston friend who had previously refused to help, along with a harsh reprimand. A barrel of flour arrived mysteriously. It was from a stranger who had been in the friend's office when Goodyear's desperate plea for help arrived. Finally $50 came from brother-in-law De Forest in New York.

Goodyear went to New York in May, 1840, and tried to persuade his brother-in-law to undertake manufacturing the vulcanized rubber. De Forest said his business was wool, but he introduced Goodyear to two brothers with money, William and Emery Rider. They put up funds to continue the experiments and insisted on his accepting money to bring Clarissa and the children to New York.

Besides money, they gave him constant enthusiastic encouragement. Convinced that he had the secret perfected, they put money into a Springfield plant, and Goodyear and his two brothers set to work with the brightest prospects.

But hardly was the plant in operation than the Riders went bankrupt. Everything was likely to be lost. Goodyear rushed to New York to see De Forest.

Again he implored his brother-in-law to get behind the venture, showing him the "shirred" goods he was making. De Forest ran the fabric through his hands, pleased and amazed. This was marketable; it could compete with wool. He put up several thousand dollars and, over the years, his total investment reached $43,000.

Good fortune rarely came to Goodyear unadulterated. He was shattered by the loss in one year of two brothers and his father. Too devastated to tend to practical manufacturing—which never appealed to him—he put the plant into the hands of his surviving brothers and turned to new experiments.

Once more he was tossed into debtors' prison. With full success in his grasp, he was again faced with ruin. He had been making payments on back debts, but now that he was in production, his creditors grew impatient. He had always refused to declare himself bankrupt in order to gain freedom, for he considered it unethical, but at this crucial juncture, he could not afford to be idle. On the outside, he could soon cover all obligations. He entered a bankruptcy plea and wiped out $35,000 of debts. Later, he paid every cent—in a few cases, double the amount borrowed.

4

His life became busy and fruitful. Goodyear's brain was on fire with ideas of ways to use rubber. One of the first things he worked on was a life preserver—the dream that had always sustained him in dark moments: to save human lives.

In the next four years, he utilized rubber in making machine belting, inkstands, hayrick covers, diving suits, knife handles, hot-water bottles, breast pumps, surgical gloves, syringes, gasbags, dolls, footballs, plates for stereotype printing, abdominal supporters, and air cushions. He worked himself to the bone, never resting, and his friends saw him only when he rushed forth exultantly, yellow and gaunt, to show them some new object he had hit upon.

Ship and windmill sails, cables for whale fishing, horse collars, daguerreotype boxes, elastics for headgear, shoestrings, air-cushion saddles, inflated boxing gloves, inflated caps for boys skating so when they fell they would not break their pates, rubber clubs for circus clowns, rain-water tanks.

He advertised chair "shoes" to prevent floor scratches; any person sitting in a chair so equipped, who wore overshoes, "need have little apprehension of danger from lightning."

He turned out pantaloons and dresses for fording streams and for baptisms. "They have been found useful," he wrote, "and have been highly approved by Baptist clergymen who are obliged to stand a long time in cold water. They are . . . similar to fishing pants, except that they are cut higher in the waist." The demand was particularly large in the South.

He took out some five hundred patents and licensed other manufacturers with exclusive sales territories. The first was the New Haven L. Candee suspenders factory, which began making rubber overshoes. So bad was the reputation of such footgear that only by door-to-door peddling was Candee able to open up a market, then demand soon exceeded supply. Years later, the United Rubber Corporation bought out Candee and moved operations to the Midwest.

From the start, Goodyear was plagued by infringements. The worst offender was Horace H. Day of New York, notorious for his unusual deals, in spite of being a close friend of President Jackson and Sam Houston of Texas, where Day was promoting land schemes. The rubber dispute was settled out of court for $5,000 cash and future royalties on stated products, chiefly "shirred" goods. But Day proceeded to turn out overshoes, poaching on another licensee, and never paid a cent of royalty.

In 1851 Goodyear filed suit against him, hiring Daniel Webster for a $25,000 fee. Day secured Rufus Choate, the cleverest lawyer of the period. "The Great India Rubber Suit"—in its day as spectacular as the later Bryan-Darrow "Monkey versus Man" suit in Tennessee—came to a dramatic hearing in March, 1852, in Trenton, New Jersey.

"No other man in the world," thundered Webster, "only the man who sits at that table—Charles Goodyear" could "stand up and say that is his invention." He would go down in that "great class of inventors at the head of which stands Robert Fulton." A cutting comparison, for Fulton never invented the steamboat! But the decision, handed down September 28, was a complete victory for Goodyear.

The suit set him to writing the story of his invention. The two-volume work of more than six hundred pages was published in 1853 with the title *Gum-Elastic*, and some copies were printed on rubber. Volume I contains the story of his long search for vulcanized rubber, proof of his claims, and a fervent description of the importance of the material. Volume II is devoted to a description of the many products he had invented and those he believed could be developed. His imagination runs over all human activities from education to military uses, from medical to mathematical instruments, objects for sports and games. He lists possible musical instruments, travel gadgets, and safety devices.

He never missed an opportunity to set before the world the utility and worth of rubber. After winning the New Jersey suit, he rushed to England and borrowed $30,000 to stage an exhibit at the international fair in the Crystal Palace. "Goodyear's Vulcanite Court" was the showiest exhibit in the place, everything rubber—walls, roof, cornices, carpet, furniture, showcases.

He called on Charles Macintosh and Company, of which Hancock had become a partner, to protest patent infringement. Macintosh advised him that the United States court decision had no validity in British courts, that Hancock had a legitimate patent.

Getting hold of early samples of Goodyear's vulcanized rubber, the British rubber man had rushed to file an intent to apply for patent—a few months before the inventor's application arrived. This blocked the granting of a patent to anybody else for a given number of years, and within that period Hancock worked out a heat-sulphur process.

But a suit brought by Goodyear would do the concern little good, and Macintosh offered to give him half the British rights. Goodyear turned down the offer.

He was prevented from pushing his claims immediately because of Clarissa's illness. The trip to England, where cold and rain kept her indoors, had been too much for her health. Goodyear attended her with great alarm. She grew steadily worse and died, March 30, 1853.

She had stood by him through years of suffering, working by his side at the bench, contributing many ideas for products. She had made maps and globes. Those harsh years had seen the death of four of their nine children.

Frantic and restless, Goodyear sold the home he had bought in London, purchased another in Norwood, lived there six months, bought a third in Sydenham. By the end of the year he was back in London.

His spirits had improved. Prosperous now, he bought a carriage, hired a valet, and acquired a splendid wardrobe. He paid off all back debts, and he gave large sums to his relatives and supported numbers of families of friends for years. He had his portrait painted—on rubber. He was half bald now and wore a luxuriant wiry beard, partly gray.

At an evening gathering, a twenty-year-old girl named

Fannie Wardell watched Goodyear, now fifty-four, come into the room on crutches—he was suffering from gout. He was presented to her and managed to bow gallantly over his crutches. The deep melancholy of his voice pierced her to the heart.

She took it upon herself to do things for him, and her solicitude and sympathy caused him to improve. They were married May 30, 1854. Both his health and financial situation continued to get better. Funds were coming in steadily from the United States; a number of French concerns using his license were beginning to show profits; a factory in Austria, one of the largest in Europe, took out a license.

His suit against Hancock came to trial in July and went against Goodyear. He moved to Paris to prepare an exhibit for the Exposition Universelle. Endeavoring to surpass his London effort, he spent $50,000 assembling every known rubber product, even rubber cannon balls.

Napoleon III and his bride Eugénie visited the exhibit and awarded him the Grand Medal of Honor and the Cross of the Legion of Honor. By then Goodyear was having serious trouble with French creditors. He was not well, and Fanny flew about trying to prevent action that would land him in debtors' prison. He was saved, it was said, by direct intervention of the Emperor, but only temporarily, for when he and Fanny returned to England, he was arrested for debt on demand of French creditors.

"Sickness and sorrow, like health and joy," he wrote to a friend, "are brief at the longest. God hath set the one over against the other." In this "snug little parlor at the 'Pavilion' ... hangs the engraving of the convalescent soldier from Waterloo, his wife and baby by his side." On the other side of the room was an "image of Christ," chiseled there by a prisoner with his fingernail. "How one would like to know that man!"

Goodyear believed these latest trials were part of God's plan for his good. "Satan was once let loose this way upon poor Job."

Following his release, with his health further undermined, he and Fanny moved to Bath. There, for the next three years, he struggled to get well. When he was able, he worked again on perfecting a life preserver. He and Fanny sailed for America in May, 1858.

They made their home in New Haven. The rubber industry was flourishing. Fortunes had been made. Thousands of men were employed. Yet Goodyear, the discoverer, when the final balance was cast—though he had lived comfortably for a few years—had nothing. His debts overbalanced his assets. In view of this showing, he was given a patent renewal for seven years.

Whenever free from gout, he worked on new rubber products. Restlessness drove him to New York, where he made objects useful for the government—blankets, mailbags, lifeboats, gun covers, and pontoons.

He went on to Washington, bought a home, and constructed a tank in which to test lifeboats, rafts, and vests—inspired by the same interest that had first focused his attention on rubber. The rubber life preserver had been an obsession all his life, the central justification for all his sufferings and those inflicted on his family. Now that his sands were nearly run out, he worked on it even more feverishly. It became the symbol of his lifetime effort.

"Must men continue to be drowned because their fathers were?" he demanded of sundry and all. "Such a state of things in the present age need not or ought not to exist." He advocated that every movable object on a ship be made of rubber: chairs, beds, stools, so that each would provide additional support for people cast into the sea.

Late in May, 1860, he was taken seriously ill, but over the protests of Fanny and his doctor, he rushed off to the bedside of his favorite daughter Cynthia in New Haven. She was thirty-three and not expected to live. Fanny could not go along because she had to care for an infant daughter, Fanny, born April 25.

He took the steamer *Montebello* to New York, where his brother-in-law De Forest met him at the dock with the news that Cynthia was dead.

Goodyear keeled over and was taken to the Fifth Avenue Hotel in a serious condition. Word was sent to Fanny to come at once.

When she arrived on June 7, his condition was hopeless. His last injunction to her was that she seek out Horace Day, who had injured him so greatly, and tell his foe he forgave him. He died Sunday, July 1, 1860, at the hour when the bells were calling people to church. He was almost sixty.

Before he died, he succeeded in making a thoroughly dependable life preserver. It was used successfully in the Civil War.

His vulcanization discovery had far-reaching effects all over the world. By finding a way to use ule sap, he created the fantastic rubber boom in Brazil that opened up the great Amazon basin and saw new cities founded there and in Peru. It brought into being the great rubber industry of southeast Asia. He widened the commerce and industry of the whole world.

Though his imagination was so great, and he hit upon so many uses for rubber and conceived of so many others, the growth and complexity of modern industry has found a hundred thousand more he never dreamed of. Without his vulcanized rubber, the wheel chairs of hospital patients would not roll gently, and the great expansion of the motor age would not have come about. Without it, automobiles would not move over the highways; planes would not fly the sky.

XVII. New England's Golden Harvest

WHEN RALPH WALDO EMERSON was thirty-six, he wrote in his journal: "I am to try the magic of sincerity, the luxury permitted only to kings and poets."

It was a belated assertion. He had followed that gleaming magic and had permitted himself that luxury from his first awareness. He was one American able to make a successful career of it, although he did not think often in terms of personal success, only of creative discovery—the inner light, wherever it might lead him.

But his success as a public figure could be gauged. He had already addressed the most scholarly gatherings in America. He had already dined tête-à-tête with a president—John Adams. He would come face to face with Lincoln. He had already met Wordsworth and Carlyle—the two beings who stood highest on his precious roster of "great souls"—and for him that really was success. But so might be the simple pleasure of skimming a stone on the ice of Walden Pond, getting the right modulation and rhythm between beats on the crystal drum. The echo of that became the jeweled perfection of his prose measuring a perfected, imperishable idea. Presently, he became the lion of the British intellectuals and aristocracy—and this, at moments, made him fretful.

Well before the declaration in his journal, he had already taken his stand publicly on "sincerity." In 1829 he had accepted a post at the Second Church in Boston. Within three years, at the age of twenty-nine, he quietly declined to observe Passover ritual—and his resignation was accepted. Thus he ended his ministerial career—though he preached many times after that—to become an unemployed citizen of the world. He nailed his thesis to the church door and walked into the freer air of a broader life.

It was more than a quibble over ritual; it was a clear-eyed determination to make his life correspond to his beliefs. It was "the best part" of him that "revolted" against being a minister, one of "God's policemen," and against "official goodness." In his journal he wrote that the Bible did not direct one to be "a Unitarian or a Calvinist or an Episcopalian." Sectarianism merely marked "the decline of religion." Religion was "the relation of the soul to God."

After his separation from the Boston church, but some years before his avowed dedication to "sincerity," he delivered the annual Cambridge Phi Beta Kappa oration that became a cornerstone of American literature and thought—"The American Scholar"—in which he set forth his credo of creative independence.

Scholarship made men free, and he sought intellectual independence for all thinking students; he sought it for the whole country, which should cease feeding on the "sere remains of foreign harvests." America's "long apprenticeship to the learning of other lands draws to a close." Put aside the past. Put aside Europe. Respond to the needs of America.

This literary chauvinism was needed at a time when the balance still dipped so far in the other direction, and it rang a bell in the spirits of men in a land beginning to discover and make use of its great potentialities. That, in time, it might be tainted and narrowed down by lesser minds to parochialism, provincialism, and jingoism was not the fault of the master.

For such emancipation, the American scholar had to become a man of integrity. The American "freeman" had become "timid, imitative, tame." There was no place any more except for "the decorous and the complacent." He warned also of decay due to overspecialization, which created only part men. Be "whole men," not "walking monsters," not just an ambulating "finger, neck, stomach, elbow." Above all, do not be "a thinker," parroting other men's ideas, but "Man Thinking." "A popgun is a popgun . . . though the honorable men of the earth affirm it is the crack of doom." Man in

America should not be afraid to seek his true spiritual allegiance and stand by his discoveries.

Sects and parties, he maintained his whole life, were merely "an elegant incognito devised to save man from the vexation of thinking." Slough off the "prison-uniform of party," he thundered. Leave off being "parlor soldiers" and do not "shun the rugged battle of fate where strength is born." Do not worry about the opinions of others; be yourself. Stand on your own feet. Create your own system. "Make your own Bible," as he had made his, from the leaves of the great thinkers, the leaves of Nature, and, above all, from the sacred leaves of inner spiritual honesty. "As fast as any man becomes great, that is [when he thinks] he becomes a new party. Socrates, Aristotle, Calvin, Luther . . . Abelard, what are these but the names of parties? . . . As fast as we use our eyes," we become "thinking corporations and join ourselves to God." Society was "a conspiracy against the manhood of every one of its members"; it "whipped the non-conformist with its displeasure," and yet each institution, for all such persecution of original ideas, was merely the lengthened shadow of the great mind of a single brave initiator. The only sacred thing was the "integrity" of one's own mind. The single man, adhering stanchly to his beliefs, could be starved or crucified, but—and here Emerson rose to inspirational self-reliance—"if the single man plant himself indomitably on his instincts, and there abide, the huge world will come round to him."

His reaffirmation of the glory and power of the individual was his *coup de grâce* to expiring Calvinism and the feudal order and rolled back the mists that had hung so darkly for so long over the New England mind, clinging there like dank cobwebs, while other parts of the country, originally nourished by New England, were growing tall in the sunlight, thinking, fighting new battles, and building in new ways. His message was a challenge to blind tradition, conformity, and complacency. It was this yawning crack between the hierarchical Calvinistic system, still so pervasive in New England, and the new world of industry and science that exposed the good soil and sunlight in which Emerson's roots could go deep and the foliage rise high and spread wide.

His truths came at an hour when men felt an uneasy emptiness, when they were facing a new kind of world, as yet only vaguely foreseen, and they were eager, many at least, to listen. New England had provided all America with schools and teachers, with the theories and mechanics of democracy, born of original thinking and acting, of town meetings, free assemblage, and representative government. It had shaped the great American documents. It had provided new vital processes that helped the nation grow great, yet it had failed to keep some of those fine instrumentalities filled with content and vigor. These seemed to have been drained off with the virile emigrating sons and the generous gifts to far places in the land.

Now New England was the very heart of the industrial revolution, the center of nascent machine production, of progress and opportunity, the theater of a new economic order, but it had no philosophy, no living faith commensurate with this new age, nothing to match its bold achievements and promise. Emerson became the articulate sounding board, on the ideal plane, of the new rampant acquisitive individualism. He provided a clean-cut, handmade philosophy and a justifying ethic for the economic order struggling into being—the era of free enterprise. His doctrine of supreme individualism helped flex the muscles of new accomplishment, not merely in New England but throughout the country, the taming of a continent, the building of new industries.

Yet, unlike Ezra Stiles, he had scant interest in the new techniques, and though he wrote, "Religion that is afraid of science dishonors God and commits suicide," he feared the evil effects of the scientific machine age on "Man Thinking," foreseeing that it might lead to a dead level of sheeplike bleating, a blundering herd of people accepting whatever was told them, angrily resenting real thought, and ever ready to stampede after the latest demagogue. He bewailed the reckless rush and lack of reflection in this strenuous new America and really believed that Oriental quietism was far superior.

Some of his fears were to be realized. Much too often the higher meaning of his ideas—independent thought, searching for truth and spiritual greatness—have gone unheeded in the new industrial exuberance. Although he nowhere expressed sympathy with such feral ruthlessness as that of the sublime *reductio ad absurdum* of individualism, Max Stirner's *The Ego and His Own*, Emerson seemed to justify for many the ruthlessness required to build a new material world out of the wilderness in the hurly-burly of early competitive America. This was the opposite of what Emerson had intended; it was precisely what he feared.

But quite apart from that, he helped free the American mind from slavish dependence on Europe, from slavish dependence on past dogmas; he brought the American mind to maturity ready to face the sunlight of science, research, and objective truth. The old medievalism takes on new colorings; it still serves the demagogues and the emotion makers, but he widened the dimensions of American thinking; he helped give it dignity, ethical content, and self-reliance.

By the time of his masterful "The American Scholar," certainly by 1840 (his declaration of sincerity), Emerson had carved out the smooth bedrock of his beliefs. Thereafter the stream of his life and thought could flow surely channeled to the goal, not often turgid, nearly always serene and strong— on rare occasions, for he was not easily aroused to indignation or deeds in the market place, a rushing torrent.

2

Emerson's father, William, was a hearty, handsome man who had become a minister because his mother wanted it so badly, but he preferred good company and playing his bass viol. His wife, Ruth Haskins, was the daughter of "Honest" John Haskins, a bluff seaman, full of pithy sayings, who settled on shore as a cooper and became a distiller to support his sixteen children. He was a Tory Episcopalian. His wife was a Congregationalist. On Sunday mornings they marched to the church with their great brood of children marshaled in two bands, and, at a given corner, executed right and left turns, each leading to his own temple of God.

Ruth chose to become an Episcopalian, and then married a Congregationalist. Thus Ralph Waldo came from a deeply religious family of mixed denominations in which rigid sectarianism was impossible. Who can doubt that this influenced his later rejection of sectarianism and intolerance?

His father was dining with Governor Strong on election day when Ralph Waldo was born, May 25, 1803. He died when Ralph Waldo was eight, one of six children under ten. Ruth had only a small church pension, and she took in boarders. The children had to help.

When he was ten, Ralph Waldo wrote to his favorite aunt, Mary Moody Emerson—a volcanic, ambitious spinster, with an "eye that went through and through you like a needle"—that he always rose at 5:55 A.M. and helped his younger brother William make fires and set the table. They called their mother at 6:15 and, while she was dressing, studied their spelling lessons. At the Latin school he learned Latin grammar and Virgil. At a private school, he wrote and ciphered. After school he ran errands for his mother and brought in firewood. When the supper dishes were cleared away and washed, he and the other children recited hymns and Bible verses—Ralph Waldo had been made to repeat holy phrases since the age of three—and then they took turns reading aloud Rollins's *History*. At eight o'clock he said his prayers and went to bed. Sometimes in the bedroom, where three brothers also slept, he pulled the blanket up about his chin in the icy chill and tried to read Plato. Ever afterward, he associated that author with the smell of wool.

None of the children were strong, though William developed a good physique. John Clarke, his oldest brother, died when a boy; his only sister at the age of three. Edward Bliss—considered the brightest—went temporarily insane in his early twenties and before long died in Puerto Rico. In 1836 Charles Chauncey, in whom Ralph Waldo always found great inspiration, was stricken with consumption and died. Robert Bulkeley was mentally defective and was kept on a farm. Ralph Waldo himself had a propensity to tuberculosis all his life.

Though subject to spells of black depression and ill health most of his life, by carefully husbanding his physical assets, Ralph Waldo accomplished more than most stronger men do. But it led him to a sedentary role of meditation and communing with Nature. "Let the glory of the world run where it will," he noted, when only twenty-three, "the mind has it own glory.... Greatness in the world and greatness of soul ... are not compatible ... I doubt not that I head on the highway that leads to Divinity."

At fourteen he entered Harvard, where he became class poet and began a journal. The first volumes have disappeared; his account begins with No. XVII in his junior year—a "Common Place Book" to record "new thoughts." He continued it until seven years before his death.

After graduating, he taught at the school for young ladies his brother William had set up in their mother's house. In the summer of 1823 he took a solitary walking trip to visit the new college of Amherst.

He was trying to decide what to do with his life. The vague romanticism that steeped his mind began to crystallize into more coherent ideas. "Opinions change. Your perceptions of right and wrong never change." (A fairly arbitrary statement; his own did). On a February day he noted, "Material beauty perishes or palls. Intellectual beauty limits admiration to seasons and ages; hath its ebbs and flows of delight ... but moral beauty is lovely, imperishable, perfect."

It was not a historic statement, or wholly true, even for him, but here was the unchanging marble at the base of his world of flux and growth.

For more than a year he debated the proper career, an agonizing self-appraisal. "We have many capacities . . . we lack the time and occasion to improve." *The Bride of Lammermoor* made him want to be a novelist. Genuine poetry awakened in his soul "a legion of little goblins," and had he time to attend to "the fine tiny rabble," he would straightway be a poet. "In my day dreams . . . I often want to be a painter." He had "spasmodic attachments" to the sciences and every province of letters. All played the "coquette" with his imagination. He feared he might die a forlorn bachelor, "jilted" by them all.

With many qualms, he chose the Church. His reasoning faculty, he declared, was "weak" and "theology was everlasting debating ground," but the vogue in preaching depended chiefly on poetic imagination. Unfortunately he was not at ease in company—"a frigid fear of offending and jealous of disrespect," but from his father he had inherited "a formality of manner and speech" and "a passionate love for eloquence," so he hoped to "thrive" in Divinity.

He enrolled in Harvard Divinity School in February, 1825, but his eyes gave out and his health failed. Hoping to get stronger, he worked on an uncle's farm. During that summer and the following winter he took private pupils.

In spite of the brevity of his divinity studies, he was appointed to preach by the Middlesex Association of Ministers but, threatened with consumption, had to go south. Even Charleston was too cold for a "luke-sick" man, and he went on to St. Augustine. He spoke little of the historical grandeurs of the place, but pined for the "genial cold" of New England.

Not strong enough to accept a regular pulpit, Emerson preached here and there, then went back to Divinity School, but grew depressed and ill. He had to rush his brother Edward Bliss south to Charleston. It was a forlorn trip. Edward's "frenzy took all forms. . . . There he lay—Edward, the admired, learned, eloquent striving boy—a maniac." He was to recover after a fashion, then wither and die.

On returning north, Emerson became engaged to sixteen-year-old Ellen Louisa Tucker, daughter of a Boston merchant, a frail girl suffering from advanced consumption. "Father in Heaven," he wrote in his journal, "strengthen and purify and prosper and eternize our affection." He accepted the call to become assistant pastor at the Boston Second Church. They were married in September, 1829.

His own health improved, but hers failed rapidly. Within six months he had to take her south. His superior fell ill, and he had to hurry back. She died February 8, 1831. There is, he wrote, "one birth, and one baptism, and one first love." Every day, rain or shine, he visited her grave in Roxbury, and for years mourned her in his journal.

It set his mind to working on a theme developed in his later "Compensation." "We cannot bring ourselves to let our angels go." But when we do, "archangels may come in." We linger on "in ruins of the old tent . . . we sit and weep in vain . . . but the death of a dear friend, wife, brother, lover . . ." he wrote, "operates revolutions in our way of life, terminates an epoch of infancy or of youth . . . breaks up a wonted occupation or a household or a style of living, and allows the formation of new ones more friendly to the growth of character." But it took time, and another wife, for him to find this out.

For more than a year, he was restless, coming to his most crucial decision. On September 9, 1832, he rose resolutely but serenely in his pulpit to announce that he could not continue to celebrate Passover. When Jesus ate with his disciples, it was not a religious rite but a "national feast." Its Oriental symbolism was "foreign and unsuited for New Englanders."

Once the break had come, briefly he felt "peace and freedom," but depression set in so deeply that his mother wrote frantically to his two brothers in Puerto Rico to hurry home. It was an ordeal—the blind trying to lead the blind; Edward was close to death, Charles seriously ill. They persuaded Ralph Waldo to visit Europe.

He sailed for Malta December 25 on the brig *Jasper*, a tiny

236-ton ship, loaded with logwood, mahogany, tobacco, sugar, coffee, beeswax, cheese, etc. The second day out, they hit a storm. The water had an "ugly sound," and he had a "harpy" feeling, "nausea, darkness, unrest, uncleanness." Not to think about his misery and the prospects of "going to the bottom," he "remembered up" nearly the whole of *Lycidas*, stanza by stanza.

3

At his first port, Valetta in Malta, he was in good spirits. "Welcome these new joys. Let my American eye become a child's again, to these glorious picture-books," he said in St. John's Church as he watched the chanting friars, the carved ceilings, the madonnas and saints. They were "living oracles, *quotidiana et perpetua*." Hearing mass at the Temple of Minerva in Syracuse, he was awed that the same walls had been devoted to divine worship for 2,500 years—"good witness to the ineradicableness of the religious principle."

In Catania he went to the opera, but the price of the ticket was "too much for the whistle." Turning his eyes inward might be a "vice," but he was his own "comedy and tragedy."

He resisted the beauty of Naples chiefly because it was so loudly acclaimed by everybody. Instead, he read Goethe, looked at Virgil's tomb, and felt homesick for "the fogs of low dense pinewoods" and "blue violets out of black loam."

Then the glory of Rome burst upon him. He was "dazzled and drunk with beauty"—the Capitoline Hill, the Dying Gladiator, Tarpeian Rock, the Vatican museum. The Apollo and Laocöon statues he already knew "by heart" from copies, and he reveled in this firsthand renewal. In the Sistine Chapel he watched the Pope bless the palms and heard the choir "chaunt the Passion." To Emerson's strict Puritan eyes the pomp and ceremony were purely "conventional . . . no true Majesty . . . only millinery and imbecility," which hid from his eyes "the gentle Son of Man who sat upon an ass amidst the rejoicing of his fickle countrymen."

But that evening, the singing of the *Miserere* by the peerless choir, the tragic notes of *"Traidor . . ."* the snuffing out of the candles, then *"miserere mei, Deus,"* coming plaintively out of the darkness, was "very touching . . . everything in good taste." The beauty and immensity of St. Peter's, the grandeur of the great circular piazza with its arcades and stone saints, the mighty façade, and the moonlight "upon the finest fountain in the world," filled him with almost painful awe.

But he grew weary. Rome was "majestic," but he would give it all for "one man fit to walk there," able to "impart the sentiment of the place."

In Florence, he visited Walter Savage Landor, one of his idols, who lived in a beautiful Fiesole villa, full of pictures, with an engaging wife and four children. Landor cut rapier-sharp into all Emerson's sacred convictions and heroes, taking delight in upsetting this too-solemn young man come forth from among the barbarians. . . . Socrates? . . . "A vulgar old sophist." In effusive terms, he praised Lord Chesterton, whom Emerson disliked for his "slippery morality."

Landor was "very decided . . . in his opinions," Emerson wrote coldly in his journal, unaware he had been spoofed, but added generously, "and a very good connoisseur in painting." Then years later, he commented of Landor's *Pericles and Aspasia,* "Honor and elegance enough to polish a nation for an age. All the elements of a gentleman . . . except holiness. Religion in a high degree he does not know."

In Florence, he saw his first ballet, fortifying himself with Goethe's injunction that judgment of a work of art should be "purely aesthetic," but again the Puritan rose in Emerson's gorge. "I could not help feeling it were better for mankind if there were no such dancers."

But the Medici Venus in the Uffizi he could not resist. His spirit rose like a bursting skyrocket. That "statue, which enchants the world!" he exclaimed—so timeless, so sculptured, yet so fluid!

On a second visit, especially to look at *her,* he tried to

"reserve" his admiration, not wanting to accept her because she was so universally praised. He "walked coolly round and round the marble lady," then planted himself at the gate to the Dutch room. "Mankind's judgment" was "right," and he gladly gave "one testimony more."

The statue became a symbol of his own creative urge, his constant search for firm but fluid expression in verse and prose. There is a discernible link between Emerson's style and the beautiful lady.

From early days he had been attracted by Solomon's Proverbs, Plutarch's *Lives*, Montaigne, and especially by Bacon, the first modern mind to become imbued with St. Francis's rich awareness of Nature. Emerson liked those writers, their clean-cut, concise, vivid style, their truths that on occasion condensed the whole universe into a glowing phrase and made a star seem like a bright pebble in the hand. When only twenty-one Emerson had written that he could emulate them and, like Bacon, perhaps add "another volume" that would similarly distill the wisdom of his own era. The glorious Venus was to art what Bacon was to thought and style. Her contours, like those of his own mind, were a perfect condensation of Nature, truth, and beauty.

The poise of the human body had always been an obsession with Emerson. When he was a boy, people remarked that he walked as if he thought the earth was not good enough for him. This might have been primness, but more likely it sprang from pride and dignity. As he might later have said, he was never the walker, but "Man Walking." The power and grace of workmen, symbolic of the virility he himself lacked and envied, which his poor health and scholarly reclusiveness denied him, always aroused his pleasure and praise. The way a man held his body mirrored his whole character—and character was everything!

In his old age, when scarcely able to remember names and faces, he visited Egypt, "coming so far, suffering discomfort, seeing so little." Mostly he was bored, but in Shepheard's

Hotel in Cairo he jotted down that what struck him most was "the erect carriage of the people . . . better and nobler than any passengers in our cities at home." He came back to this a few days later. "The people are a perpetual study for the excellence and grace of their forms and motion. No people walks so well, so straight . . . strong and flexible; and for studying the nude, our artists should come here and not to Paris."

"Strong and flexible"—this was his ideal for himself and for his writing, the qualities he most admired. It was there in Bacon. It was in the Medici Venus. He achieved this ideal better than most authors did. His firm prose, sculptured for all time like the Venus, fluid yet self-contained and balanced, walked like the straight-backed, swaying Egyptians beside the Nile, graceful and free and unashamed, each sentence a proud individual, perfectly endowed, perfectly poised, moving across the page strong and exquisite.

Thus it was that he did in actuality become the Bacon of his age in America. Out of the even-flowing stream of his reading, his experience, and his meditations over the years, he drew forth those pithy aphorisms like jewels to glisten forever. They come fresh from the cool dipper of his careful, sinuous prose. Like limpid carved gems, their form forever set, having fire at the core, they explode in the brain with rainbow spray. In spite of his sheer intellectuality, Emerson penetrates to the human heart as great truth always does, creating the desire to achieve full awareness of self and the world.

4

Except by spells—some vision like St. Peter's or the Venus—Emerson was not happy those early days in Europe. He grew ever more irritated at being pulled this way and that by mere sights and mediocrities. He longed constantly for New England, for that precise, cold discipline where he could feel the inner warmth of his own undisturbed thoughts.

He did have one more moment of uplift in Italy: the sight of the Milan cathedral, with its "exquisitely sculptured pin-

nacles," the snowy Alps in the background—"one of the grandest views on earth." But everything else was anticlimax. In
"disagreeable" Venice, the stink of bilgewater pervaded everything. Italy, he summarized, had "charm" only because of its
historic names. He had seen as fine days from his own window
at home. "Illustrate, eternize your own woodhouse," he
counseled. "It is much cheaper, and quite possible to any
resolute thinker."

Years later, in his essay "Self-Reliance," he was to call
traveling "a fool's paradise." The sad self always went along.
Ingrained prejudice and smugness were merely deepened. It
was a story of "ruins to ruins." It was "want of self-culture,"
a peculiar snobbishness, that drove most "educated Americans" in stampeding herds for quick tours on which they could
learn nothing of importance about the people they visited.

In Geneva he visited Ferney, the chateau of Voltaire, "king
of scoffers." It would be "a sin against faith and philosophy"
to exclude him from "toleration." He did his work "as the
bustard and tarantula do theirs." Evidently he did not appreciate Voltaire's towering genius.

In Paris, he found inspiration only at the Jardin des Plantes,
and exclaimed, "I will be a naturalist." Everything else made
him weary and nervous. The gardens of the Louvre looked
"pinched," wind drove dust into his eyes, and before his party
got to the Champs Elysées, he insisted on turning around. He
would not give his inkstand for all of Paris, just "another loud,
modern New York of a place." His trip, he grieved, was all
waste. If he did not see Thomas Carlyle in Edinburgh, he
would go back to America without having said "anything in
earnest."

In London, "an immense . . . very dull place," he saw Cole-
ridge, a short, thick old man with merry blue eyes, who greeted
him with messy pinches of snuff and a diatribe against Uni-
tarians. "Quackery!" William Ellery Channing loved the good
in Christianity, not its truth. The poet recited his own verses.

The visit, remarked Emerson ruefully, was "a spectacle, not a conversation."

On Mount Rydal in Ambleside near the Scottish border, he sought out Wordsworth—"the high watermark which the intellect has reached in this age," he said, too extravagantly. The poet turned out to be "a plain, elderly white-haired man ... nothing striking about his appearance," though Emerson was startled by his green goggles.

At once Wordsworth harped on the "foolishness" of American schools ... "superficial tuition ... unrestrained by moral culture." He railed against American vulgarity, the lack of "gentlemen," and America's preoccupation with sordid money-making. The poet had little use for Emerson's love of Virgil, and he thought Carlyle "sometimes insane." He denounced Goethe. *Wilhelm Meister* was "full of fornication." He struck a valiant pose and recited his own sonnets. Emerson could hardly keep from "giggling," but he did not find the poet's egoism too "displeasing." Wordsworth's ideas, his poetry, his fresh Franciscan glorification of Nature fed Emerson's deepest wellsprings.

He found Carlyle in a lonely house on the Hill of the Hawk, sixteen miles out in "the wild and desolate heathery," not another house in sight. Shaggy Carlyle turned out to be the most amiable man he had ever met, and Jane was "a most accomplished and agreeable woman."

Carlyle was a raging critic of nearly everything, a series of passionate diatribes. He did extol Mirabeau, for Emerson a mere "scrub." Rousseau's *Confessions* proved that the Frenchman was not such an "ass" after all. John Stuart Mill was the greatest intellect on earth, all "purity" and "force." But Carlyle shattered most of Emerson's idols.... Plato? ... Socrates? ... "Despicable!" For real genius he preferred pigs to men and praised the clever tricks of the half-wild one he owned. He ridiculed all religious sects, the magazines that published him, the newspapers, the publishers—in the end all England, although he allowed that London was the only place in the world fit to live in, despite its tart-eating level of brains.

Emerson suddenly "pitied" the blustering Scot for his lack of "reverence" but basked in his bluff kindness. He respected Carlyle's extraordinary mind, expanded in the wide, daring embrace of his vision, and continued to admire him.

There was real stuff in both, and cynical, shaggy Carlyle, with his craggy brows and booming voice, was charmed by Emerson's half-innocent earnestness; he knew real sincerity when he encountered it. After the New Englander left, Carlyle said gently, "I saw him go up the hill. I didn't go with him to see him descend. I preferred to watch him mount and vanish like an angel."

5

Emerson's mind was truly eclectic. He snatched his pearls from the lore of the East, the Persian poets, the Greeks, the essayists of every clime; from Wordsworth, "cold passionless Swedenborg," and Goethe, always Goethe. He could appreciate talents remote from his own. Years later, in 1855, he perceived the illumination of Whitman's *Leaves of Grass*, issued that year, although Whitman's roistering genius, his earthiness, his sex symbolism ran counter to Emerson's own attitudes. But Whitman's gemlike flashes of poetic truth and his celebration of the "uniqueness of individual man"—this was close to Emerson's way of looking at life. He recognized the volume as a towering landmark in American literature, thus showing more discernment than most of his contemporaries. The poet owed much to Emerson. He said he was "simmering, simmering, simmering" until Emerson brought him "to boil." The New Englander did not know this, but wrote generously, "I greet you at the beginning of a great career." He hastened to send a copy to Carlyle, describing it as "a nondescript monster with terrible eyes and buffalo strength ... indisputably American."

Emerson also derived much from his friends at home and the marvels of Nature about him. He was very much in rapport with young Thoreau, Orientalist and child of Nature, who carried the sovereign rights of the conscience against the claims of the State, even to the point of going to jail. He got much from Alcott, "the tedious archangel"; from masculine Margaret Fuller, whose busybody bustling appalled him; from William Ellery Channing, shining light of Unitarianism. Hawthorne was a neighbor, and Emerson was impressed by his intense dissection of Puritan sin and remorse.

From little men, too, he learned; from the villagers of his beloved Concord, for he respected everybody who could do things well on any level; he envied practical men. Once he and his boy were tugging unsuccessfully at a calf, trying to get it into the barn. An Irish servant girl put her finger into the calf's mouth to suck, and it followed her docilely. Emerson always marveled at any such simple effective knowledge, close to Nature's own wisdom.

In spite of his seclusion, he won the love of such people; when late in life his house burned down, they pitched in and rebuilt it, even providing replicas of the furnishings and the pictures.

Emerson owed much indirectly to many Americans who had broken ground for him, loosening up the soil, breaking down the clods of prejudice: those valiant, often suffering thinkers long forgotten, like John Wise; those clear-sighted ministers of the gospel who found their own tortured way out of the maze of superstition and rigid dogma and creed, who lopped off the gangrened members of Calvinism, one by one, and who were usually persecuted and died young. They harrowed the ground and fertilized it, so that Emerson's seed, at the right moment, could take root and flourish and grow great. Or men like Stiles, who hit upon perfectionism so early and stuck by his guns without fanfare or controversy, quietly spreading his enlightenment to his congregation, his pupils and associates.

Until Emerson, most American intellectuals, particularly in New England, had hotly rejected French ideas, violently so

after the French Revolution, but the new thought answered a
need, and it slipped quietly in through the pulpits as Unitarianism. Calvinism had taught predestination and implacable punishment. Man was sinful, his fate sealed, the human
serf must grovel, which might save him a few cuffs but did not
alter his final fate—a doctrine growing increasingly distasteful
to virile New England shipowners and traders. They had
taken it as a wry Sunday catharsis, then had gone about their
business in their own way the rest of the week. But when
William Ellery Channing told them God was kind and man
was good, a sharer with God, not a whipped vassal, it found
lodging in the most respectable pulpits, and, though Channing
had his bouts with hidebound ministers and shoddy politicians
and was often misunderstood by the public, his Unitarianism
became a fad.

Though often vacillating, the Unitarian leader was a broader
if less brilliant thinker than Emerson, for he was interested in
every aspect of society and human rights, and saw man's
grandeur, not merely as an independent courageous thinker,
but as a thinker in connection with society and its problems.
Particularly did he fight bravely for the right of all men to
express their opinions, for he saw clearly that this right did
not depend entirely on the individual, that nursing great ideas
in enforced solitude was not enough. No man, no group of
men, he insisted, was wise enough to determine what should
be suppressed. Often "the greatest truths" were the most unpopular and exasperating, at war with "the habits, prejudices
and immediate interests of a large class of the community,"
but if blacked out, "time-honored abuses" could not be exposed, society could not progress. Anybody who would rob
his neighbor of "free discussion" should have "a mark set
upon him as the worst enemy of freedom."

Perfectionism, the essence of Stiles's beliefs, the postulate
that each individual could and should seek spiritual perfection
and thereby win his ticket to heaven, not to a predestined fate,
also plowed up fertile new ground for Emerson. That creed

burst forth during the first quarter of the new century—a noisy, militant movement of parading banners and panacea seekers —and provided a ferment of new ideas. The perfectionists also helped widen the free space between static colonial society and the new, rapidly growing America, the space Emerson occupied, where he grew taller than them all.

He symbolized the striking off of medieval chains, the emergence of free men and of an authentic American culture, and he wished this new freedom to be reflected in grandeur of spirit, faith, and mind.

6

For all his genius, like most Americans of his day, Emerson was a belated eddy in the wake of a great main current already gone by, part of the world-wide intellectual movement started the previous century by the French utopians and freethinkers, carried on by the German idealists, a movement to free the human mind from the dark ages, remove the heavy chains of superstition, and let in the new light of industry and science and philosophy and promote man's welfare.

Emerson opened up this great subterranean stream, which flowed powerfully underneath contemporary reaction, which had so alarmed most American "thinkers," and channeled the gushing founts through his own mind and spirit to make it palatable and profitable for his countrymen. Thereby he irrigated and revitalized the whole of American intellectual life.

Other Americans before Emerson—not many—had drunk deeply of the French font and had made important contributions: Ezra Stiles, Thomas Jefferson, Tom Paine, Philip Freneau, America's first important poet, who was also a New Englander; Samuel Adams of Boston and other promoters of independence; and, to a lesser degree, Roger Sherman of New Haven. In practical form, the great purposes of French thought were in the American Declaration of Independence. But Emerson found rich, untapped veins. For him what most appealed in the slogan of Liberty, Fraternity, and Equality was not the humanitarian or the social and political facets, but the right of all men to think for themselves, to be children of Nature and commune with God face to face.

German idealism was the more influential in his thinking. He always gave great credit to Goethe. "A genius . . . wholly so . . . well alive . . . no pedant." Goethe's falling in love in old age was proof of his "delicate and noble sentiments." Goethe was "the cow" who had given "milk" to the whole New England intellectual renaissance. Anyone who failed to read him was "an old fogey" and belonged to the "antediluvians," for Goethe was the "pivotal" man of "the old and new times. . . . He shuts out the old, he opens the new."

But mostly for Emerson, Continental thought was sieved through the minds of Carlyle, "blessed" for his "Germanick" philosophizing and belief in human greatness, and Wordsworth, who had discovered, as had St. Francis five centuries earlier, God in Nature and in man.

For all his independent genius, Emerson became primarily the popularizer of this mighty torrent of European thought, which had taken so long to reach provincial America. He strained away its muddiness and, from the liquid residue, drew off everything suitable for his own intellectualized Puritanism and for the particular needs of America and the new individualism, channeling it through his New England ethic, tinging everything with moral fervor, religious essence, and explosive ideas. A condenser, a synthesizer, he worked French and German thought into palatable homeopathic pills for his compatriots. Thus did he achieve his youthful ambition to become a modern Bacon.

Much of his popularity was due to his extraordinary ability, like that of Benjamin Franklin, to reduce truth to incisive, pungent apothegms, many of which have become American proverbs. He provided philosophy "on the run," ready made, for, as Will Durant also found to his great profit, Americans prefer reading "about" philosophy in pithy form to reading the original work. Though Emerson had no wish to cater to superficiality, he sought simplicity in his writing, and his method and style were patterned to the short-cut American way. Actually his gemlike sentences cost him years of search, reading, agonizing thought, revision, and endless polishing before they emerged sharp-edged. The results were well suited to the American mood.

In calling upon each man to discover the glory of his own powers—in terms of his own life, his own home, his town, his country—Emerson insisted that all the truth about self and the universe was inside each human being, nowhere else, for all of God resided there within if man would but pause to look for Him. For Emerson, all human beings were like the sparkling, concise phrases he concocted, ruled by eternal principle, truth, the inner Godhead, complete in each, there to be taken and understood if the effort was made. Thus all truth—which he identified with morality—lay in each man's deepest intuition of what was right.

This, of course, is considered poppycock by modern behaviorists and psychologists, the cart before the horse, an entirely too limited, romantic, and unhistorical view of the evolution of morality, thought, and conduct.

Post-Emerson philosophy contends that the individual's ideas, prejudices, doctrines, knowledge of what is right or wrong, are not primarily the product of his own intuition and reason but are molded by family, school, society, press, radio, television, incessant propaganda—not to mention heredity, climate, altitude, food, and medical treatment.

An army can brain-wash a recruit very quickly, erasing everything in his individualism that is not helpful to army purposes. Modern governments, using the techniques of semantics and propaganda, are able to brain-wash vast herds of men and hold them in mental bondage for long periods, thus delaying the process of objective truth-finding. No one ever set forth more sardonically how even great philosophers and their ideologies have been the product of their "particular kind of breakfast food" than Giovanni Papini in his vitriolic *Beheadings* and *Twenty-Four Brains*.

Emerson's reply would be: all the more need for brave spirits to sever their chains. Few men ever severed them more thoroughly than he, but for all his independence and originality, his discoveries did not come solely from his own inner resources but were also the product of his ministerial background, his tolerant, divided, religious family, the growing force of perfectionism and Unitarianism, the crumbling away of Calvinism, the forces of modernity and the machine age— the whole trend of his time. His truths could have found no similar expression at any other hour or under any other circumstances. His philosophy also derives directly from his frail health, his inability to sustain the active battles of the market place. He was driven by his own temperament and physical handicaps into solitary study. This freed him from parties and system, which he considered to be the death of mind and spirit; it led to sublime truths denied lesser men; but it closed off from him vast areas of knowledge and experience. It intensified his thought and feelings, but it also limited the dimensions and direction of his thought. He set a great, eternal beacon on the highest mountaintop, but he rarely told men how they might reach it, nor did he often warn them they might perish trying to do so, nor even counsel them how to avoid the bloodhounds set to prevent men from reaching it.

This made him faintly disdainful of those who broke such good ground for him, those who did face the bloodhounds, some of whom were torn to pieces. He actually accused a number of such as lacking "nerve and dagger," they lacked "character." Yet Channing and William Cullen Bryant, two to whom he applied these phrases, were among the bravest men of New England and America. What Emerson really meant—and this was fastidious and also unfair—was, not that they lacked courage, but that they were too much of the market place to dedicate themselves unremittingly to the refinement of inner truth. After all, this is a luxury the world allows only to a few.

Though so tremendously messianic, yet he could rarely be induced to support the needed reforms that his fellow messiahs sought to bring about. But he was probably correct in not joining the efforts to "organize" the new transcendentalism, of which he was founder and father, in order to make it serve social needs directly. The "Social Plans" of those good souls, the Alcotts, Margaret Fuller, and others, made him want to be made "nobly mad by the kindling of a new dawn of human piety," but the proposed Brook Farm experiment, he felt, was mere "arithmetic and comfort . . . a hint borrowed from . . . the United States Hotel [in Saratoga] . . . not the cave of persecution which is the palace of spiritual power." He preferred his own prison a little longer. He wanted to break "all prisons." But he had not yet "conquered his own house," so why should he "raise the siege of this hencoop to march away to the pretended siege of Babylon"? To "join a crowd" would "traverse" all his "long-trumpeted theory." He gave the cherished project of his most beloved friends its death-laughter—"the Age of Reason in a patty-pan."

7

In 1634, after his brother Edward Bliss died, Emerson moved with his mother and brother Charles to the home of his step-grandfather, Dr. Ripley, the "Old Manse" in Concord immortalized by Hawthorne. It was one of the momentous changes of his life.

He preached around. In Plymouth, he found "families and faces almost as tranquil as their pines." He stood on the "Rock" and observed "all the fair objects . . . from men and women down to vegetables." Among the "fair objects" was Lydia Jackson, sister of Dr. Charles Jackson, discoverer of anesthesia. She was sturdier than his first wife, but also tubercular.

He and Lydia—"Lydian" she became, for euphony—were

married September 14, 1835, in the old Edward Winslow House in Plymouth. She was a gracious, dignified girl whom her friends called "the Abbess" and whom Emerson came to call "Mine Asia" and "Queenie." Modest, unexacting, competent, she was retiring in the sunlight of her husband's fame. He took her to a house he had just bought on the edge of Concord. Its two acres looked out upon the blue Lincoln Hills and was near the Musketaquid, or Good Grass, River. A meadow path led to Walden Pond, made famous by Thoreau. Besides that, he got a "bargain" in "bluebirds, bobolinks and thrushes." There, with Lydian and his children, he lived out the rest of his days except when lecturing far and wide across the country.

Concord had been founded by a Puritan refugee, the Reverend Peter Bulkeley, one of Emerson's ancestors. During King Philip's War, when all the villages around had been burned, a chieftain, looking at it from a hilltop, ordered it spared. "The Great Spirit loves that town," he said. Though some residents could still recall the violent Shays's Rebellion, put down in blood, which had been its one outburst, it was a quiet place of meadow and lovely Nature. It lacked all resources for industry, and Emerson suggested to the townsfolk they ought to manufacture teachers—"the best in the world."

He never tired of its beauties, the eternal new dress of Nature: the sky-blue river and the river-blue sky; the yellow meadow spotted with sacks and sheets of cranberry pickers; the red bushes; the iron-gray house with just the color of the granite rock; the paths of the thicket, in which the only engineers were the cattle grazing on yonder hill; the wide, straggling, wild orchard in which Nature had deposited every possible flavor in the apples of different trees. "Whole zones and climates she has concentrated into apples," and he thought of "the benefactors," the townspeople, who had "conquered these fields"—old man Moore, dying, who had "absorbed volumes of sunshine like a huge melon or pumpkin in the sun." Nature, Emerson remarked about this time, "is the food in my basket." An American Shakespeare, he noted, could save all these beauties for all men—not with stereotyped European phrases, but with fresh American vision and fresh, meaningful words.

That November he delivered ten Boston lectures on English literature and on Michelangelo, Luther, Milton, Fox, and Burke. Early in 1836, he wrote an introduction for Carlyle's *Sartor Resartus* and paid part of the cost of getting it published in Boston, for no British publisher would bring it out.

His favorite brother, Charles, died, the one brother close to him spiritually and intellectually—"his life all healing, uplifting, fragrant." To keep going and forget the sorrow, Emerson lectured more and prepared his essay on Nature for publication. His essay had many "cracks," but so did "Nature." The little azure-bound book was his most thorough presentation of transcendentalism. He called for a fresh appraisal of Nature and Self. Give up seeing Nature through the eyes of past masters and see it for yourself. These "are new lands, new men, new thoughts. . . . Let us demand our own work and laws and worship." He sent a copy to Carlyle, calling it a "slight thing." But Carlyle thundered back, it was the "Apocalypse," the "Foundation and Ground Plan" on which Emerson could build whatsoever of "great and true" was given him to build.

It sold only 495 copies in twelve years, but "the good of publishing one's thoughts," Emerson remarked, "is that of hooking on to you like-minded men. . . . Yet how few! Who in Concord cares for the first philosophy in a book? The woman whose child is to be suckled? The man at Nine-Acre Corner who is to cart six loads of gravel on his meadow?"

That year Emerson's son Waldo was born—"makes the universe look friendly to me."

The year 1837 was a depression year: "Cold April; hard times, men breaking who ought not to break; banks bullied into the bolstering of desperate speculators, all the newspapers a chorus of owls."

For once Emerson slipped out of his studious role and gave

an antislavery talk. He also went to a meeting to protest the brutal expulsion of the Cherokee Indians from their homes and penned an indignant letter to President Van Buren: "Does the government think that the people of the United States are become savage and mad?"

That August, he delivered his famous Phi Beta Kappa address, which for the first time gave him real stature. In a Harvard Divinity School lecture he struck at the creeds and praised Oriental religions—the "devout contemplative East" to which so much was owed. Jesus himself was proof of that. He was bitterly attacked by the ministers. At Dartmouth, he tried to break down easy complacency. "Land, place, name, money" were not true goals. He learned a bit more about the imperviousness of human minds.

But when published, the three lectures were extravagantly praised. He was uneasy. "As long as all that is said is *against* me, I feel a certain sublime assurance of success. . . . Whosoever would be a man must be a nonconformist. . . . To be great is to be misunderstood."

In 1839 his daughter Ellen was born—"a soft swarthy little creature." He was lecturing in Boston and preparing his first volume of *Essays*. He was despondent that his lectures seemed cold and decorous and that he was unable to evoke the customary warm response.

The next year opened the "Roaring 'Forties." He noted down that the Greeks had "cleaner wits than any people in the Universe." The *Dial* was founded, edited by transcendentalist Margaret Fuller—one of the great landmarks in American literary history. Emerson was a copious contributor.

Two events added greatly to his happiness the following year. Henry Thoreau, then twenty-four, came to live with them for two years. He was an intellectual peer, a scholar, a true child of Rousseau, but, more to the point, a fine, willing handy man about the house, which Emerson had not the talent to be. That November, Emerson's daughter Edith was born. "There came into the house a young maiden, but she seemed . . . more than a thousand years old . . . naked . . . help-less, but she had the defence more than the strength of mil-lions."

He went to see Fanny Elssler in the ballet "Naphthalie" in Boston and forgot his youthful Puritanical strictures. Raptur-ously he wrote of "her softest graces of motion . . . the wisdom of her feet." Time was loosening up other early rigidities, making him more mellow, less provincial. Now he could even enjoy sitting in a Catholic church and reveling in the ritual. "The Presbyterians forgot that men are poets." He revised many early judgments. Spinoza, once a "hobgoblin," had become a "saint." But Machiavelli, Voltaire, Rabelais—"pig-lead trying to fly"—remained on his black list. Shelley (curious blindness) was only "mica glitter."

He was in the full tide of his powers when tragedy struck in 1842 with the death of five-year-old Waldo. "With his majestic deportment" and "perfect gentleness," the child had decorated for him "the morning star, the evening cloud." Emerson wrote his throbbing *Threnody*, and he lectured on, pain cracking his voice.

In March he had to take over the thankless burden of edit-ing the *Dial*, for he wished it to live and not fall into the hands of the "Humanity and Reform" men—"they trample on let-ters and poetry"—or the scholars—"they are dead and dry." The magazine died anyway the following year; a bright flame in the long, dreary history of America's journalistic mediocrity was snuffed out. But a second son, Edward Waldo, was born.

Emerson lectured on Napoleon, who "deserved the crown." He "won his victories in his head before he won them on the battlefield," and he quoted the Corsican: "What is history but a fable agreed upon?"

To Emerson, history was the record of reasoning men who had altered man's destiny; thus any man "admitted to the right of reason" could understand history and was "a freeman of the whole estate." "What Plato has thought, he may think; what a saint has felt, he may feel; what at any time has befallen man, he can understand." All history was in each and every man. It could germinate there, just as a whole forest could be found in one acorn. Unfortunately man imitated not only past nobility but the same old degradations, such as "the Salem hanging of witches."

Emerson's fame, fanned abroad by Carlyle and other friends and by his own writings, brought him an invitation to lecture in England. The notables of the land turned out to hear him, including Carlyle, who "grunted and snorted" his vast approval. They saw much of each other. Carlyle said "the same things over and over," but his "guiding genius" was his "moral sense," and Emerson was invigorated by him.

He was entertained lavishly. At one dinner he met Thomas De Quincey, a small old man of seventy, "with a very handsome face . . . marked with great refinement." He arrived soaked to the skin. Two street girls had successively rifled him of his eight shillings and his umbrella, and he had had to walk ten miles in the rain, not wanting to miss the Concord sage.

Although the Revolution of '48 was scarcely over, Emerson could not leave Europe without a glance at France, where he had been so unhappy. He displayed little enthusiasm this time either. He found the boulevards denuded of trees, cut down for barricades, and very much doubted if the uprising had been worth their loss.

Emerson was growing more interested in the antislavery movement, though he heartily disliked the noisy Abolitionists, showing his usual fastidiousness toward those who bore the brunt of the fight. Wendell Phillips had "only a platform existence . . . no personality." Emerson had no desire to meet him. William Lloyd Garrison was "a virile speaker, but lacking the "feminine element we find in genius." Take away the egotism of this "son of thunder," and he would be "castrated."

His advice to such do-gooders indulging in far-off charity was: "Go love thy infant; love thy wood-chopper . . . never varnish your hard uncharitable ambition with this incredible tenderness for black folk thousands of miles off. Thy love afar is spite at home."

But the 1854 Fugitive Slave Law made him boil. It was "odious news . . . detestable . . . I will not obey it by God," and he told his neighbors to break it on the slightest occasion. "Save the Union? . . . By such cowardly compromises?" Honor was more important than Union. Of Daniel Webster, so responsible for its passage, Emerson wrote bitterly, "The word *liberty* in the mouth of Mr. Webster sounds like *love* in the mouth of a courtezan."

For years he had looked upon Daniel Webster, in whose office his brother Charles had worked, as "the acme of American achievement." That towering giant from Vermont, with his fine knowledge of the law and of right, his great eloquence and charity, had been the most promising figure ever to appear in American politics. But as early as 1843 Emerson had written that Webster had missed "the opportunity of making himself the darling of the American world" by not "putting himself at the head of the Anti-Slavery movement." Increasingly after that, he criticized Webster's equivocal actions. Presidential ambition had ruined his moral grandeur, making him the spokesman of unsavory special interests, cloaking their deeds with fine, righteous phrases. In the end, he sold his talents to the highest bidder. Emerson's disillusion was complete.

As the nation drifted toward domestic conflict, Emerson came out of his shell to deliver several antislavery lectures and got howled down for his pains. John Brown spoke in Concord—"gave a good account of himself," noted Emerson, and he felt special grief in his later execution.

The war cut off nearly all Emerson's income, and had not a friend come forward with ample money, he would have been unable to continue his work. He lectured in Washington and met Lincoln.

He had formed prejudices because of tales of the President's off-color stories, his vulgar, intimate way with crowds, his petty quarrels with nonentities. But Lincoln made a better impression than the Concord sage had expected. Somewhat condescendingly he noted that Lincoln was "a frank, sincere, well-meaning man, with a lawyer's habit of mind, good clear statement of fact, a sort of boyish cheerfulness." But his taste was not good; he was too much the clown.

Then came the Emancipation Proclamation. Deeply stirred, Emerson celebrated it by reading to a Boston gathering his *Boston Hymn*—his best political poem—and when Lincoln died, Emerson had caught the full grandeur of the man.

"Step by step, he walked before them—slow with their slowness, quickening his march with theirs, the true representative of the continent . . . father of his country—the pulse of twenty millions throbbing in his heart, the thought of their minds articulated by his tongue."

Emerson was sixty-nine when he wanted artists to go to the Nile to paint nudes, and he was still engaged in the luxury—or better said—the anguish of sincerity. His hair had slipped back on his forehead, his eyes were more deeply sunken, some of the vast benignity of his countenance had vanished into sadness as he struggled with the difficulties of age. Few people had ever noticed his great beak of a nose because of the penetrating power and understanding of his eyes, but now it dominated his face. Lines, cut deep into his cheeks, as they had been for years, deepened, giving his expression greater austerity, emphasizing more his straight mouth, his squarish chin. "He was like a steel spring," remarked a man who met him shortly before he went to Egypt.

Not since Roger Williams had New England produced such a man—so fine a thinker, so great a heart. The deep-rooted tree of New England life had at last borne its finest fruit.

He became the brain and conscience of America in the days of its first intellectual awakening after independence. He wished America to cut loose from Europe and stand bravely on its own resources and develop its own mind and philosophy. He was the prophet of nineteenth-century America on the march toward wealth and power. He foresaw all that, but he knew better than any other American who ever lived that its true wealth and power would always lie in its moral courage, its freedom of thought, its creative achievements, its greatness of soul; that these could be achieved only with free, honest citizens not afraid to think. If this light failed, then America, however great its wealth, however mighty, would fail.

"Man Thinking!" America will always have to face that great challenge. The contribution of this American seer to all American civilization was great. He built a mighty mansion for the mind and soul of America. He added splendid new rooms. Many still have to be furnished and occupied by America. They are there forever for those who wish to enter. They belong to America, to all the world.

XVIII. The Ongoing

To STRESS between the covers of a single book some of the significant material, intellectual, and spiritual contributions New England has made to American civilization is not to belittle or ignore the great contributions from other sources and other regions.

American civilization is the product of varied places and climes, a composite created by the people of many nations and races, all of whom have made rich, far-reaching contributions without which today we would scarcely recognize this country of ours. The experience and benefits of numerous older cultures have gone into the making, and others besides the men of New England have gradually changed over from being the sons of other lands and other continents to being Americans. It was a continuing process that helped build the country during the entire frontier period.

Others, too, have adapted the fine things of their own traditions to the requirements of New World life. The multiplicity, the diversity, the variations both of origin and of the on-flow of American life provide much of its adaptability and strength and hope for the future. If it is to remain strong and creative, it can never close its doors to new peoples, new ideas, new ways of life from beyond its borders.

Much of its power to grow and expand and create the good life for its citizens—after all the only justification for any nation—is due to the great fluidity and freedom within its own borders that has enabled each region, old and new, to make contributions to every other region and the whole.

For that, too, is much of the American story, the changing life along its expanding frontier, which made for freedom, adaptability, ingenuity, new ideas, experimentation, and growth. Onto the New England way of life, transported to the open spaces of the West, were grafted many new important things, including some aspects of human freedom overlooked by New Englanders.

Thus, still another book could be written about America's contributions to New England. It was inevitable, for instance, that New England's skills and industries would move west with the growing up of the country. To those who know the long history of New England, the recent wailing and gnashing of teeth over the loss of much of its textile industry is an old story. Such worries and fears absorbed New England from the very first years, even when the Reverend Thomas Hooker, Jack Oldham, John Steele, and William Pynchon led the clans to western Massachusetts and Connecticut. From the beginning, men with special aptitudes and skills moved out—emigrants who sought, as the first comers had sought, wider opportunities, new horizons. But it was never any real loss, for with the development of the western country, the rise of industry in the Midwest, New England benefited in many ways, and not merely by a wider free market for its goods.

For every industry New England has lost, numbers more have emigrated there from West and South to take advantage of resources, close markets, and the special skills and crafts of the area. For New England these gifts from the rest of the land have resulted in a more varied pattern, a reinvigoration of men and methods, and greater diversification. This has provided greater stability and balance. Such wide diversification gives a firmer economic base for the whole region than in the days when a single factory or industry ruled the life of a community, as when New Haven was the carriage capital of the world. Today the loss of a shoe factory or a textile mill can scarcely hurt the over-all industrial strength of the area.

New England remains one of the most highly industrialized parts of the land. Some skills it has never lost. They were never successfully transplanted, and for many specialized products the great auto and aviation industries must still turn to New England factories.

As with industry, so with ideas, political and social doc-

trines. Without such constant interplay, both New England
and other places would have received lesser benefits. Today,
the democratic processes in New England have as fine a substance as anywhere in America—a great tolerance for races,
religions, and ideas, where individual integrity is still respected
more than in some other sections of the nation.

The fact also remains that much of the essential framework, the basic structure of American life, owes its origin and
its survival to New England—to the wisdom, the experiments,
the struggles of the first men and their descendants in shaping free institutions to the needs of this New World of ours.
New England provided a basic strength and optimism for
much of the country during the hurly-burly years of western
growth when men had few opportunities to do more than
battle for the material requirements of existence and had little
time to chart their course. New England provided the great
guideposts. It furnished the country with an enduring pattern,
a universal concept of social and political relationships. Thus
it provided the earlier years of the Republic, the years of
active western settlement, with purpose, direction, and meaning, and the strength of some of those early ideas and institutions, however altered or added to over the years, still repre-
sents much of the true strength and glory of America. We
discard them at our peril for, even more than any specific
provisions, they provide a method of orderly progress and free,
representative government. To the extent that we abridge
those basic freedoms, to that extent we may endanger our
future, destroy our national unity, and exchange violence and
bitterness for a harmonious political system.

In this hour of storm and stress, every idea, every institution of the land is under great strain. In the general hysteria
of our times, New England has maintained a greater equa-
nimity and steadfastness than some other parts of the land.
Proud of its schools, bred to a tradition of reason and proper
evidence, dignified in its exchange of arguments, it has, with
exceptions, resisted the blandishments of the latest breed of

demagogues who have tried to set aside long-tested individual and democratic rights, who have substituted trickery and false slogans for the habits of fair play and justice. New England's schools and colleges, beginning with such great conservative institutions as Yale and Harvard, have quietly resisted encroachments on traditional academic freedom better than some institutions elsewhere. Perhaps one of New England's contributions to American civilization in the days to come will be the level-headed preservation of those American ways that guarantee our freedoms and our progress under peace and law, the ongoing of the great truths of Roger Williams and Thomas Hooker, of Ezra Stiles, Roger Sherman, and Ralph Waldo Emerson, the eternal concepts of human freedom, their defense, and their fresh application to the needs of our own day.

	DATE
MAY 2 4 1977	
NO 5 '84	
GAYLORD	